SIMON & SCHUSTER
WORKBOOK
for WRITERS

FOURTH EDITION

SIMON & SCHUSTER
WORKBOOK
for WRITERS

Lynn Quitman Troyka
Emily R. Gordon

Prentice Hall
Upper Saddle River, New Jersey 07458

Executive Editor: Alison Reeves
Production Editor: Andrew Roney
Prepress and Manufacturing Buyer: Mary Ann Gloriande
Assistant Development Editor: Kara Hado
Creative Design Director: Leslie Osher
Designers: Anne Bonanno Nieglos and Susan Walrath

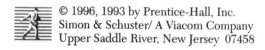

Printed in the United States of America

10 9 8 7 6 5 4 3 2 1

ISBN 0-13-455396-9

Prentice-Hall International (UK) Limited, *London*
Prentice-Hall of Australia Pty. Limited, *Sydney*
Prentice-Hall Canada Inc., *Toronto*
Prentice-Hall Hispanoamericana, S.A., *Mexico*
Prentice-Hall of India Private Limited, *New Delhi*
Prentice-Hall of Japan, Inc., *Tokyo*
Simon & Schuster Asia Pte. Ltd., *Singapore*
Editora Prentice-Hall do Brasil, Ltda., *Rio de Janeiro*

Contents

Writing When English Is a Second Language

Preface

The *Simon & Schuster Workbook for Writers, Fourth Edition* continues our tradition, established by prior editions, of serving dual purposes. It is designed foremost as a supplement of exercises and writing activities that parallel its parent, the *Simon & Schuster Handbook for Writers, Fourth Edition*. Also, it is designed as a self-contained textbook with concise explanations of key concepts followed by copious opportunities for practice. To those ends, this *Workbook* offers:

- Complete coverage of all basic topics: grammar, punctuation, mechanics, the writing process, and critical thinking. Technical terms are defined and explained simply and directly.

- Matching section heads and section numbers for easy cross-reference to the *Simon & Schuster Handbook for Writers*. **New for this edition,** all changes in the fourth edition of the *Handbook* now appear in the *Workbook*.

- **New for this edition,** many pages on English as a second language, with special emphasis on count and noncount nouns, articles, verbals, prepositions, word order, and modal auxiliary verbs.

- Attention to using quotations and writing paraphrases and summaries—topics not usually included in workbooks on writing.

- Charts and checklists throughout to summarize and highlight key information. Photographs as occasional writing prompts are included to stimulate visual as well as linguistic thinking.

- Exercise sequencing that leads to independent work, allowing users to move from simpler tasks, such as identifying sentence elements; to guided writing, such as sentence combining; and on to original sentences, paragraphs, and essays.

- Exercise content in connected discourse to replicate more closely the activities of revising and editing real writing. The topics from across the curriculum are chosen for their engaging interest. **New for this edition,** new subject matter appears in many exercises to keep the material fresh and up-to-date.

One person, above all, was indispensable to the completion of the fourth edition of the *Workbook:* Marcia Songer, East Tennessee State University. She brought an impressive combination of skill, teaching savvy, and dedication to the project. We appreciate, too, the influence of these colleagues who advised on English as a second language for the *Handbook*—and thus indirectly for the *Workbook:* Warren Herendeen, Mercy College; Alice Maclin, DeKalb College; and Mary Ruetten, University of New Orleans. Colleagues who served as reviewers include Judith Kohl, Duchess Community College of the State University of New York; David Mair, University of Oklahoma; Thomas Orr, Ball State University; and Marilyn Terreault, Macomb Community College.

At Prentice Hall/Simon & Schuster, a top team worked doggedly to see the project completed. We thank Alison Reeves, former Executive Editor for English, for her clear vision, high professional standards, and unfailing moral support; Joyce F. Perkins, Senior Development Editor for English, for her keen mind and patient attention to detail; Kara Hado, Assistant Development Editor for English, not only for attending to the daily details of coordination and communication but also for monitoring the quality of the work; Andrew Roney, Senior Project Manager, for his high standards and terrific sense of humor; and Phil Miller, President, Humanities and Social Science, for his leadership. And, once again, we renew our thanks to David Troyka, for being, as always, extraordinary.

Lynn Quitman Troyka
Emily R. Gordon

SIMON & SCHUSTER WORKBOOK
for WRITERS

1, 2, and 3 | *Thinking about Purposes and Audiences; Planning and Shaping; Drafting and Revising*

1: THINKING ABOUT PURPOSES AND AUDIENCES

Why write? In this age of telephones and tape recorders, television and film, why should you bother with writing? The answer has many parts.

Writing is a way of thinking and learning. Writing gives you opportunities to explore ideas and obtain information. By writing, you come to know subjects well and make them your own. When you write what you know, you are also teaching the reader.

Writing is a way of discovering. The act of writing allows you to make unexpected connections among ideas. As you write, thoughts develop and interconnect in new ways.

Writing creates reading. Writing creates a permanent record of your ideas for others to read and think about.

Writing ability is needed by educated people. College work demands that you write many different types of assignments. Most jobs require writing skills for preparing letters, memos, and reports. Throughout your life, your writing will reveal your ability to think clearly and use language to express ideas.

1a Understanding the elements of writing

Writing is a way of communicating a message to a reader for a purpose.

Let us look at the key words in this definition. **Communication** means that a message has a destination, a reader. The **message** of writing is its content. You need a thesis, a central idea that unites your writing. You also need enough content to support that thesis. Finally, the **reader** of your writing is your audience.

1b Understanding purposes for writing

Students often think their **purpose** for writing is to complete a class assignment. However, purpose means more than that: It refers to what the writing seeks to achieve. Although writing to express yourself and to create a literary work are important, this workbook concentrates on the two purposes most frequently found in academic writing: **to provide information for your reader** and **to persuade your reader**.

Expressive writing is usually the private recording of your thoughts and feelings. A personal journal is an example of expressive writing.

Informative writing (also known as **expository writing**) seeks to give information and, when necessary, to explain it. Informative writing focuses on the subject being discussed. Informative writing includes reports of observations, ideas, scientific data, facts, and statistics. It can be found in textbooks, encyclopedias, technical and business reports, nonfiction books, newspapers, and magazines.

CHECKLIST FOR INFORMATIVE WRITING

1. Is its major focus the subject being discussed?
2. Is its primary purpose to inform rather than to persuade?
3. Is its information complete and accurate?
4. Is its information verifiable?
5. Is its information arranged for clarity?
6. Is it interesting to read?

Persuasive writing (also known as **argumentative writing**) seeks to convince the reader about a matter of opinion. Persuasive writing focuses on the reader whom the writer wants to influence. Examples of persuasive writing include editorials, letters to the editor, reviews, sermons, business or research proposals, opinion essays in magazines, and books that argue a point of view.

CHECKLIST FOR PERSUASIVE WRITING

1. Is its major focus the reader?
2. Is its primary purpose to convince?
3. Does it offer information or reasons to support its point of view?
4. Is its point of view based on sound reasoning and logic?
5. Are the points in the argument arranged clearly?
6. Does it move the reader to act or to think in the desired way?

1c Understanding audiences for writing

Good writing is often judged by its ability to reach its intended **audience**. The more information you have about your audience's background, beliefs, and concerns, the better you can think about how to reach that audience.

CHECKLIST OF AUDIENCE CHARACTERISTICS

WHO ARE THEY?

Age/sex/education?
Ethnic background/political philosophy/religious beliefs?
Role(s): student/veteran/parent/wage earner/voter/etc.?
Employment/economic status?
Interests/hobbies?

WHAT INFORMATION DO THEY HAVE?

Level of education?
Experience with reading academic or business writing?
Amount of general knowledge about the subject?
Amount of specialized knowledge about the subject?
Set ideas they bring to the material?

1d Understanding the effect of tone

As an adult writing to an adult audience, you are expected to sound sensible and even-tempered. This stance is reflected in your **tone**—*what you say* and *how you say it.* Tone can be broadly described as **informal** or **formal.** Tone is informal in journals and freewriting. As you move from writing for the private you to **writing for an audience,** you are expected to move toward a more formal tone. This does not mean that you should use overblown language or put on airs that make you sound artificial (see 21e). Most audiences expect a tone midway between informal and highly formal. Your tone should take into account the topic, purpose, and audience of your piece.

1e Using sources for writing

You are your first source for writing. For many college writing assignments, you can draw on your own prior knowledge. For others, you will be expected to use outside sources, sources outside of what you already know.

2: PLANNING AND SHAPING

Experienced writers know that **writing is a process,** a series of activities that starts the moment they begin thinking about a subject and ends when they complete a final draft. Experienced writers also know that good writing is rewriting. Their drafts are filled with additions, cuts, rearrangements, and rewordings.

2a Understanding the writing process

For the sake of explanation, the different parts of the writing process are discussed separately in this chapter. In real life, you will find that the steps loop back and forth as each piece of writing develops.

AN OVERVIEW OF THE WRITING PROCESS

Planning calls for you to gather ideas and think about a focus.

Shaping calls for you to consider ways to organize your material.

Drafting calls for you to write your ideas in sentences and paragraphs.

Revising calls for you to evaluate your draft and rewrite it by adding, deleting, changing, moving—and often totally reworking material.

Editing calls for you to check the correctness of your grammar, spelling, punctuation, and mechanics.

Proofreading calls for you to read your final copy for typing errors or handwriting legibility.

2b Adjusting for each writing situation

As you think through and gather ideas (2d) for your topic, your task is to establish a **focus**, or a point of view, about the topic, and **support** for that focus. You also need to think about the purpose for your writing (1b) and the audience (1c).

2c Choosing a topic for writing

Some assignments leave no room for making choices. You may be given very specific instructions, such as "Explain how plants produce oxygen." Your job with such assignments is to do exactly what is asked and not go off the topic.

Some instructors will ask you to write on whatever topic you wish. In such situations, you need to select a topic that is suitable for informative or persuasive writing in college, one that reflects your ability to think through ideas. You need to demonstrate that you can use specific, concrete details to support what you want to say. Be careful not to choose a topic that is too narrow, or you will not have enough to say.

When you choose or are assigned a topic that is very broad, you have to **narrow the subject**. To do this, you must think of different areas within the subject until you come to one that seems workable for an essay.

Any broad subject may contain hundreds of possible essay topics. Do not try to think of them all, but also do not jump on the first topic that occurs to you. Consider the purpose of the assignment, the audience, the word limit, the time available to you, and your own interests and knowledge. A suitably narrowed topic will enable you to move back and forth between general statements and specific details.

2d Gathering ideas for writing

Techniques for gathering ideas, sometimes called **invention techniques**, can help you while you are narrowing your topic. For example, they help you to discover how much you know about a topic before you decide whether or not to write on it. Experienced writers use many techniques for gathering ideas; we will discuss the most common ones in this chapter.

2e Keeping an idea book and writing in a journal

Many writers carry an **idea book**—a small notebook—with them at all times so that they can jot down ideas that spring to mind.

A **journal**, like an idea book, is a record of your ideas, but it is built from daily writing sessions. In your journal you can write about your opinions, beliefs, family, friends, or anything else you wish. The content and tone can be as personal and informal as you wish. Nevertheless, a journal is not a diary for merely listing things done during the day. It is a book for you to fill with what you want to think about.

Keeping a journal can help you in three ways. First, writing every day makes it easier for you to write. Second, a journal encourages close observation and thinking. Third, a journal is an excellent source of ideas when you need to write in response to an assignment.

2f Using freewriting

Freewriting is writing down whatever comes into your mind without stopping to worry about whether the idea is good or the spelling is correct. You do nothing to interrupt the flow. Do not go back to review. Do not cross out. Some days your freewriting might seem mindless, but other days it can reveal interesting ideas. Freewriting works best if you set a goal, such as writing for ten minutes or until one page is filled. Sometimes you may decide to do focused freewriting—writing on a set topic—in preparation for an essay.

2g Using brainstorming

In **brainstorming**, you make a list of all the ideas you can think of associated with a topic. The ideas can be listed as words, phrases, or complete sentences. List making, like freewriting, produces its best results when you let your mind work freely, producing many ideas before analyzing them.

Brainstorming is done in two steps. First make your list. Then go back and try to find patterns in the list and ways to group the ideas into categories. Set aside any items that do not fit into groups. The groups with the most items are likely to reflect the ideas that you can write about most successfully.

2h Using the journalist's questions

Another commonly used method for generating ideas is the **journalist's questions**: *who? what? where? why? when?* and *how?* Asking such questions forces you to approach a topic from several different points of view.

2i Using mapping

Mapping is much like brainstorming, but it is more visual. When you map, begin by writing your subject in a circle in the middle of a sheet of unlined paper. Next draw a line out from the center and name a major division of your subject. Circle it, and from that circle move out to further subdivisions. Keep associating to further ideas and to details related to them. When you finish with one major division of your subject, go back to the center and start again with another major division. As you go along, add anything that occurs to you for any section of the map. Continue the process until you run out of ideas.

2j Using incubation

When you allow your ideas **to incubate,** you give them time to grow and develop. Incubation works especially well when you need to solve a problem in your writing (for example, if material is too thin and needs expansion, if material covers too much and needs pruning, or if connections among your ideas are not clear for your reader). Time is a key element for successful incubation. You need time to think, to allow your mind to wander, and then to come back and focus on the writing.

One helpful strategy is to turn attention to something entirely different from your writing problem. After a while, guide your mind back to the problem you want to solve. Another strategy is to allow your mind to relax and wander, without concentrating on anything special. Later, return to the problem you are trying to solve. At this point you might see solutions that did not occur to you before.

2k Shaping ideas

To shape the ideas that you have gathered (2d), you need to group them (see 2l) and sequence them (see 2m).

An essay has three basic parts: an introduction, a body, and a conclusion. The body consists of a number of paragraphs. The introduction and conclusion are usually one paragraph each. Chapter 4 discusses and illustrates various types of paragraphs.

2l Grouping ideas

Effective writing includes both general statements and specific details. In both informative and persuasive writing, general statements must be developed with facts, reasons, examples, and illustrations.

To group ideas, review the material you accumulated while gathering ideas. Look for general ideas. Next group under them related, but less general ideas. If you find that your notes contain only general ideas, or only very specific details, return to gathering techniques to supply what you need.

2m Sequencing ideas for writing

Shaping ideas for writing also means placing them into a logical structure. You need to decide what should come first, second, and so on. Within the essay, and within individual body paragraphs, you can order ideas in various ways. The most common organizational strategies are generalization to specifics, climactic order (from least to most important), chronological order (from beginning to end), and spatial order (following a pattern in space, such as top to bottom).

2n Shaping writing by drafting a thesis statement

A **thesis statement** is the main idea of an essay. Because it prepares your reader for what you will discuss, the thesis statement must accurately reflect the content of the essay. Following is a list of the basic requirements for a thesis statement.

BASIC REQUIREMENTS FOR A THESIS STATEMENT

1. It states the essay's main idea—the central point you are making to your readers.
2. It is in the form of a complete sentence, not a fragment or a question.
3. It is a generalization.
4. It reflects the essay's purpose—either to give your readers information or to persuade your readers to agree with you.
5. It includes a focus—your assertion that conveys your point of view.
6. It *may* briefly state the major subdivisions of the essay's topic.

Many instructors also require that the thesis statement appear as a single sentence at the end of the introductory paragraph.

In most writing situations you cannot be certain that a thesis statement accurately reflects what you say in the essay until you have written one or more drafts. To start shaping your essay, however, you can use a preliminary thesis statement. Even if it is too broad, it can guide you as you write. When the essay is completed, be sure to revise so that your final thesis statement accurately reflects the content of your essay.

Here are some thesis statements written for 500- to 700-word essays. The first two are for essays with an informative purpose, and the last two are for essays with a persuasive purpose.

TOPIC	rain
No	Rain is important. [too broad]
YES	Rain is part of the earth's water cycle.

TOPIC	radio
No	Everyone listens to the radio. [too broad]
YES	The variety of radio programming ensures there is a program for every taste.

TOPIC	drunk driving
No	Drunk driving is dangerous. [too broad]
YES	Unless drunk drivers are taken off our roads, they will continue to kill and injure thousands of people each year.

TOPIC	adoption
No	Sometimes, adopted children have problems. [too broad]
YES	Adopted children should be able to find out about their birth-parents for psychological, medical, and moral reasons.

2o Knowing how to outline

Many writers find outlining to be a useful planning strategy. An **outline** helps pull together the results of gathering and ordering ideas and preparing a thesis statement. It also provides a visual guide and checklist. Some instructors require outlines because they want you to practice the discipline of thinking through the arrangement and organization of your writing.

An **informal outline** does not have to follow all the formal conventions of outlining. It simply *lists* the main ideas of an essay—the major subdivisions of the thesis statement—and the subordinate ideas and details.

A **formal outline** follows strict conventions concerning content and format. The material must be displayed so that relationships among ideas are clear and so that the content is orderly. A formal outline can be a **topic outline** or a **sentence outline**: each item in a topic outline is a word or phrase, whereas each item in a sentence outline is a complete sentence.

Here are the conventions to follow in a formal outline.

1. **Numbers, letters, and indentations**: All parts of a formal outline are systematically indented and numbered or lettered. Capitalized Roman numerals (I, II, III) signal major divisions of the topic. Indented capital letters (A, B) signal the next, more specific level of information. Further

indented Arabic numbers (1, 2, 3) show the third, even more specific level of information, and so on.

2. **Grouping in pairs**: At all points on an outline there is no I without a II, no A without a B, and so on. If a heading has only one subdivision, you need either to eliminate that subdivision or expand the material so that you have at least two subdivisions.

3. **Levels of generality**: All items in a subdivision are at the same level of generality. A main idea cannot be paired with a supporting detail.

4. **Overlap**: Headings do not overlap. What is covered in A, for example, must be quite different from what is covered in B.

5. **Parallelism**: All entries are grammatically parallel. For example, all items might start with *-ing* forms of verbs or all might be adjectives and nouns (see 18h).

6. **Capitalization and punctuation**: Capitalize only the first word of each heading. In a sentence outline, end each sentence with a period. Do not put periods at the end of items in a topic outline.

7. **Introductory and concluding paragraphs**: The introductory and concluding paragraphs are not part of an outline. Place the thesis statement above the outline.

Here is a formal topic outline of an essay on living alone.

THESIS STATEMENT

Chances are high that adult men and women will have to know how to live alone, briefly or longer, at some time in their lives.

I. Living alone because of circumstances

   A. Grown children moving to other cities

      1. Going away to school
      2. Taking jobs

   B. Married people not being married forever

      1. One out of two marriages ending in divorce
      2. Eight out of ten married women becoming widowed, usually late in life

II. Taking care of practical matters

   A. Opening a checking account

      1. Comparing bank services
      2. Comparing advantages of different kinds of checking accounts

   B. Making major purchases

      1. Replacing a refrigerator
      2. Buying a car

III. Establishing new friendships

   A. Students getting used to going to classes without old friends

      1. Being able to concentrate better
      2. Being able to meet new friends

   B. Single adults going to the beach or parties

➔

3b

IV. Dealing with feelings of loneliness

    A. Understanding the feeling

    B. Avoiding depression

        1. Not overeating

        2. Not overspending

        3. Not getting into unwanted situations

            a. Taking the wrong job

            b. Going into the wrong relationship

    C. Keeping busy

3: DRAFTING AND REVISING

Drafting is getting ideas onto paper in rough sentences and paragraphs. **Revising** is taking a draft from its first to its final version by evaluating, adding, cutting, moving material, editing, and proofreading.

3a Getting started

If you have trouble getting started when the time arrives for drafting, you are not alone. Even professional writers sometimes have trouble getting started. Here are some time-proven methods experienced writers use to get started when they are blocked.

1. Don't stare at a blank page. Fill up the paper. Write words, scribble, or draw while you think about your topic. The movement of filling the paper while thinking can stimulate your mind to turn to actual drafting.

2. Picture yourself writing. Imagine yourself in the place where you usually write, with the materials you need, busy at work.

3. Picture an image or a scene. Start writing by describing what you see or hear.

4. Write your material in a letter to a friend. Doing this gives you a chance to relax. The letter can serve as a rough draft.

5. Write your material as if you were someone else: You can be a friend writing to you, an instructor writing to a class, a person in history writing to you or to someone else. Once you take on a role, you may feel less inhibited about writing.

6. Start in the middle. If you do not know what to write in your introduction, start with a body paragraph.

7. Use "focused freewriting" (2f).

8. Switch your method of writing. If you usually typewrite or use a word processor, try writing by hand. If you usually use a pen, switch to a pencil.

3b Knowing how to draft

First drafts are not meant to be perfect; they are meant to give you something to revise. The direction of drafting is forward: **keep pressing ahead**. Do not stop to check spelling or grammar. If you are not sure a word or sentence is correct, circle it or put an *X* in the margin so that you can return to that spot later.

No single method of drafting an essay works for everyone. Following are a pair of methods you might try—or you might prefer to use another method that you have developed for yourself.

1. Put aside all your notes from planning and shaping. Write a "discovery draft." As you write, be open to discovering ideas and making connections that spring to mind during the physical act of writing. When you finish a discovery draft, you can decide to use it either as a first draft or as part of your notes when you make a structured first draft.

2. Keep your notes from planning and shaping in front of you and use them as you write. Write a structured first draft, working through all your material. If you are working on a long essay, you may want to draft in chunks, a few paragraphs at each sitting.

3c Knowing how to revise

To revise your essay, you must first evaluate it. Then you make improvements and in turn evaluate them in the context of the surrounding material. This process continues until you are satisfied that the essay is in final draft.

STEPS FOR REVISING

1. Shift mentally from suspending judgment (during idea gathering and drafting) to making judgments.
2. Read your draft critically to evaluate it. Be guided by the questions on the Revision Checklist below.
3. Decide whether to write an entirely new draft or to revise the one you have.
4. Be systematic. You need to pay attention to many different elements of a draft, from overall organization to choice of words. Most writers work better when they concentrate on specific elements during separate rounds of revision.

MAJOR ACTIVITIES DURING REVISION

Add. Insert needed words, sentences, and paragraphs. If your additions require new content, return to idea-gathering techniques (see 2d–k).

Cut. Get rid of whatever goes off the topic or repeats what has already been said.

Replace. As needed, substitute new words, sentences, and paragraphs for what you have cut.

Move material around. Change the sequence of paragraphs if the material is not presented in logical order (see 2l–m). Move sentences within paragraphs, or to other paragraphs, if arrangements seem illogical (see 4e).

THINKING ABOUT PURPOSES AND AUDIENCES

When you revise, you need to pay special attention to your essay's title and thesis statement. Both of these features can help you stay on track, and they tell your reader what to expect.

The **title** of an essay plays an important organizing role. A good title can set you on your course and tell your readers what to expect. A title always stands alone. The opening of an essay should never refer to the essay's title as if it were part of a preceding sentence. For example, after the title "Knowing How to Live Alone," a writer should not begin the essay with the words, "This is very important." The title sets the stage, but it is not the first sentence of the essay.

The **thesis statement** expresses the central idea that controls and limits what the essay will cover. A thesis statement contains the **topic**, narrowed appropriately; the **focus**, which presents what you are saying about the topic; and the **purpose**. If your **thesis statement** does not match what you say in your essay, you need to revise either the thesis statement or the essay—sometimes both (see 2m).

A revision checklist can help you focus your attention as you evaluate your writing. Use a checklist provided by your instructor or compile your own based on the Revision Checklist below.

Revision checklist

The answer to each question on this checklist should be yes. If it is not, you need to revise.

THE WHOLE ESSAY

1. Is the topic of the essay suitable for college writing and is it sufficiently narrow? (2c)
2. Does your thesis statement clearly communicate the topic and focus of the essay? (2n)
3. Does your thesis clearly reflect the purpose of the essay? (1b)
4. Does the essay reflect an awareness of its audience? (1c)
5. Does the essay take into account special requirements—the assignment's time limit, word limit, and other factors?
6. Does your essay have a logical organization pattern? (2l, 2m)
7. Is the tone of the essay suitable for its audience? Is the tone consistent? (1d)
8. Is your thesis well supported by the main ideas of the paragraphs? (3c, 6c)
9. Do the paragraphs cover separate but related main ideas? (2l, 2m)
10. Have you covered all the material promised by your thesis statement? (2n)
11. Are the connections among the paragraphs clear? (4d, 4g)
12. Does your introduction lead into the thesis statement and the rest of the essay? (4g)
13. Does your conclusion provide a sense of completion? (4g)
14. Have you cut any material that goes off the topic?

15. Does your essay have a title? Does it reflect the content of the essay? (3c)

Paragraphs

1. Does the introduction help your audience make the transition to the body of your essay? (4g)
2. Does each body paragraph express its main idea in a topic sentence as needed? (4b)
3. Are the main ideas—and topic sentences—clearly related to the thesis statement of the essay? (4)
4. Are your body paragraphs developed? Is the development sufficient? (4b, 4c, and 4f)
5. Does each body paragraph contain specific and concrete support for its main idea? Do the details provide examples, reasons, facts? (4c)
6. Are your facts, figures, and dates accurate?
7. Is each body paragraph arranged logically? (4e)
8. Have you cut all material that goes off the topic?
9. Have you used necessary transitions? (4d, 4g)
10. Do the paragraphs maintain coherence with pronouns (4d), selective repetition (4d), and parallel structures (4d, 18)?

Sentences

1. Have you eliminated sentence fragments? (Chapter 13)
2. Have you eliminated comma splices and fused sentences? (14)
3. Have you eliminated confusing shifts? (15a)
4. Have you eliminated misplaced modifiers? (15b)
5. Have you eliminated dangling modifiers? (15c)
6. Have you eliminated mixed sentences? (15d)
7. Have you eliminated incomplete sentences? (15e)
8. Are your sentences concise? (16)
9. Have you used coordination correctly? (17a–17d)
10. Have you used subordination correctly? (17c–17h)
11. Have you used parallelism as needed to help your sentences deliver their meaning? (18)

Words

1. Does your word choice reflect your intentions in denotation and connotation? (20b)
2. Have you used specific and concrete language to bring life to general and abstract language? (20b)
3. Does your word choice reflect a level of formality appropriate for your purpose and audience? (21a)
4. Have you avoided sexist language? (21b)
5. Have you avoided slang and colloquial or regional language not appropriate to your audience and purpose? (21a)

➜

6. Have you avoided slanted language? (21a)
7. Have you avoided clichés and artificial language? (21d–21e)

3d Knowing how to edit

When you **edit**, you check the correctness of your writing. You pay attention to grammar, spelling, and punctuation, and to correct use of capitals, numbers, italics, and abbreviations. You are ready to edit once you have a final draft that contains suitable content, organization, development, and sentence structure. Once you have edited your work, you are ready to transcribe it into a final copy.

As you edit, be systematic. Use a checklist supplied by your instructor or one you compile from the following Editing Checklist.

Editing checklist

The answer to each question on this checklist should be yes. If it is not, you need to edit.

1. Is the grammar correct? That is, have you used correct verb forms (Chapter 8); have you used the correct case of nouns and pronouns (9); do pronouns refer to clear antecedents (10); do subjects and verbs agree (11a–l); do pronouns agree with their antecedents (11m–r); have you distinguished between adjectives and adverbs (12)?
2. Is the spelling correct? (22)
3. Have you correctly used hyphens? (22)
4. Have you correctly used commas? (24)
5. Have you correctly used semicolons (25), colons (26), apostrophes (27), and quotation marks (28)?
6. Have you correctly used other marks of punctuation? (29)
7. Have you correctly used capital letters, italics, numbers, and abbreviations? (30)

3e Knowing how to proofread

When you **proofread**, you check a final version carefully before handing it in. You need to make sure your work is an accurate and clean transcription of your final draft. Proofreading involves a careful, line-by-line reading of an essay. You should proofread with a ruler so that you can focus on one line at a time. Remember that no matter how hard you have worked on other parts of the writing process, if your final copy is inaccurate or messy, you will not be taken seriously.

Adapting to Your Audience and Purpose

Look at this picture of a flood. Describe the scene as part of your response to each of the four different audiences described below. Use your own paper.

David Wells/The Image Works

1. You have just walked home through this flood, and there is a message on your answering machine from your parents (in another state). They want to know if you are all right because they heard about the flood on the radio.

2. You are a businessperson whose basement has been flooded. Write a letter to your insurance company requesting particular action and explaining how you are not to blame for the damage.

3. You are a college senior whose finals have been postponed because of the flood. Write a letter home explaining what has happened on campus and asking your parents to handle the situation at their end (contacting your new employer, notifying your girlfriend/boyfriend, etc.).

4. You are the city official in charge of emergency preparations. Write a bulletin

to be read on the radio announcing the extent of the emergency and the availability of shelters. Explain who may use the shelters and what people may bring with them. Use language the general public can understand.

Using Idea-Gathering Techniques

Select four topics from this list, and prepare to write by narrowing each one. Use a different idea-gathering technique for each: freewriting, brainstorming, the journalist's questions, and mapping. Use your own paper, but record your narrowed topic on the line next to each subject you use.

1. talent _____

2. someone I can count on _____

3. traveling alone _____

4. happiness _____

5. graduation _____

6. breakfast _____

7. the beach _____

8. my grandparents _____

9. a personal loss _____

10. choosing a car _____

Grouping and Ordering Ideas

Select two of the topics you explored in Exercise 2-2. For each, group ideas in clusters of related material and then order the clusters. Remember that not every item in an idea-generating exercise has to appear in the final essay. Feel free to omit items that do not fit your pattern. If there are gaps, return to idea-gathering techniques to get more material. Your end products will be informal outlines. Use your own paper.

Writing Thesis Statements

A: Most of the following thesis statements are unacceptable because they are too broad or too narrow. Label each thesis *acceptable* or *unacceptable*. Then revise each unacceptable thesis to make it suitable for an essay of about 500 words.

EXAMPLE   Canada is a nice place to visit.
Its nearness to the United States, its cultural variety, and the lack of a language barrier make Canada an attractive choice for a family vacation.

1. Planned budget cuts will do terrible damage to the university.

   _____

2. Many students do not study as much as they should.

   _____

3. My parents blame today's violence on movies, but I blame it on society.

   _____

4. I saw several interesting auto races last week.

   _____

5. I fell in love when I was seventeen.

   _____

6. In interviews a job applicant should not beat around the bush.

   _____

7. The local post office provides services that I use regularly.

   _____

8. Remodeling an older home involves three major steps.

   _____

9. In May I visited Turkey.

   _____

10. The Norman Conquest occurred in 1066.

    _____

B: Write thesis statements for the four topics you narrowed in Exercise 2-2 and for six original topics. Be sure that each topic is suitably narrow for an essay of about 500 words and that the thesis statement shows a purpose and a point of view.

EXAMPLE   Topic: *how shopping has been changed by the development of closed malls*

Thesis Statement: *The development of closed malls has led to a revolution in the way Americans shop: we can shop easily at night and in rough weather, we see a greater variety of goods than in any single store, and we are encouraged to think of shopping as fun rather than as a chore.*

1. Topic _____

   Thesis Statement _____

2. Topic _____

   Thesis Statement _____

3. Topic _____

   Thesis Statement _____

4. Topic _____

   Thesis Statement _____

5. Topic _____

   Thesis Statement _____

6. Topic _____

   Thesis Statement _____

7. Topic _____

   Thesis Statement _____

8. Topic _____

   Thesis Statement _____

9. Topic _____

   Thesis Statement _____

10. Topic _____

   Thesis Statement _____

Planning a Formal Outline

The following topic outline contains twelve errors in form and logic. Revise the outline, using the guidelines listed in 2o. Draw a single line through each error and write your revision beside it.

Thesis Statement: Leaving a roommate for a single apartment can have definite drawbacks.

I. Unsatisfactory Furnishings
   A. Appliances
      1. Major
         a. Stove
         b. Refrigerator
      2. Minor
         a. Microwave
         b. Blender
         c. Toaster
         d. Mixer
      3. Washer
   B. Furniture
      1. Futon
      2. Living room
         a. Sofa
         b. Chairs
         c. Tables
      3. Kitchen
         a. Table
         b. Chairs
   C. Equipment
      1. For entertainment
         a. VCR
      2. Exercise
II. Not enough money to pay the bills
   A. Rent
   B. Utilities
      1. Gas
      2. Electricity
      3. Phone
   C. Food
      1. Groceries
   D. Entertainment

➜

III. Inadequate companionship
    A. Loneliness is a frequent problem
    B. Occasional fear
    C. Friendly neighbors

Making a Formal Outline

Convert one of the informal outlines you developed in Exercise 2-3 into a formal outline. Write a sentence outline or a topic outline, but be sure not to mix the two types. Begin by placing the thesis statement you developed in Exercise 2-4B at the top of your page. Use the list of conventions in 2o for guidance and as a checklist when you are done.

Revising, Editing, and Proofreading Essays

A: Here is a middle draft of a short essay. It has already been revised, but it has not yet been edited. Edit the essay, using the Editing Checklist in 3d. If you like, you may also make additional revisions. When you are done, submit a carefully proofread copy of the completed essay to your instructor.

Forks, knives, and spoons seam so natural to most of us that its hard to imagine eaten diner with out them. Yet many people, such as the chinese, use chopsticks instead, and other's use their hands to eat.

Knives are the oldest western utensils. The first ones were made of stone 1.5 million years ago. It was originally use to cut up dead animals after a hunt. The same knife were used to: butcher game slice cooked food, and kill enemies. Even later in History, nobles was the only ones who could afford separate knives for different uses. People use all-purpose knives, pointed like todays steak knives. The round-tipped dinner knife is a modern invention. It became popular in 17th cen. France because hosteses want to stop guests from picking they're teeth with the points of there dinner knives.

The spoon is also an anceint tool. Wooden spoons twenty thousand years old have been found in Asia; spoons of stone, wood, ivory, and even gold have been found in Egyptian tombs. Spoons scoop up foods that were to thick to sip from a bowl.

The fork is a newcomer. Forks did not become widely accepted until the eighteenth century; when the French nobility adopted the fork as a status symbol, and eating with ones hands became un-fashionable. At about the same time, individual place setings became the rule to. Previous, even rich people had shared plates and glasses at meals, but know the rich demanded individual plates, glasses, forks, spoons, and knives. Today in America, a full set of utensils is considered a necesity. We forget that as recently as the american revolution some people still considered anyone who use a fork to be a fussy showoff.

B: Here is the first draft of an essay. It needs a great deal of work, as most first drafts do. Revise the essay, using the Revision Checklist in 3c. Then edit your work, using the Editing Checklist in 3d. Finally, submit a carefully proofread copy of the completed essay.

The Suburbs

This morning at registration the clerk who was reviewing my program insulted me when she said, "Why do you live all the way out there?" She said it as if I was a fool to live in the suburbs. It was really crowded, so I didn't tell her what was on my mind. In this essay I will tell you why I like living in the suburbs.

City slickers always have pity on me. "Your so far away from everything" they say. This remark only shows how stupid they are. First, I am not as isolated as they think. To get to school, I drive about 40 minutes on a smooth highway. The highway is uncrowded too. My city friends take an overcrowded bus for forty minutes. Or longer, if there is a traffic jam. When I graduate and begin to work, I probably will not have even the forty-minute drive because local businesses are growing by leaps and bounds. There are factories, shopping malls, and large insurance, law, and advertising firms. All within twenty miles of my home.

I think that if my classmates knew how pleasent suburban life can be, they would join me in a flash. People here are friendlier. First moving onto my block, people I didn't recognize waved to me as I walked my dog. I thought they had me confused with someone else. I later found out that they were just been friendly. I use to live in the city. The only people who notice me when I was walking my dog were the ones who sternly reminded me to "keep the dog off their lawns." Neighbors here keep an eye on one another. Once when I did not move my car for three days a nieghbor knocked on my door to see if I was feeling alright. When I lived in the city, no one cared what I did or how I was, as long as I kept the volume down on the stereo.

Maybe I do not live in the most sophisticated area in the world, but I am not deprived. My stores carry the same fashions as stores in the city, my television recieves the same programs, and my radio carries the same stations. So everything is equal except the suburbs have some advantages I have described to you in this essay. The city is a nice place to visit, but I wouldn't want to live there.

4 | *Rhetorical Strategies in Paragraphs*

4a Understanding paragraphs

A **paragraph** is a group of sentences that work together to develop a unit of thought. Paragraphing permits you to subdivide material into manageable parts and, at the same time, to arrange those parts into a unified whole that effectively communicates its message.

To signal a new paragraph, you indent the first line five spaces in a typewritten paper and one inch in a handwritten paper.

A paragraph's purpose determines its structure. In college, the most common purposes for writing are *to inform* and *to persuade* (as discussed in 1b). Some paragraphs in informative and in persuasive essays serve special roles: they introduce, conclude, or provide transitions (see 4g). Most paragraphs, however, are **body paragraphs**, also called **developmental paragraphs** or **topical paragraphs**. They consist of a statement of a main idea and specific, logical support for that main idea.

4b Writing unified paragraphs

A paragraph is **unified** when all its sentences relate to the main idea. Unity is lost if a paragraph contains sentences unrelated to the main idea.

The sentence that contains the main idea of a paragraph is called the **topic sentence.** The topic sentence focuses and controls what can be written in the paragraph. Some paragraphs use two sentences to present a main idea. In such cases, the first is the topic sentence and the second is the **limiting** or **clarifying sentence** which narrows the focus of the paragraph.

Topic sentence at the beginning of a paragraph: Most informative and persuasive paragraphs have the topic sentence placed first so that a reader knows immediately what to expect. Placing the topic sentence first also helps to ensure that the entire paragraph will be unified.

1   **Many first-jobbers suffer from the "semester syndrome."** Students can usually count on being "promoted" at least twice a year—into the next semester. "Promotions" came regularly and at fixed intervals in school. At work, it's a different story. Promotions don't necessarily occur with any regularity, and sometimes they don't occur at all. This point may seem like a very obvious one, but the fact that students are used to rapid advancement can make their transitions to work harder. Since as students they become so conditioned to advancement at a fixed rate, many first-

23

jobbers become impatient when they are required to remain in one job or at one task without a promotion for longer than a "semester." They begin to feel they're not moving anywhere, and as a result many leave their first jobs much too soon.

—The staff of *Catalyst, Making the Most of Your First Job*

Topic sentence at the end of a paragraph: Some informative and persuasive paragraphs present the supporting details before the main idea. The topic sentence, therefore, comes at the end of the paragraph. This technique is particularly effective for building suspense, but it should be used sparingly. In the following paragraph, notice how concrete details build up to the main idea.

2   I read Dreiser's *Jennie Gerhardt* and *Sister Carrie* and they revived in me a vivid sense of my mother's suffering: I was overwhelmed. I grew silent, wondering about the life around me. It would have been impossible for me to have told anyone what I derived from these novels, for it was nothing less than a sense of life itself. **All my life had shaped me for the realism, the naturalism of the modern novel, and I could not read enough of them.**

—RICHARD WRIGHT, "The Library Card," from *Black Boy*

Topic sentence implied: Some paragraphs make a unified statement without the use of a topic sentence. Writers must construct such paragraphs carefully, so that a reader can easily see the main idea. Paragraphs with implied topic sentences are rare in academic writing.

4c Supporting the main idea of a paragraph

A topic sentence is usually a generalization. A topical paragraph is **developed** by the sentences that support the topic sentence, offering specific, concrete details. Without development, a paragraph fails to make its point or capture a reader's interest.

The key to successful development of topical paragraphs is detail. Details bring generalizations to life by providing concrete, specific illustrations. A paragraph developed with good detail often has RENNS—an acronym that stands for *r*easons, *e*xamples, *n*umbers, *n*ames, and appeals to the five *s*enses. Use RENNS as a memory device to help you check the development of your paragraphs, but do not feel that every paragraph must have a complete menu of RENNS to be well-developed. Here is a paragraph with two of the five types of RENNS.

3   However, the first ride I got took me on the way to New York rather than Washington. It was a big Standard Oil truck, heading for Wellsville. We drove out into the wild, bright country, the late November country, full of the light of Indian summer. The red barns glared in the harvested fields, and the woods were bare, but all the world was full of color and the blue sky swam with fleets of white clouds. The truck devoured the road with high-singing tires, and I rode throned in the lofty, rocking cab, listening to the driver telling me stories about all the people who lived in places we passed, and what went on in the houses we saw.

—THOMAS MERTON, *The Seven Storey Mountain*

This paragraph offers concrete, specific illustrations which describe Merton's first ride on the way to New York. It has *names* such as Standard Oil truck (not the general term *truck*), Wellsville, November country, and red barns (not the general term *buildings*). It appeals to the *senses* by including many references to light and specific colors, as well as to the rocking motion of the cab and the sound of the tires.

4d Writing coherent paragraphs

A paragraph is coherent when its sentences are related to each other, not only in content but also in grammatical structures and choice of words. The techniques of coherence are transitional expressions, pronouns, repetition of key words, and parallel structures. Though they are discussed separately in this section for the sake of clear example, techniques of coherence usually work in unison.

Transitional expressions—words and phrases that signal connections among ideas—can help you achieve coherence in your writing. Here are the most commonly used transitional expressions.

TRANSITIONAL EXPRESSIONS	
SIGNAL	**WORDS**
Addition	also, in addition, too, moreover, and, besides, further, furthermore, equally, important, next, then, finally,
Example	for example, for instance, thus, as an illustration, namely, specifically,
Contrast	but, yet, however, on the other hand, nevertheless, nonetheless, conversely, in contrast, on the contrary, still, at the same time, although,
Comparison	similarly, likewise, in like manner, in the same way, in comparison,
Concession	of course, to be sure, certainly, naturally, granted,
Result	therefore, thus, consequently, so, accordingly, due to this,
Summary	as a result, hence, in short, in brief, in summary, in conclusion, finally, on the whole,
Time sequence	first, firstly, second, secondly, third, fourth, next, then, finally, afterwards, before, soon, later, during, meanwhile, subsequently, immediately, at length, eventually, in the future, currently,
Place	in the front, in foreground, in the back, in the background, at the side, adjacent, nearby, in the distance, here, there,

Notice how transitional expressions (shown in boldface) help to make the following paragraph coherent.

4   The role of stress in the development of schizophrenic symptoms is particularly hard to study **since** what is stressful for one person may not be stressful for another. **Nonetheless**, two conclusions can be drawn. **First**, the biological predisposition to become mentally disorganized lowers a schizophrenic's resistance to stress in general, although some people who are so predisposed can tolerate more stress than others. **Second**, the issue of becoming independent from one's family of origin appears to pose special difficulties for individuals predisposed to schizophrenia. This is not surprising in view of the fact that mental, emotional, and social competence are requirements of successful completion of this task. The predisposed individual may be impaired in each of these areas.

—Kayla F. Bernheim and Richard R. J. Lewine, *Schizophrenia*

When you use **pronouns** that clearly refer to nouns and other pronouns, you help your reader move from one sentence to the next. Notice how the pronouns (shown in boldface) help make the following paragraph coherent.

5   The men and women who perform the daring and often dangerous action that is part of almost every television and motion-picture story today are special people. **They** are professional stunt men and women. **They** know precisely what **they** are doing and how to do it. **Most** are extraordinary athletes with the grace and timing of dancers. **They** plan ahead what **they** must do. And **they** have no intention of getting hurt, although sometimes **they** do.

—Gloria D. Miklowitz, *Movie Stunts and the People Who Do Them*

You can achieve coherence by repeating **key words** in a paragraph. Notice how the careful repetition of the words *demand, difficulty, game(s), fun*, and *rules* (shown in boldface) help make this paragraph coherent.

6   We **demand difficulty** even in our **games**. We **demand** it because without **difficulty** there can be no **game**. A **game** is a way of making something hard for the **fun** of it. The **rules** of the **game** are an arbitrary imposition of **difficulty**. When the spoilsport ruins the **fun**, he always does so by refusing to play by the **rules**. It is easier to win at chess if you are free, at your pleasure, to change the wholly arbitrary **rules**, but the **fun** is in winning within the **rules**. No **difficulty**, no **fun**.

—John Ciardi, "Is Everybody Happy?"

Parallel structures (see Chapter 18) can help you achieve coherence. Using the same form of phrase or clause several times sets up a rhythm which gives unity to the paragraph. Notice how the parallel structures (shown in boldface) make this paragraph coherent.

7   **This is** our hope. **This is** the faith with which I return to the South. **With this faith we will be able to** hew out of the mountain of despair a stone of hope. **With this faith we will be able to** transform the jangling discords of our nation into a beautiful symphony of brotherhood. **With this faith we will be able to work together, to pray together, to struggle together, to go to jail together, to stand up for freedom together**, knowing that we will be free one day.

—Martin Luther King, "I Have a Dream"

4e Arranging a paragraph

Here are some of the most common ways to organize paragraphs.

From general to specific: An arrangement of sentences from the general to the specific is the most common organization for a paragraph. Such paragraphs often begin with a topic sentence and end with specific details.

8   **Gifts from parents to children always carry the most meaningful messages.** The way parents think about presents goes one step beyond the objects themselves—the ties, dolls, sleds, record players, kerchiefs, bicycles and model airplanes that wait by the Christmas tree. The gifts are, in effect, one way of telling boys and girls, "We love you even though you have been a bad boy all month" or, "We love having a daughter" or, "We treat all our children alike" or, "It is all right for girls to have some toys made for boys" or, "This alarm clock will help you get started in the morning all by yourself." Throughout all the centuries since the invention of a Santa Claus figure who represented a special recognition of children's behavior, good and bad, presents have given parents a way of telling children about their love and hopes and expectations for them.

—MARGARET MEAD and RHODA METRAUX, *A Way of Seeing*

From specific to general: A less common arrangement moves from the specific to the general. The paragraph ends with a topic sentence and begins with the details that support the topic sentence.

9   They live up alongside the hills, in hollow after hollow. They live in eastern Kentucky and eastern Tennessee and in the western part of North Carolina and the western part of Virginia and in just about the whole state of West Virginia. They live close to the land; they farm it and some of them go down into it to extract its coal. Their ancestors, a century or two ago, fought their way westward from the Atlantic seaboard, came up on the mountains, penetrated the valleys, and moved stubbornly up the creeks for room, for privacy, for a view, for a domain of sorts. **They are Appalachian people, mountain people, hill people. They are white yeomen, or miners, or hollow folk, or subsistence farmers**.

—ROBERT COLES, "A Domain (of Sorts)"

From least to most important: A sentence arrangement that moves from the least to the most important is known as a **climactic sequence**. This arrangement holds the reader's interest because the best part comes at the end.

10   Joseph Glidden's invention, barbed wire, soon caught on—though not with everyone. Indians called it "devil's rope." Ranchers often cut it down so their cattle could graze freely. Most farmers, however, liked barbed wire. It kept cattle away from their crops. Cattle could break through most wire fences. With barbed wire, they quickly got the point. Eventually, ranchers started using barbed wire. With it, they separated the best cattle from the others to produce better breeds. Barbed wire helped railroads keep cattle off the tracks. As a result, the railroads expanded into new territory. **Glidden probably didn't realize it at the time,**

but the few hours he spent twisting wires would help speed the taming of the West.

—*Small Inventions That Make a Big Difference,*
National Geographic Society

According to location: A paragraph that describes the relative position of objects to one another, often from a central point of reference, uses **spatial sequence**. The topic sentence usually gives the reader the location that serves as the orientation for all other places mentioned.

11   The bay in front of the dock was framed by the shores of the mainland, which curved together from both sides to meet in a point. At that vertex another island, rocky and tall, rose from the water. It looked uninhabited; and although a few cabins were scattered along the mainland, between and behind them was unbroken forest. It was my first sight of a natural wilderness. Behind our tent too, and several other tents here and a house in their midst, was the forest. Over everything, as pervasive as sunshine, was the fragrance of balsam firs. It was aromatic and sweet and I closed my eyes and breathed deeply to draw in more of it.

—SALLY CARRIGHAR, *Home to the Wilderness*

According to time: A paragraph arranged according to time uses a **chronological sequence**.

12   About 30 years ago, a prince in India found a rare white tiger cub whose mother had been killed. The prince decided to raise the cub, which he named Mohan. When Mohan grew up, he fathered some cubs that were white. One of his cubs, Mohini, was sent to the National Zoo in Washington, D.C. Mohini was used to breed more white tigers for other zoos in the United States.

—"Who-o-o Knows?" *Ranger Rick*

4f Knowing patterns for developing a paragraph

If you know a variety of patterns for paragraph development, you have more choices when you are seeking ways to help your paragraphs deliver their meanings most effectively. Although, for the purpose of illustration, the patterns shown here are discussed in isolation, in essay writing paragraph patterns often overlap. Be sure to use the paragraph pattern that communicates your meaning most effectively.

Narration: Narrative writing tells about what is happening or what happened. Narration is usually written in chronological sequence.

13   During the 1870s, the business world was not yet ready for the typewriter. Inventor C. Latham Sholes and his daughter Lillian faced two major objections as they demonstrated Sholes's writing machine. "Too expensive and too slow," the businessmen protested. The response discouraged the inventor, but he didn't give up. At his home in Milwaukee, Wisconsin, he designed improvements for his machine. He also invented touch-typing, a system that enables a person to type fast without looking at the keys. Touch-typing was faster than handwriting. It could

save both time and money. That caused businessmen's interest to perk up. By 1900, in offices all over the United States, the *clickety-clack* of typewriters was replacing the scratching of pens.

—*Small Inventions That Make a Big Difference,*
National Geographic Society

Description: Descriptive writing appeals to a reader's senses—sight, sound, smell, taste, and touch—creating a sensual impression of a person, place, or object.

14   The forest was quiet except for the shrill cries of faraway toucans. Then many leaves began to rustle nearby. Seconds later crickets and cockroaches were hopping and crawling frantically in my direction. *What could be causing these creatures to run for their lives?* I wondered. Then I saw them: Tens of thousands of *army ants* were marching toward their fleeing prey—and me! The swarm of ants looked like a huge moving triangle, with the ants at the head of the swarm forming the widest part. And this part was as long as a school bus.

—DOUG WECHSLER, "I Met the Rambo Ants"

Process: A process describes a sequence of actions by which something is done or made. It is usually developed in chronological order. If it is to be effective, a process must include all steps. The amount of detail included depends on whether you want to teach the reader how to do something or you merely want to offer a general overview of the process.

15   To keep the big teams as nearly even as possible in the level of performance, a system called the draft has been devised. This is the way it works. Names of top college players who are graduating and want to turn pro are listed. Team representatives meet for a few days, usually in New York, to select the players they wish from this list. The team that placed last in the standings that year, gets first choice. The team next lowest in the standings gets the next choice, and so on. Naturally the representative will select the player the team needs the most. If one team gets a player that another team wants, that other team may trade an established team member or members for the draft choice. Naturally, a lot of wheeling and dealing goes on at this time.

—BOB and MARGUITA McGONAGLE, *Careers in Sports*

Example: A paragraph developed by example uses one or more illustrations to provide evidence in support of the main idea.

16   Getting right down to the gory details, ever since the earliest days of movie making, stars have been gushing, oozing, trickling, or dripping blood, as the case may be, on screen. Victims in silent movies "bled" chocolate syrup, which looked just like the real McCoy on the kind of black-and-white film used then. If a cowboy in a Western was to get shot, just before the scene was filmed a little chocolate syrup would be poured into the palm of his hand. Then, when the cameras started rolling and the cowboy got "blasted," he merely slapped his hand to his chest and what audiences saw was the bloody aftermath.

—JANE O'CONNOR and KATY HALL, *Magic in the Movies*

Definition: A paragraph of definition explains the meaning of a word or concept. Because it is more thorough than the definition offered by a dictionary, such a paragraph is called an **extended definition**.

An extended definition may contain any of several elements, but it rarely includes all of them: (1) a dictionary definition, (2) a negative definition—what the term is *not*, (3) a comparison and contrast of definitions used by other people, (4) an explanation of how this term differs from terms with which it is often confused, and (5) an explanation of how the term originated. If the subject is a human quality, the definition may include (6) a discussion of how a person develops the quality and how the quality shows up in the individual's personality.

17   Now, consider for a moment just exactly what it is that you are about to be handed. It is a huge, irregular mass of ice cream, faintly domed at the top from the metal scoop, which has first produced it and then insecurely balanced it on the uneven top edge of a hollow inverted cone made out of the most brittle and fragile of materials. Clumps of ice cream hang over the side, very loosely attached to the main body. There is always much more ice cream than the cone could hold, even if the ice cream were tamped down into the cone, which of course it isn't. And the essence of ice cream is that it melts. It doesn't just stay there teetering in this irregular, top-heavy mass; it also melts. And it melts *fast*. And it doesn't just melt—it melts into a sticky fluid that *cannot* be wiped off. The only thing one person could hand to another that might possibly be more dangerous is a live hand grenade from which the pin had been pulled five seconds earlier. And of course if anybody offered you that, you could say, "Oh. Uh, well—no thanks."

—L. Rust Hills, *How to Do Things Right*

Analysis and classification: **Analysis** divides things up, and **classification** puts things together. A paragraph developed by analysis, also known as **division**, divides one subject into its component parts. Paragraphs written in this pattern usually start by identifying the one subject and then explain that subject's distinct parts. For example, a football team can be divided into its offensive and defensive teams, which can be divided further into the various positions on each.

A paragraph developed by classification discusses the ways that separate groups relate to one another. The separate groups must be *from the same class*; that is, they must have some underlying characteristic in common. For example, different types of sports—football, Rugby, and soccer—can be classified *together* according to their handling of the ball, their playing fields, the placement of their goals, and the like.

18   **There are three kinds of book owners.** The **first** has all the standard sets and best sellers—unread, untouched. (This deluded individual owns wood-pulp and ink, not books.) The **second** has a great many books—a few of them read through, most of them dipped into, but all of them as clean and shiny as the day they were bought. (This person would probably like to make books his own, but is restrained by a false respect for their physical appearance.) The **third** has a few books or many—every one of them dog-eared and dilapidated, shaken and loosened by continual use, marked and scribbled in from front to back. (This man owns books.)

—Mortimer J. Adler, "How to Mark a Book"

Comparison and contrast: **Comparison** deals with similarities, and **contrast** deals with differences between two objects or ideas. Paragraphs using comparison and contrast can be structured in two ways. A **point-by-point structure** allows you to move back and forth between the two items being compared. A **block structure** allows you to discuss one item completely before discussing the other.

POINT-BY-POINT STRUCTURE
Student body: college A, college B
Curriculum: college A, college B
Location: college A, college B

BLOCK STRUCTURE
College A: student body, curriculum, location
College B: student body, curriculum, location

Here is a paragraph structured point-by-point for comparison and contrast.

19   Some people say the business about the jolly fat person is a myth, that all of us chubbies are neurotic, sick, sad people. I disagree. Fat people may not be chortling all day long, but they're a hell of a lot *nicer* than the wizened and shriveled. Thin people turn surly, mean, and hard at a young age because they never learn the value of a hot-fudge sundae for easing tension. Thin people don't like gooey soft things because they themselves are neither gooey nor soft. They are crunchy and dull, like carrots. They go straight to the heart of the matter while fat people let things stay all blurry and hazy and vague, the way things actually are. Thin people want to face the truth. Fat people know there is no truth. One of my thin friends is always staring at complex, unsolvable problems and saying, "The key thing is...." Fat people never say that. They know there isn't any such thing as the key thing about anything.

—SUZANNE BRITT JORDAN, "That Lean and Hungry Look"

Here is a paragraph structured block style for comparison and contrast.

20   Many people think that gorillas are fierce and dangerous beasts. Stories have been told about gorillas attacking people. Movies have been made about gorillas kidnapping women. These stories and movies are exciting, but they are not true. In real life, gorillas are gentle and rather shy. They rarely fight among themselves. They almost never fight with other animals. They like to lead a quiet life—eating, sleeping, and raising their young.

—SUSAN MEYERS, *The Truth about Gorillas*

Analogy: Analogy is a type of comparison. By comparing objects or ideas from different classes, an analogy explains the unfamiliar in terms of the familiar. For example, the fight to find a cure for a disease might be compared to a war. Often a paragraph developed with analogy starts with a simile or metaphor (see 21c).

21   If clothing is a language, it must have a vocabulary and a grammar like other languages. Of course, as with human speech, there is not a single language of dress, but many: some (like Dutch and German) closely related and others (like Basque)

almost unique. And within every language of clothes there are many different dialects and accents, some almost unintelligible to members of the mainstream culture. Moreover, as with speech, each individual has his own stock of words and employs personal variations of tone and meaning.

—ALISON LURIE, *The Language of Clothes*

Cause-and-effect analysis: Cause-and-effect analysis involves examining the origin or outcome of something that happened or might happen. Causes are what lead up to an event; effects are what result.

22   When a person is weightless, the slightest exertion causes motion. For example, if you pushed yourself away from a chair, you would continue to move away from it. There would be nothing to stop the motion. You would float in space. Should you let go of your book, it would hang in space. Push it ever so slightly, and the book would move in a straight line. Splash water, and it would form into round drops moving in all directions.

—FRANKLYN M. BRANLEY, *Mysteries of Outer Space*

4g Writing introductory, transitional, and concluding paragraphs

Introductory paragraphs, concluding paragraphs, and transitional paragraphs have special roles in an essay. **Introductions** prepare a reader for the topical paragraphs that follow, **conclusions** bring the topical paragraphs to a close for a reader, and **transitional paragraphs** help the reader move through complex material. Generally, special paragraphs are shorter than topical paragraphs.

Introductory paragraphs: In informative and persuasive writing, an introductory paragraph prepares readers for what lies ahead. For this reason, your introduction must relate clearly to the rest of your essay. If it points in one direction and your essay goes off in another, your reader will be confused—and may even stop reading.

In college writing, many instructors want an introductory paragraph to include a statement of the essay's **thesis**—its central idea. Although professional writers do not always use thesis statements in their introductory paragraphs, they can help student writers who need to practice clear essay organization. Here is an example of an introductory paragraph ending with a thesis statement.

23   Basketball is a team game. Individual stars are helpful, but in the end, the team that plays together is the team that wins. No one player can hog the ball; no one player should do all the shooting. Every player, every coach and every fan knows that. But once in a while, a team needs a super effort by an individual. **In a National Basketball Association playoff game between Boston and Syracuse, Boston's Bob Cousy made one of the most spectacular one-man shows ever seen.**

—HOWARD LISS, *True Sports Stories*

An introductory paragraph often includes an **introductory device** to lead into the thesis and to stimulate reader interest. To be effective, an introductory device must relate clearly to the essay's thesis and to the material in the topical paragraphs. Some of the most common introductory devices are listed below.

SELECTED DEVICES FOR INTRODUCTORY PARAGRAPHS

Provide relevant background information.
Tell an interesting brief story or anecdote.
Give a pertinent statistic or statistics.
Make a stimulating statement.
Ask a stimulating question or questions.
Use an appropriate quotation.
Make a useful analogy.
Define a term used throughout the essay.

Here is a guide to what to avoid in introductory paragraphs.

WHAT TO AVOID IN INTRODUCTORY PARAGRAPHS

1. Don't be too obvious. Avoid bald statements such as "In this paper I will discuss the causes of falling oil prices."
2. Don't apologize. Avoid self-critical statements such as "I do not have much background in this subject" or "I am not sure if I am right, but here is my opinion."
3. Don't use overworn expressions. Avoid empty statements such as "Love is what makes the world go round" or "Haste makes waste."

Transitional paragraphs: A transitional paragraph usually consists of one or two sentences that help the reader move from one major point to another in long essays. Here is a transitional paragraph that moves the reader between a series of details and an explanation of their possible source.

24   Now that we've sampled some of the false "facts" that clutter our storehouse of knowledge, perhaps you'd like to consider some of the possible reasons why we seem so susceptible to misinformation.

—William P. Gottlieb, *Science Facts You Won't Believe*

Concluding paragraphs: In informative and persuasive writing, a conclusion brings discussion to a logical and graceful end. Too abrupt an ending leaves your reader suddenly cut off, and a conclusion that is merely tacked onto an essay does not give the reader a sense of completion. In contrast, an ending that flows gracefully and sensibly from what has come before it reinforces your ideas and increases the impact of your essay. The most common ways of concluding an essay are listed below.

SELECTED WAYS TO CONCLUDE AN ESSAY

Use the devices suggested in this chapter for introductory paragraphs—but avoid using the same device in the introduction and conclusion of an essay.

Summarize the main points of an essay.

Call for awareness and action.

Point toward the future.

The concluding paragraph below summarizes Cousy's "show." (See page 34.)

25   In that game Bob Cousy scored a total of 50 points. He made 25 of them in regulation time, and 25 more in the four overtime periods. And he made 30 out of 32 foul shots. Even more important, he had scored his points at the right time. Four times he scored in the final seconds to keep the game going. Then he helped his team pull away. Basketball may be a team game, but most teams would not be sorry to have an individual performer like Bob Cousy.

—Howard Liss, *True Sports Stories*

Here is a list of what to avoid when writing concluding paragraphs.

WHAT TO AVOID IN WRITING CONCLUDING REMARKS

1. Don't go off the track. Avoid introducing an entirely new idea or adding a fact that belongs in the body of the essay.

2. Do not merely reword your introduction. Also do not simply list the main idea in each topic sentence or restate the thesis. While a summary can refer to those points, it must tie them into what was covered in the essay. If the introduction and conclusion are interchangeable, you need to revise.

3. Don't announce what you have done. Avoid statements such as "In this paper I have tried to show the main causes for the drop in oil prices."

4. Don't use absolute claims. Avoid statements such as "This proves that. . ." or "If we take this action, the problem will be solved." Always qualify your message with expressions such as "This seems to prove. . ." or "If we take this action, we will begin working toward a solution of the problem."

5. Don't apologize. Avoid casting doubt on your material by making statements such as "I may not have thought of all the arguments, but. . ."

Identifying Sentences That Do Not Fit the Topic Sentence

Identify the topic sentence in each paragraph, and write its number in the first column. Then, identify any irrelevant sentences (ones that do not fit the topic sentence), and write their numbers in the second column.

	Topic Sentence	Irrelevant Sentences
EXAMPLE [1]The flute is a very old instrument. [2]It existed as long ago as 3500 B.C. [3]My brother plays the flute. [4]Archaeologists digging in the cities of ancient Sumeria and Egypt have found well-preserved flutes. [5]When these flutes were tested, they sounded much like modern flutes. [6]However, they look different. [7]My brother's flute is silver. [8]Ancient flutes were played vertically, and they were 1½ feet long but only a ½ inch wide.	1	3, 7
1. [1]Many people associate the clarinet with jazz or the Big Bands of the forties. [2]However, the clarinet has been around since ancient times. [3]The clarinet can be hard to play. [4]The first clarinet appeared in Egypt before 2700 B.C. [5]The double clarinet appeared about eight hundred years later. [6]The first modern Westerner to compose for the clarinet was a sixteenth century German, Johann Christoph Denner. [7]He improved the clarinet by making it of wood, using a single rather than a double reed, and increasing its length from one foot to two feet.	_____	_____

2. [1]The lute is the ancestor of many modern stringed instruments. [2]There is even a mural, dating from 2500 B.C., that shows a Babylonian shepherd playing a lute. [3]The guitar, the ukulele, and the sitar are descendents of the lute. [4]The sitar became popular in the West after the Beatles' George Harrison studied with Indian musician Ravi Shankar. [5]The violin, fiddle, and cello also are descended from the lute. [6]The bows used to play these instruments are an eighth century Islamic addition to the tradition of stringed instruments.

    _____ _____

3. [1]The trumpet is another instrument with a long history. [2]The first trumpets were made of bamboo cane or eucalyptus branches. [3]The eucalyptus tree is found in Australia and is the chief food source for koalas. [4]The first metal trumpets, made of silver, were found in the tomb of King Tutankhamen of Egypt, who died about 1350 B.C. [5]The Greek trumpets of the fifth century B.C. were made of carved ivory. [6]Like us, the Romans had both straight and J-shaped trumpets. [7]The Romans are often depicted in paintings as enjoying music.

    _____ _____

4. [1]The first bagpipes were very unusual instruments. [2]They were made from the complete hide of a sheep or goat. [3]The chanter, a pipe with finger holes, was set in a wooden plug placed in the animal's neck. [4]The drones, the pipes that produced the bagpipe's sound, were set in wooden plugs placed in the forelegs. [5]Then as now, a blowpipe was used to fill the bag with air. [6]The player pressed the bag under one arm, forcing air out the drones, and fingered the chanter, making

    _____ _____

the bagpipe's famous sound. [7]The bagpipe originally came from Asia.

5. [1]Many people assume the piano is an improved version of some older keyboard instrument, such as the harpsichord. [2]Actually, the harpsichord, the clavichord, and the piano are widely different. [3]In a harpsichord, the strings are plucked. [4]This plucking enables the instrument to sustain a note. [5]In the clavichord, the strings are struck by blades of metal. [6]Once a blade moves off a string, the note stops. [7]The first clavichord dates back to about 1385. [8]In the piano, the strings are struck by small hammers that rebound immediately. [9]The piano did not become popular until the eighteenth century.

_____ _____

Identifying Transitions

Underline all the transitional words and expressions in these paragraphs. Then list the transitions on the lines provided.

1. The lion is called the King of Beasts, but the tiger really deserves the title. Male lions are six to eight feet long, not counting their tails. They are about three feet high at the shoulder, and they weigh four to five hundred pounds. In contrast, the tiger can grow up to a foot longer, several inches taller, and a hundred pounds heavier.

   _____

2. Most people think the boomerang is found only in Australia; however, this is not so. People use curved hunting sticks in four other parts of the world: Indonesia, eastern Africa, the Indian subcontinent, and the southwestern United States. In the United States, the Hopi, Acoma, and Zuni Indians use such sticks to hunt small animals. Few boomerangs are designed to return to their owners, but the Australian aborigines have perfected a kind that does return. In fact, the word "boomerang" comes from the aborigines' name for such a hunting stick.

   _____

3. Despite its name, The *Encyclopaedia Britannica* is not a British enterprise, nor has it ever been. The *Britannica* was founded in 1771 by a group of "Gentlemen in Scotland" who ran it until 1815, when a second group of Scotsmen took over. The British finally became involved in 1910, but as partners to Americans. Since the 1920s, the *Britannica* has been a completely American project. From 1928 to 1943, it was owned by Sears, Roebuck. Since 1943, the *Britannica* has been owned by the University of Chicago.

   _____

4. Everyone knows the story of Cinderella. She was treated as a servant by her stepmother and stepsisters, helped by a fairy godmother, and finally rescued by a prince who identified her because her small foot fit the glass slipper that his "mystery woman" had left behind at the ball. Were glass slippers fashionable centuries ago, or did someone make a mistake? Someone certainly made a mistake. In 1697, Charles Perrault translated Cinderella from Old French into English. Unfortunately, he mistranslated *vair* as "glass." Actually, *vair* means "white squirrel fur." So, Cinderella's shoes were much more comfortable than we had been told.

   _____

5. Dr. Joseph Guillotin did not invent the guillotine, although it was named after him. The guillotine had been in use throughout Europe since at least the early fourteenth century. In most places, the guillotine was reserved for executing nobility. During the French Revolution, Dr. Guillotin suggested to the French National Assembly that the machine become the country's official form of capital punishment. He wanted it to be used on criminals regardless of their social class. The Assembly agreed. The first victim of the French guillotine was a highwayman in 1792. Within a year, the heads of the nobility began to fall in the infamous Reign of Terror.

Identifying Devices that Provide Coherence EXERCISE 4-3

(4d)

Read this paragraph carefully, and then answer the questions that follow.

[1]Have you ever wondered how the painted lines in the road are made straight? [2]No one painting freehand could consistently keep lines straight, so machines are used. [3]Before a small road or street is painted, a highway crew marks it at twenty-foot intervals, following an engineer's plan. [4]Then a gasoline-powered machine, about the size of a large lawnmower, is pushed along by one person. [5]The operator follows the marks on the road, while air pressure forces out a stream of paint or hot plastic. [6]Hot plastic lasts from eighteen months to three years; paint lasts from three to six months. [7]Of course, this machine is too slow for use on highways. [8]Instead, four-person crews use a large truck equipped with a pointer that can be used to follow the median strip, so there is no need to mark the road before painting. [9]The truck is faster than the one-person machine for other reasons as well: it has *two* adjustable sprayguns that paint lines at the required distances apart, and it moves at five miles an hour. [10]Crew members must have great skill. [11]In fact, they receive up to a year of training.

1. Which words and phrases serve as transitional devices?

2. What key words are repeated (include all forms of the words)?

3. How does parallelism function in sentences 6 and 9?

4. What key words are later replaced by pronouns? List the nouns and the pronouns that substitute for them.

Organizing Sentences to Create a Coherent Paragraph

Rearrange the sentences in each set to create a coherent paragraph. Write the letters of the sentences in their new order on the lines given. Then write out the paragraph.

1. a. Second, compare fees for special services, such as stopping checks.
    b. Always compare several banks before you open a checking account.
    c. Finally, make sure the bank's hours are convenient for you.
    d. First, find out the monthly fee each bank charges.
    e. Next, see if you will be earning interest on your account.

2. a. Early humans imitated these "natural bridges" by chopping down tall trees and placing them across water.
    b. It was built of many logs tied together with rope.
    c. The first bridges were simply trees that had, by chance, fallen across streams.
    d. The bridge over the Euphrates River lasted for decades.
    e. The first genuine bridge was laid across the Euphrates River at Babylon about 700 B.C.

3. a. Sir Alexander Fleming discovered the penicillin mold, the first modern antibiotic, by accident in 1928.
    b. For the next 200 years, scientists sought a cure for infection.
    c. The Chinese used this soybean mold to treat skin infections.
    d. The first antibiotic was made from moldy soybeans around 500 B.C.
    e. Soon after, other cultures began using moldy bread and cobwebs to treat infected wounds.
    f. Strangely, they never looked into these folk remedies.

4. a. Two years later, Long's wife became the first woman to deliver a baby under anesthesia.
    b. Before the introduction of ether by Long, doctors had relied on crude methods of anesthesia.
    c. The use of ether in surgery started in 1842.
    d. In 1846 in Boston, the word "anesthesia," meaning "lack of feeling," was coined after the first use of ether in major surgery.
    e. In that year, Dr. Crawford W. Long used ether to anesthetize a young man who was having a cyst removed from his neck.
    f. These early methods included alcoholic intoxication, freezing the area of the operation, and having the patient inhale the fumes from burning narcotic plants.

Supporting the Topic Sentence

For each topic sentence below, supply three to five relevant details. Then, using your own paper, write a unified and coherent paragraph using the topic sentence and your supporting details.

1. Topic Sentence: Parenting class should (should not) be required for high school graduation.

   Details:

2. Topic Sentence: Buying on credit can be disastrous.

   Details:

3. Topic Sentence: The _____ have contributed many
   (members of an ethnic group)
   things to American culture.

   Details:

4. Topic Sentence: _____ is an exciting spectator sport.

   Details:

5. Topic Sentence: The laws regarding _____ should be changed.

   Details:

6. Topic Sentence: Choosing a college can be difficult.

   Details:

Organizing Details
within Paragraphs

Details in a paragraph are often organized in one of four patterns: chronological order (time), spatial order (location), general to specific, or climactic order (least important to most important). For each pattern, select a subject from the ones given, construct a topic sentence, and list three to five supporting details. Then, on your own paper, use the topic sentence and details to write a unified and coherent paragraph of at least four sentences. It may be possible to combine two closely related details in one sentence.

1. CHRONOLOGICAL ORDER: the steps in applying to college; preparing for vacation; painting a room
   Topic Sentence:
   > Details:

2. SPATIAL ORDER: the view from the classroom window; the floor plan of the local video rental store; the layout of a basketball court
   Topic Sentence:
   > Details:

3. GENERAL TO SPECIFIC: the advantages (disadvantages) of working while attending school full time; the mood on New Year's Eve; the reasons _____ is my favorite meal
   Topic Sentence:
   > Details:

4. CLIMACTIC ORDER: why I've chosen my career; how I control anger; how I would raise responsible children
   Topic Sentence:
   > Details:

Using Examples in Paragraphs

Write two paragraphs in which examples are used to support your topic sentence. In the first paragraph, use three to five short examples; in the second, use one extended example. First compose a topic sentence. Next, list the supporting example(s) you will use. After that, write your paragraph, using your own paper.

Select your topics from this list: the risks of walking alone at night; my favorite actor/ actress; the advantages (disadvantages) of playing on a school team; how peer pressure can be hard to resist; professional athletes are overpaid (underpaid); the difficulty of adjusting to a new neighborhood, school, or job.

1. MULTIPLE EXAMPLES

   Topic Sentence: _____

   Examples: a. _____

   b. _____

   c. _____

   d. _____

   e. _____

2. EXTENDED EXAMPLE

   Topic Sentence: _____

   Example: _____

Using Paragraph Development Strategies

Most paragraphs are developed through a combination of several of the strategies discussed in this chapter. Usually one strategy predominates, however. For each development strategy listed below, select a topic from the list; compose a topic sentence; list three to five details, examples, or other pieces of support; and then, using your own paper, write the paragraph.

1. NARRATIVE

   Topics: a time I surprised my friends; a success story; meeting someone special; recovering from a tragedy

   Topic Sentence: _____

   Events: a. _____

          b. _____

          c. _____

          d. _____

          e. _____

2. DESCRIPTION

   Topics: the locker room between classes; a weekend evening at a local dance club; Michael Jackson or Duke Ellington (see photographs on pages 48 and 49); an odd person in my neighborhood

   Topic Sentence: _____

   Details: a. _____

         b. _____

         c. _____

         d. _____

         e. _____

3. PROCESS

   Topics: how to study for a test; how to plan a Halloween party; how to select a pet; how to read a map

   Topic Sentence: _____

   Steps: a. _____

        b. _____

        c. _____

        d. _____

        e. _____

Name _____ Date _____

4. DEFINITION
   Topics: my ideal job; a perfect day; fear; science fiction

   Topic Sentence: _____

   Qualities: a. _____

   b. _____

   c. _____

   d. _____

   e. _____

5. ANALYSIS AND CLASSIFICATION (pick one)
   Topics for Analysis: types of sports shoes; types of cars; types of fear; types of dreams

   Topic Sentence: _____

   Subgroups: a. _____

   b. _____

   c. _____

   d. _____

   e. _____

   Topics for Classification: movies; desserts; baby sitters; bosses

   Topic Sentence: _____

   Individual
   Components: a. _____

   b. _____

   c. _____

   d. _____

   e. _____

AP/Wide World Photos

AP/Wide World Photos

6. COMPARISON AND CONTRAST

Topics: my brother (sister) and I; being a high school senior and a college freshman; team sports and individual competition; Michael Jackson's stage personality and that of another performer

Topic: _____

Points of Comparison
and Contrast: a. _____

b. _____

c. _____

d. _____

e. _____

7. ANALOGY

Topics: a possessive person and a spider in its web; starting a new job (attending a new school) and jumping into a cold pool; a lie and a forest fire; daydreaming and going for a walk

Topic Sentence: _____

Similarities: a. _____

b. _____

c. _____

d. _____

e. _____

8. CAUSE AND EFFECT

Topics: why I chose the college I am now attending; why I dropped an old friend; how a new baby affects a family; the effects that Michael Jackson or Duke Ellington has had on popular music

Topic Sentence: _____

Causes
or Effects: a. _____

b. _____

c. _____

d. _____

e. _____

Revising Introductions and Conclusions

EXERCISE 4-9

(4g)

Each of these introductions and conclusions is inadequate as part of a 500-word essay. Determine what is wrong with each. Then, using your own paper, revise each paragraph. Some may need to be completely rewritten.

1.
THE EXPLORATION OF THE ANTARCTIC

Introduction: I think the Antarctic is very interesting, so even though I didn't have time to do a lot of research I'm going to tell you what I know about its exploration.

Conclusion: In this paper I have tried to show how brave all these explorers were to face the terrible cold and loneliness of Antarctica. By the way, Antarctica is the *South* Pole.

2.
THE CAUSES OF VOLCANIC ERUPTIONS

Introduction: There are 850 active volcanoes in the world. More than 75 percent of them are located in the "Ring of Fire," an area that goes from the west coasts of North and South America to the east coast of Asia, all the way down to New Zealand. Twenty percent of these volcanoes are in Indonesia. Many are also in Japan, the Aleutian Islands (off Alaska), and Central America. Other big groups of volcanoes are in the Mediterranean Sea and Iceland. In contrast, there are only six volcanoes in Africa and three in Antarctica.

Conclusion: So this is why volcanoes erupt.

3.
SHOULD CAPITAL PUNISHMENT BE RESTORED IN OUR STATE?

Introduction: Yes, I agree with the question. Every year the rate of serious crime in our state rises. Now is the time to get the murderers and rapists off the streets.

Conclusion: In this essay, I have proven beyond any doubt that the death penalty will discourage people from committing violent crimes, that it will save the taxpayers a lot of money, and that hardly anybody will be executed by accident.

4.
LET'S NOT LIMIT PRESIDENTS TO TWO TERMS

Introduction: The twenty-second amendment to the Constitution, limiting presidents to two elected terms, should be repealed.

Conclusion: Fourth, the twenty-second amendment was ratified in 1951 as a Republican reaction to the earlier four-term election of Democrat Franklin Roosevelt. Now the strategy has backfired; although the American people may be very happy with a president, they cannot keep him in office long enough to successfully put all his policies to work.

5.

Introduction: In this essay I will discuss why it is important for Americans to speak and read more than one language. Knowing a second language helps people to explore another culture, keeps them in touch with their roots, and can make traveling abroad much easier and more interesting. Therefore, all Americans should learn a second language.

Conclusion: There are, then, three good reasons to learn a second language. First, knowing a language such as French or German enables a person to read some of the world's most important literature, philosophy, and science. Second, learning the language of our ancestors may help us to learn about our families and ourselves and may help us to preserve vanishing ways. Third, travel in Europe, Asia, or South America is easier when the traveler is able to speak to the inhabitants in their own language. Finally, once we have struggled to learn a new language we can understand how newcomers struggle to learn English. This can make us more patient and understanding, leading to better relations with our neighbors and co-workers.

Writing Introductions and Conclusions

EXERCISE **4-10**

(4g)

Write introductory and concluding paragraphs for three of the topics listed here. Refer to the chapter for suggested strategies. Before writing, list your thesis statement and strategies on the lines below. Use a different strategy for each paragraph. Use your own paper.

TOPICS: selecting a sensible diet for life; violence in the stands at sports events; applying for a student loan; dealing with difficult neighbors; noise pollution; motorcycles; old movies; talking to your doctor; teenage marriage; computers in the classroom; science fiction monsters

ESSAY 1

Thesis Statement: _____

Strategy for Introduction: _____

Strategy for Conclusion: _____

ESSAY 2

Thesis Statement: _____

Strategy for Introduction: _____

Strategy for Conclusion: _____

ESSAY 3

Thesis Statement: _____

Strategy for Introduction: _____

Strategy for Conclusion:_____

5 and 6 | *Critical Thinking, Reading, and Writing; Writing Argument*

5: CRITICAL THINKING, READING, AND WRITING

5a Understanding critical thinking

Although thinking comes naturally to you, awareness of *how* you think does not. Thinking about thinking is the key to thinking critically.

The word **critically** here has a neutral meaning. It does not mean taking a negative view or finding fault. Critical thinking is an attitude. If you face life with curiosity, you are a critical thinker. If you do not believe everything you read or hear, you are a critical thinker. If you enjoy contemplating the puzzle of conflicting theories and facts, you are a critical thinker.

5b Engaging in critical thinking

Critical thinking is a process that evolves from becoming fully aware of something, to reflecting on it, to reacting to it. The general process of critical thinking used in academic settings is described in the following chart.

STEPS IN THE CRITICAL THINKING PROCESS

1. **Analyze:** Consider the whole and then break it into its component parts so that you can examine them separately.
2. **Summarize:** Extract and restate the material's main message or central point at the literal level.
3. **Interpret:** Make inferences about unstated assumptions implied by the material. Evaluate it for underlying currents.
4. **Synthesize:** Pull together what you have summarized, analyzed, and interpreted to connect it to what you know or are currently learning.
5. **Assess critically:** Judge the quality of the material on its own and as compared with related material.

5c Understanding the reading process

Purposes for reading vary. In college, most reading involves reading to learn new information, to appreciate literary works, or to review notes on classes or assignments. These types of reading involve rereading.

Your purpose in reading determines the speed at which you can expect to read. When you are hunting for a particular fact, you can skim the material until you come to what you want. When you read material about a subject you know well, you can move somewhat rapidly through most of it, slowing down when you come to new material. When you are unfamiliar with the subject, your brain needs time to absorb the new material, so you have to read slowly.

5d Reading critically

The full meaning of a passage develops on three levels: the literal, the inferential, and the evaluative. Most people stop reading at the literal level, but unless you move on to the next two steps you will not fully understand what you read.

1. Reading for **literal** meaning means understanding what is said. The literal level involves (a) the key facts, the central points in an argument, or the major details of plot and character, and (b) the minor details that fill out the picture.
2. Reading to make **inferences** means understanding what is implied (that is indicated indirectly) but not stated. Often you have to infer information, or background, or the author's purpose.
3. **Evaluative** reading, necessary for critical thinking, occurs after you know an author's literal meaning and you have drawn as many inferences as possible from the material.

A major evaluative reading skill is **differentiating fact from opinion**. The difference between fact and opinion is sometimes quite obvious, but at other times telling fact from opinion can be tricky. Keep in mind that facts (numbers, statistics, dates, quotations) can be proven. Opinions, in contrast, reflect individual biases. Consider these examples:

OPINIONS	FACTS
California is too crowded.	California has the largest population of any U.S. state—over 29 million people.
Living in Alaska must be lonely.	Alaska has a population density of only .96 persons per square mile.

| New Jersey has the best scenery on the East Coast. | New Jersey's official nickname is the Garden State. |

5e Engaging in critical reading

To read critically is to think about what you are reading while you are reading it. You can use some specific approaches such as reading systematically and reading actively and closely.

To **read systematically** is to use a structured plan for delving into the material. First preview the material. Then read it carefully, seeking full meaning at all levels. Finally, review what you have read.

To **read actively and closely** is to annotate as you read. Annotation means writing notes in a book's margin or in a notebook, underlining or highlighting key passages, or using other codes that alert you to special material. Experiment to find what works best for you.

5f Distinguishing between summary and synthesis

A crucial distinction in critical thinking, critical reading, and writing resides in the differences between summary and synthesis. In the process of critical thinking, summary comes before synthesis.

To **summarize** is to condense the main message or central point of a passage. It is the gist of what the author is saying.

To **synthesize** is to connect what you are reading to what you already know or are currently learning. You cannot synthesize effectively until you have first summarized the material.

5g Writing a critical response

A critical response essay has two missions: to summarize what a source says and then to discuss the main idea by giving your thoughts and opinions. A well-written critical response accomplishes these two missions with grace and style.

5h Assessing evidence critically

The most important part of reasoning is **evidence**—facts, statistics, examples, and expert opinion.

GUIDELINES FOR USING EVIDENCE EFFECTIVELY

1. **Evidence should be plentiful.** In general, the more evidence, the better. A survey that draws upon 100 people is more likely to be reliable than a survey involving only ten.
2. **Evidence should be representative.** Do not trust a statement if it is based on only some members of the group being discussed; it must be based on a truly *representative*, or typical, sample of the group.
3. **Evidence should be relevant.** Be sure the evidence you present truly supports your point and is not simply an interesting but irrelevant fact. For example, declining enrollment at a college *might* indicate poor teaching—but it also might indicate a general decline in the student population of the area, a reduction in available financial aid, higher admissions standards, or any number of other factors.
4. **Evidence should be accurate.** Evidence must come from reliable sources.
5. **Evidence should be qualified.** Avoid words such as *all, certainly, always,* or *never.* Conclusions are more reasonable if they are qualified with words such as *some, many, a few, probably, possibly, may, usually,* and *often.*

5i Assessing cause and effect critically

Cause and effect is a type of thinking that seeks the relationship between two or more pieces of evidence. You may seek either to understand the effects of a known cause or to determine the cause or causes of a known effect.

GUIDELINES FOR EVALUATING CAUSE AND EFFECT

1. **Clear relationship.** Causes and effects normally occur in chronological order: *First* a door slams; *then* a pie that is cooling on a shelf falls. However, a cause-and-effect relationship must be linked by more than chronological sequence. The fact that B happened after A does not prove that it was caused by A.
2. **A pattern of repetition.** To establish the relationship of A to B, there must be proof that every time A was present, B occurred.
3. **No oversimplification.** The basic pattern of cause and effect—single cause, single effect—rarely gives the full picture. Most complex social or political problems have *multiple causes*, not a single cause and a single effect.

```
GUIDELINES FOR EVALUATING CAUSE AND EFFECT (continued)

     cause 1
     cause 2  ──────────────→   produce   ──────────────→   effect B
     cause 3

Similarly, one cause can produce multiple effects:

                                                             effect 1
     cause A  ──────────────→   produces  ──────────────→   effect 2
                                                             effect 3
```

5j Assessing reasoning processes critically

Induction and **deduction** are reasoning processes. They are natural thought patterns that people use every day to think through ideas and to make decisions.

Induction is the process of arriving at general principles from particular facts or instances. Suppose you go to the supermarket and when you get home you notice that the eggs are smashed because the packer put a melon on top of them. The next week you come home from the market after the same person has bagged your groceries to find that a package of spaghetti has split open. The week after that the same packer puts a container of yogurt in upside down. It opens and you have to wash your groceries before you can put them away. You decide never to go on that person's line again because you want your groceries packed properly. You have arrived at this conclusion by means of induction.

Once you have become convinced that a certain grocery packer at your supermarket does a sloppy job, you will probably stay off that person's line—even if it is the shortest one. Your reasoning might go like this:

A. That grocery packer smashes groceries.
B. I can choose to get on that person's line or not.
C. If I choose to get on that person's line, my groceries will get smashed.

You reached this decision by means of deduction. Deduction moves from two or more general principles (A and B above) to a conclusion (C) about a specific instance.

A COMPARISON OF INDUCTIVE AND DEDUCTIVE REASONING		
	INDUCTION	DEDUCTION
Where the argument begins	with specific evidence	with a general claim
Type of conclusion	a general claim	a specific statement
Main use	to discover something new	to apply what is known

5k Recognizing and avoiding fallacies

Logical fallacies are flaws in reasoning that lead to illogical statements. They tend to occur most often when ideas are being argued. Mots logical fallacies masquerade as reasonable statements, but they are in fact attempts to manipulate readers. Logical fallacies are known by labels that indicate how thinking has gone wrong during the reasoning process. Some examples of logical fallacies are *hasty generalization, false analogy, begging the question, irrelevant argument, false cause, self-contradiction, red herring, argument to the person, guilt by association, bandwagon, irrelevant authority, card-stacking, the either-or fallacy, appeal to ignorance,* and *ambiguity*.

6: WRITING ARGUMENT

When **writing argument** for your college courses, you seek to convince a reader to agree with you concerning a topic open to debate. A written argument states and supports one position about the debatable topic. Support for that position depends on evidence, reasons, and examples chosen for their direct relation to the point being argued.

Written argument differs from everyday, informal arguing. Informal arguing often originates in anger and might involve bursts of temper or unpleasant emotional confrontations. An effective written argument, in contrast, sets forth its position calmly, respectfully, and logically.

6a Choosing a topic for a written argument

When you choose a topic for written argument, be sure that it is **open to debate**. Be careful not to confuse facts with matters of debate. A fact is the name of a college course or how many credits are required in a college curriculum. An essay becomes an argument when it takes a position concerning the fact or other pieces of information. For example, some people might think that college students should be free to choose whatever courses they want, while other people might think that certain courses should be required of all students.

A written argument could take one of these opposing positions and defend it. If you cannot decide what position to agree with because all sides of an issue have merit, do not get blocked. Instead, concentrate on the merits of one position, and present that position as effectively as you can.

6b Developing an assertion and a thesis statement for a written argument

An **assertion** is a statement that reflects a position about a debatable topic that can be supported by evidence, reasons, and examples (see 4c). The assertion acts as a preliminary form of your thesis statement. Although the wording of the assertion often does not find its way into the essay itself, the assertion serves as a focus for your thinking and your writing.

TOPIC	Buying on credit
ASSERTION	Buying on credit can be helpful.
ASSERTION	Buying on credit can be dangerous.

Next, based on your assertion, you compose a **thesis statement** (see 2n) to use in the essay. It states the *exact* position that you present and support in the essay.

THESIS STATEMENT	Buying on credit enables people to make necessary purchases without straining their budgets.
THESIS STATEMENT	Buying on credit causes people to go dangerously into debt.

To stimulate your thinking about the topic and your assertion about the topic, use the techniques for gathering ideas explained in 2d–k. Jot down your ideas as they develop. Many writers of arguments make a list of the points that come to mind. Use two columns to visually represent two contrasting points of view. Head the columns with labels that emphasize contrast: for example, *agree* and *disagree* or *for* and *against*.

6c Considering the audience for written argument

When a topic is emotionally charged, chances are high that any position being argued will elicit either strong agreement or strong disagreement in the reader. For example, topics such as abortion, capital punishment, and gun control arouse very strong emotions in many people.

The degree to which a reader might be friendly or hostile can influence what strategies you use to try to convince that reader. For example, when you anticipate that many readers will not agree with you, consider discussing common ground before presenting your position. Common ground in a debate over capital punishment might be that both sides agree that crime is a growing problem. Once both sides agree about the problem, there might be more tolerance for differences of opinion concerning whether capital punishment is a deterrent to crime.

6d Using the classical pattern for written argument

No one structure fits all written argument. However, for college courses, most written arguments include certain elements.

ELEMENTS IN THE CLASSICAL PATTERN FOR WRITTEN ARGUMENT

1. **Introductory paragraph**: Sets the context for the position that is argued in the essay. (See 4g.)

2. **Thesis statement**: States the position being argued. In a short essay, it often appears at the end of the introductory paragraph. (See 2n.)

3. **Background information**: Gives the reader basic information needed for understanding the position being argued. This information can be part of the introductory paragraph or can appear in its own paragraph.

4. **Reasons or evidence**: Supports the position being argued. This material is the heart of the essay. The discussion of each reason or type of evidence usually consists of a general statement backed up with specific details or specific examples. Depending on the length of the essay, one or two paragraphs are devoted to each reason or type of evidence. The best order for presenting support depends on the impact you want to achieve. (See 4c.)

5. **Anticipation of opposing positions**: Mentions positions in opposition to the one being argued and responds to them briefly. This counter-argument can appear in its own paragraph, just before the conclusion or immediately after the introduction.

6. **Concluding paragraph**: Brings the essay to a logical end. It does not cut off the reader abruptly. (See 4g.)

6e Using the Toulmin model for argument

The Toulmin model for argument has recently gained popularity among teachers and students because it clarifies the major elements in an effective argument.

The terms used in the Toulmin model may seem unfamiliar, but the concepts are ones you have encountered before.

ELEMENTS IN THE TOULMIN MODEL OF ARGUMENT

Toulmin's Term	More familiar term
the claim	the main point
the support	data or other evidence
the warrant	underlying assumptions

6f Defining terms in written argument

When you **define terms**, you clarify the meaning of key words. Key words are terms that are central to your message. Key words that are **open to interpretation** should be replaced with other, more specific words.

No	Buying on credit is **bad.**
YES	Buying on credit **encourages people to buy things they do not need.**
YES	Buying on credit **makes it hard to see how much one is actually spending.**

Some key words might **vary with the context** of a discussion and should be explained. Abstract words such as *love, freedom*, and *democracy* have to be explained because they have different meanings in different situations.

Many students wonder whether they should use actual dictionary definitions in an essay. Looking up words in the dictionary to understand precise meanings is a very important activity for writers. Quoting a dictionary definition, however, is rarely wise. Using an **extended definition** is usually more effective. See the extended definition of an ice cream cone in 4f.

6g Reasoning effectively in written argument

The basis for a debatable position is often personal opinion or belief, and in such cases it is unrealistic to expect to change someone's mind with one written argument. Nevertheless, you still have an important goal: to convince your reader that your point of view has value. You can achieve this by combining three strategies:

1. **Be logical**: use solid evidence; analyze cause and effect carefully; and distinguish between fact and opinion.
2. **Enlist the emotions of the reader**: appeal to the values and beliefs of the reader, usually by arousing the "better self" of the reader.

3. **Establish credibility**: show that you can be relied upon as a knowledge-able person with good sense by being accurate and not distorting facts.

6h Establishing a reasonable tone in written argument

To achieve a reasonable tone, **choose your words carefully**. Avoid exaggerations and artificial language (see 21e). No matter how strongly you disagree with opposing arguments, never insult the other side. Name-calling is impolite, shows poor self-control, and demonstrates poor judgment.

Distinguishing Fact from Opinion

Identify each passage as *fact* or *opinion. Be prepared to explain your answers.*

Examples Once people had little choice in what they ate.   *fact*

They would have preferred our food.   *opinion*

A.   1. The diet of prehistoric people was confined to what they could gather or catch. _____

    2. Control of fire enabled people to cook their food. _____

    3. Cooking undoubtedly improved the taste. _____

    4. Gradually people learned to plant seeds and tame animals. _____

    5. Planting and herding allowed people to settle in one place. _____

    6. Some people must have longed for their former nomadic life. _____

    7. Early civilizations sprang up in areas that could produce bountiful crops. _____

    8. The fact that some could produce more than they needed freed others for nonagricultural chores. _____

    9. Farming cannot have been very difficult if one person could produce so much food. _____

  10. With such abundance I imagine many became wasteful. _____

  11. People gradually learned to preserve food by curing, drying, and pickling. _____

  12. My favorite pickle is the sweet gherkin. _____

  13. Bacon is a form of cured meat still popular today. _____

  14. Dried fruit does not taste as good as fresh fruit. _____

  15. Some dehydration machines on today's market are great. _____

B.   1. In 1781 Nicolas Appert developed the first canning method. _____

    2. He sealed cooked food in glass bottles. _____

    3. Today's stores are filled with cans of every kind of food. _____

4. The canning industry should give Appert more credit than it does. . _____

5. Refrigeration, one of the oldest methods of food preservation, is increasingly popular. _____

6. Cave dwellers kept food in cool recesses. _____

7. Ancient Romans imported ice to cool food. _____

8. Most of it probably melted before it got to Rome. _____

9. In the United States ice used to be delivered door to door. _____

10. Today electricity has made refrigerators and freezers common. _____

11. In fact, living without a refrigerator would be impossible. _____

12. Refrigeration enables many grocery stores to offer fruits and vegetables grown far away. _____

13. Grocery freezer sections are kept too cold. _____

14. The different methods of food preservation have added variety to the contemporary diet. _____

7 | *Parts of Speech and Structures of the Sentence*

PARTS OF SPEECH

Knowing grammar helps you understand how language works. Grammar describes the forms and structures of words. In this way, it offers an explanation of how language operates and how words make meaning to deliver their messages. Grammar also sets down the standards accepted by people who write and speak for educated audiences.

If you know the parts of speech, you have a basic vocabulary for identifying words, their various forms, and the sentence structures they build. The first part of this chapter explains each part of speech to help you identify words and their functions. Being able to do this is important because sometimes the same word can function as more than one part of speech. To identify a word's part of speech, you have to see how the word functions in a sentence.

We drew a **circle** on the ground. [*Circle* is a noun.]

Sometimes planes **circle** the airport before landing. [*Circle* is a verb.]

Running is good exercise. [*Running* is a noun.]

Running shoes can be very expensive. [*Running* is an adjective.]

7a Recognizing nouns

A **noun** names a person, place, thing, or idea.

Most nouns change form to show number: *week, ox* (singular); *weeks, oxen* (plural) (see 22c). Nouns also change form for the possessive case: *the **mayor's** decision* (see 27a). Nouns function as subjects (7k), objects (7l), and complements (7m): ***Marie** saw a **fly** in the **soup*** (subject, direct object, object of preposition); ***Marie** is a **vegetarian*** (subject, subject complement).

NOUNS		
TYPE	**FUNCTION**	**EXAMPLE**
Proper	Names specific people, places, or things (first letter is always capitalized)	**John Lennon** **Paris** **Buick**
Common	Names general groups, places, people, things, or activities	**singer** **city** **car** **talking**
Concrete	Names things that can be seen, touched, heard, smelled, tasted	**landscape** **pizza** **thunder**
Abstract	Names things *not* knowable through the five senses	**freedom** **shyness**
Collective	Names groups	**family** **team** **committee**
Noncount or Mass	Names "uncountable" things	**water** **time**
Count	Names countable items	**lake** **minutes**

Articles often appear with nouns. The articles are *a, an*, and *the*, and they signal whether a noun is meant generally or specifically in a particular context.

Give me **a** pen. [General: any pen will do.]
Give me **the** pen on the desk. [Specific: only one pen will do.]

7b Recognizing pronouns

A **pronoun** takes the place of a noun.

Peter is an engineer. [noun]
He is an engineer. [pronoun]

The word (or words) a pronoun replaces is called its **antecedent**.

Some pronouns change form to show **number**: *I, she, yourself* (singular); *we, they, themselves* (plural). Many pronouns change form to show **case**: *I, who* (subjective); *me, whom* (objective); *my, mine, whose* (possessive) (see Chapter 9).

PRONOUNS

Type	Function	Example
Personal *I, you, they, we, her, its, our,* and others	Refers to people or things	**I** saw **her** take **your** books to **them**
Relative *who, which, that, what, whomever,* and others	Introduces certain noun clauses and adjective clauses	**Whoever** took the book **that** I left must return it.
Interrogative *who, whose, what, which,* and others	Introduces a question	**Who** called?
Demonstrative *this, these, that, those*	Points out the antecedent	Is **this** a mistake?
Reflexive; Intensive *myself, yourself, herself, themselves,* and all *-self* or *-selves* words	Reflects back to the antecedent; intensifies the antecedent	They claim to support **themselves**. **I myself** doubt it.
Reciprocal *each other, one another*	Refers to individual parts of a plural antecedent	We respect **each other.**
Indefinite *all, anyone, each*	Refers to nonspecific persons or things	**Everyone** is welcome here.

7c Recognizing verbs

A **verb** expresses an action, an occurrence, or a state of being.

I **leap**. [action]
Claws **grab**. [action]
The sky **becomes** cloudy. [occurrence]
He **seems** sad. [state of being]

A **linking verb** connects a subject with one or more words—called a **subject complement**—that rename it or describe it.

Eleanor Roosevelt **was** First Lady. [*Eleanor Roosevelt* = subject, *was* = linking verb, *First Lady* = subject complement]

Eleanor Roosevelt **was** popular. [*Eleanor Roosevelt* = subject, *was* = linking verb, *popular* = subject complement]

<table>

VERBS

TYPE	FUNCTION	EXAMPLE
Main *ask, begin, choose, dangle, eat, follow, go, hear, investigate,* and thousands more	Delivers verb meaning	I **drove** yesterday.
Linking *be, appear, become, look, seem,* and others	Acts as main verb but delivers meaning by linking a subject (7k) to a complement (7m)	You **seem** angry.
Auxiliary *can, could, may, might, must, should, would,* and others	Combines with main verb to make a verb phrase (7n) that delivers information about tense (8g–h), mood (8l), and voice (8n)	If I **had** driven last week, you **would be** driving now.

</table>

The most common linking verb is *be* (8e). Verbs describing the workings of the senses sometimes function as linking verbs: *feel, smell, taste, sound, look,* and so on. Other linking verbs include *appear, seem, become, remain,* and *grow.*

Auxiliary verbs, also known as **helping verbs,** are forms of *be, do, have,* and several other verbs that combine with main verbs to make verb phrases.

This season many new television series **have imitated** last year's hit shows. [*have* = auxiliary, *imitated* = main verb, *have imitated* = verb phrase]

Programs **are becoming** more and more alike. [*are* = auxiliary, *becoming* = main verb, *are becoming* = verb phrase]

Soon we **may** not **be able to tell** the programs apart. [*may be able* = auxiliary verb, *to tell* = main verb, *may be able to tell* = verb phrase]

7d Recognizing verbals

Verbals are made from verb parts but they cannot function as verbs, because they do not change form to show time (tense) changes. They function as nouns, adjectives, or adverbs.

VERBALS		
Type	**Function**	**Example**
Infinitive *to* + simple form of verb	1. Noun: names an action, state, or condition 2. Adjective or adverb: describes or modifies	**To eat** now is inconvenient. Still, we have far **to go**.
Past participle *-ed* form of regular verb	Adjective: describes or modifies	**Boiled, filtered** water is usually safe to drink.
Present participle *-ing* form of verb	1. Adjective: describes or modifies 2. Noun; see *gerund,* below	**Running** water may not be safe.
Gerund *-ing* form of verb	1. Adjective: describes or modifies 2. Noun: names an action, state, or condition	**Hiking** gear is expensive. **Hiking** is healthy.

7e Recognizing adjectives

An **adjective** modifies—that is, describes—a noun or a pronoun. Adjectives also modify word groups—clauses and phrases—that function as nouns.

He received a **low** grade on the first quiz. [*Low* modifies noun *grade.*]
His second grade was **higher**. [*Higher* modifies noun phrase *his second grade.*]
That he achieved a B average was **important**. [*Important* modifies noun clause *that he achieved a B average.*]

Descriptive adjectives such as *low* and *higher* show levels of "intensity," usually by changing form (*low, lower, lowest*). For more information about these changes, see Chapter 12.

Determiners are sometimes called **limiting adjectives**. **Articles**, one type of these limiting adjectives, are discussed in 7a. The chart that follows lists types of determiners.

DETERMINERS (LIMITING ADJECTIVES)

Articles
a, an, the

The students made **a** bargain.

Demonstrative
this, these, that, those

Those students rent **that** house.

Indefinite
any, each, other, some, few, and
others

Few films today have complex plots.

Interrogative
what, which, whose

What answer did you give?

Numerical
one, first, two, second, and others

The **fifth** question was tricky.

Possessive
my, your, their, and others

My violin is older than **your** cello.

Relative
what, which, whose, whatever,
whichever, whoever

We don't know **which** road to take.

7f Recognizing adverbs

An **adverb** modifies—that is, describes—a verb, an adjective, another adverb, or a clause.

In winter the ice on ponds may freeze **suddenly**. [*Suddenly* modifies verb *may freeze*.]

It is **very** tempting to go skating. [*Very* modifies adjective *tempting*.]

People die **quite** needlessly when they fall through the ice. [*Quite* modifies adverb *needlessly*.]

Always wait until the ice has thickened enough to hold your weight. [*Always* modifies entire clause.]

Most adverbs are easily recognized because they are formed by adding *-ly* to adjectives (*wisely, quickly, devotedly*). Yet some adjectives also end in *-ly* (*motherly, chilly*). Also, many adverbs do not end in *-ly* (*very, always, not, yesterday, well*). See Chapter 12 for an explanation of how confusion between adverbs and adjectives can be avoided.

Conjunctive adverbs are a group of adverbs that function (1) to modify the sentences to which they are attached, and (2) to help create logical connections in meaning between independent clauses.

CONJUNCTIVE ADVERBS (WORDS OF TRANSITION)

Function	Examples
Indicate addition	**also, furthermore, moreover**
Indicate contrast	**however, still, nonetheless, nevertheless, conversely**
Indicate comparison·	**similarly**
Indicate summary or result	**therefore, thus, consequently**
Indicate time	**next, then, meanwhile, finally**
Indicate emphasis	**indeed, certainly**

Construction has slowed traffic on the interstate; **therefore**, people are looking for other routes to work.

People have been complaining for weeks. **Finally**, one more lane has been opened during rush hour.

7g Recognizing prepositions

A **preposition** signals the beginning of a prepositional phrase. It is followed by a noun or pronoun (called the **object of the preposition**), and it indicates the relationship of that noun or pronoun to another word. The object of the preposition is never the subject of the sentence. Here is a complete list of prepositions.

about	despite	over
above	down	past
across	during	regarding
after	except	round
against	excepting	since
along	for	through
among	from	throughout
around	in	till
as	inside	to
at	into	toward
before	like	under
behind	near	underneath
below	next	unlike
beneath	of	until
beside	off	up
between	on	upon
beyond	onto	with
but	out	within
by	outside	without
concerning		

Prepositional expressions are formed by combinations of single-word prepositions.

according to	due to	instead of
along with	except for	in the midst of
apart from	in addition to	on account of
as for	in back of	on top of
as regards	in case of	out of
as to	in front of	up to
because of	in lieu of	with reference to
by means of	in place of	with regard to
by reason of	in regard to	with respect to
by way of	in spite of	with the exception of

A **prepositional phrase** consists of a preposition (or prepositional expression), its object, and any modifying words. A prepositional phrase always starts with a preposition: *above their heads, in the pool, in front of the store.*

7h Recognizing conjunctions

A **conjunction** connects words, phrases, or clauses. **Coordinating conjunctions** join two or more grammatically equivalent structures.

COORDINATING CONJUNCTIONS

and	or	for
but	nor	so
		yet

And, but, yet, or, and *nor* can join structures of any kind: two or more nouns, verbs, adjectives, adverbs, phrases, and all types of clauses.

> Joe is majoring in Computer Technology **and** Engineering. [nouns]
>
> He finds his course interesting **but** demanding. [adjectives]
>
> In his spare time, he works on his car, **and** he helps care for his grandfather. [independent clauses]

For and *so* can connect only independent clauses.

> Joe helps his grandfather, **for** he does not want the man to move to a nursing home.

Correlative conjunctions function in pairs, joining equivalent grammatical constructions.

CORRELATIVE CONJUNCTIONS

both . . . and	neither . . . nor
either . . . or	not only . . . but (also)
whether . . . or	

Both industrialized *and* agricultural nations are developing new strategies to protect the environment.

Subordinating conjunctions begin certain dependent clauses that function as modifiers.

SUBORDINATING CONJUNCTIONS

after	even though	though	where
although	if	unless	wherever
as	once	until	whether
because	since	when	while
before	so that	whenever	

Because of the unpredictability of hurricanes, many lives are lost each year.

People sometimes refuse to evacuate *although* they are warned in plenty of time.

7i Recognizing interjections

An **interjection** is a word or expression used to convey surprise or other strong emotions. An interjection can stand alone, usually punctuated with an exclamation point, or can be part of a sentence, usually set off with commas. Interjections occur only rarely in academic writing.

Oh no!
Darn! I lost my keys.
Well, how much will it cost to fix my car?

STRUCTURES OF THE SENTENCE

7j Defining the sentence

The *sentence* can be defined in several ways. On its most basic level, a sentence starts with a capital letter and finishes with a period, question mark, or exclamation point. Sentences can be classified according to purpose. Most sentences are **declarative**; they make a statement:

Pizza is fattening.

Some sentences are **interrogative**; they ask a question:

How fattening is pizza?

Some sentences are **imperative**; they give a command:

Give me a pizza!

Some sentences are **exclamatory**; they exclaim:

What a large pizza!

Grammatically, a sentence contains at least one **independent clause**, that is, a group of words that can stand alone as an independent unit, in contrast to a **dependent clause**, which cannot stand alone. Sometimes a sentence is described as a "complete thought," but the concept of "complete" is too vague to be useful.

To begin your study of the sentence, consider its basic structure. A sentence consists of two parts: a subject and a predicate.

7k Recognizing subjects and predicates

1 Recognizing subjects

The **simple subject** is the word or group of words that acts, is acted upon, or is described. In the sentence *The saxophonist played*, the simple subject is the one word *saxophonist*. The **complete subject** is the simple subject and all the words related to it.

THE SENTENCE

Complete Subject	+	Complete Predicate
The talented saxophonist		played.

↑
SIMPLE
SUBJECT

The **pianist** sang. [simple subject]
The new pianist sang. [complete subject]

A subject can be **compound**, that is, can consist of two or more nouns or pronouns and their modifiers.

THE SENTENCE

Complete Subject	+	Complete Predicate
The talented saxophonist and the trumpeter		played.

↖ ↗
COMPOUND SUBJECT

The audience and **the club manager** applauded. [compound subject]

2 Recognizing predicates

The **predicate** is the part of the sentence that says what the subject is doing or experiencing, or what is being done to the subject. The predicate usually comes after its subject, and it always contains a verb. The **simple predicate** contains only the verb. The **complete predicate** is the simple predicate and all the words related to it.

THE SENTENCE		
Complete Subject	+	**Complete Predicate**
The talented saxophonist		played passionately. ↑ SIMPLE PREDICATE

The pianist **sang**. [simple predicate]

The pianist **sang beautifully**. [complete predicate]

A predicate can be **compound**, that is, consisting of two or more verbs.

THE SENTENCE		
Complete Subject	+	**Complete Predicate**
The talented saxophonist		strutted and played. ↖ ↗ COMPOUND PREDICATE

The pianist **sang** and **swayed**. [compound predicate]

7l Recognizing direct and indirect objects

1 Recognizing direct objects

A **direct object** occurs in the predicate of a sentence. It receives the action of a transitive verb (8f), completing its meaning.

```
THE SENTENCE

Complete Subject                    +                    Complete Predicate
─────────────                                            ──────────────────

Their agent                                              negotiated a contract.
                                                              ↑           ↑
                                                            VERB       DIRECT
                                                                       OBJECT
```

Their agent called **the music critics**. [direct object]

To find the direct object, make up a *whom?* or *what?* question about the verb. (The agent negotiated what? *A contract.* The agent called whom? *The music critics.*) A direct object may be compound:

They played **their hit** and **a new song**.

2 **Recognizing indirect objects**

An **indirect object** occurs in the predicate of a sentence. It answers a *to whom?, for whom?, to what?*, or *for what?* question about a verb.

```
THE SENTENCE

Complete Subject                    +                    Complete Predicate
─────────────                                            ──────────────────

Their agent                        got                   the group    a contract.
                                    ↑                        ↑            ↑
                                   VERB                   INDIRECT      DIRECT
                                                          OBJECT        OBJECT
```

He tried to get **them** an album deal. [indirect object]

7m Recognizing complements, modifiers, and appositives

1 **Recognizing complements**

A **complement** occurs in the predicate of a sentence. It renames or describes the subject or object. A **subject complement** is a noun or adjective that follows a linking verb, such as *was* or *seems*, and renames or describes the subject.

THE SENTENCE

Complete Subject	+	Complete Predicate

The club manager   was   the owner.
                                ↑   ↑

                              LINKING   SUBJECT
                               VERB   COMPLEMENT

The owner was **a jazz lover**. [noun as subject complement]

The owner was **generous**. [adjective as subject complement]

An **object complement** is a noun or adjective that immediately follows the direct object and either renames or describes it.

THE SENTENCE

Complete Subject	+	Complete Predicate

The owner   called   himself   Artie.
                          ↑   ↑   ↑

                         VERB   DIRECT   OBJECT
                                   OBJECT   COMPLEMENT

The group considered itself **lucky**. [adjective as object complement]

Artie called them **exceptional**. [adjective as object complement]

He began to consider himself **a patron of the arts**. [noun phrase as object complement]

---

2   Recognizing modifiers

Modifiers are words or groups of words that describe other words. There are two basic kinds of modifiers: adjectives and adverbs.

Adjectives modify only nouns or words acting as nouns, such as pronouns, noun phrases, or noun clauses. They may appear in the subject or the predicate of a sentence.

THE SENTENCE

Complete Subject	+	Complete Predicate

The talented saxophonist   played a mellow tune.
↑   ↑
ADJECTIVE   ADJECTIVE

Adverbs modify verbs, adjectives, other adverbs, or independent clauses. They may appear in the subject or the predicate of a sentence.

THE SENTENCE

Complete Subject	+	Complete Predicate

The saxophonist   played very passionately.
                                        ↖   ↗
                                          ADVERBS

The audience responded **warmly**. [Adverb *warmly* modifies verb *responded*.]

They swayed **quite** excitedly in their seats. [Adverb *quite* modifies adverb *excitedly*.]

Enthusiastically, they demanded more. [Adverb *enthusiastically* modifies independent clause.]

3 | Recognizing appositives

An **appositive** is a word or group of words that renames the word or group of words preceding it. Generally, appositives are nouns used to rename other nouns, although adjectives and verbs are also sometimes renamed by appositives.

THE SENTENCE

Complete Subject	+	Complete Predicate

The group, Diamond in the Rough,   looked like a hit.
                 ↗
             APPOSITIVE

Their manager, **Jon Franklin**, was ready to take the next step. [*Jon Franklin* renames the noun *manager*.]

He picked his targets: **the record companies and the television shows**. [*The record companies and the television shows* renames the noun *targets*.]

7n Recognizing phrases

A **phrase** is a group of words that lacks a subject (7k–1) or a predicate (7k–2). Phrases function as parts of speech. They cannot stand alone as sentences.

A **noun phrase** functions as a noun in a sentence.

Some political terms have unusual histories.

The seating plan in the French congress during their Revolution gives us our names for political radicals, conservatives, and moderates.

A **verb phrase** functions as a verb in a sentence.

The members **were seated** in a semicircular room. The most radical members **were located** to the left of the chairperson's platform, the more conservative to the right.

A **prepositional phrase** functions as an adjective or adverb. It is formed by a preposition (7g) followed by a noun or pronoun.

This arrangement enabled members **with similar views** to talk **during meetings**. [*with similar views* modifies *members*; *during meetings* modifies *to talk*.]

An **absolute phrase**, which consists of a participle (7d, 8b) preceded by a subject, modifies the entire sentence to which it is attached. An absolute phrase cannot stand alone as a sentence because it lacks a true verb.

The moderates being in the center, physical fights were avoided. [*Being* is the present participle of *to be; the moderates* acts as a subject.]

Verbal phrases use forms of verbs that do not express time (7d), so they cannot function as verbs in sentences. Instead, they function as nouns or modifiers. Verbal phrases are formed with infinitives, past participles, or present participles.

Infinitive phrases contain a verb's simple form preceded usually, but not always, by the word *to*. Infinitive phrases function as nouns, adjectives, or adverbs.

Politicians love **to debate every issue**. [infinitive phrase = noun as object of verb *love*]

Physically separating politicians works **to prevent debates from becoming fist fights**. [infinitive phrase = adverb modifying verb *works*]

Gerund phrases use the present participle—a verb's *-ing* form—as nouns.

Understanding the origin of certain terms helps us recognize the repetition of historical patterns. [gerund phrase = noun functioning as sentence subject]

(In the preceding example, notice *recognize the repetition of historical patterns* too. It is an infinitive phrase, but one that does not use *to*.)

Participial phrases function as adjectives. They are formed from a verb's present participle—its *-ing* form—or from its past participle—the *-ed* form of a regular verb.

> **Imitating the French plan**, we now call radicals leftists, conservatives right-wingers, and moderates centrists. [present participle phrase = adjective modifying *we*]

> These labels, **copied by many governments**, continue long after the revolution that gave them birth. [past participle phrase = adjective modifying *labels*]

Telling the difference between a gerund phrase and a present participle phrase can be tricky because both contain a verb form that ends in *-ing*. Remember that a gerund phrase functions *only* as a noun, and a participial phrase functions *only* as an adjective.

> **Seeing liver on the dinner menu**, I decided to fast. [participial phrase as adjective describing *I*]

> **Seeing liver on the dinner menu** made me want to fast. [gerund phrase as subject of sentence]

7o Recognizing clauses

A **clause** is a group of words that contains a subject and a predicate (7k–1, k–2). Clauses are divided into two categories: **independent clauses** (also known as **main clauses**) and **dependent clauses** (including **subordinate clauses** and **relative clauses**).

1 Recognizing independent clauses

An **independent clause** contains a subject and a predicate. It can stand alone as a sentence. However, it cannot begin with a subordinating conjunction (7h) or a relative pronoun (7b) because those words make a clause dependent (7o–2).

THE SENTENCE		
Complete Subject	**+**	**Complete Predicate**
The saxophonist		played.

2   Recognizing dependent clauses

A **dependent clause** contains a subject and a predicate and usually starts with a word that makes the clause unable to stand alone as a sentence. A dependent clause must be joined to an independent clause.

Some dependent clauses start with **subordinating conjunctions** such as *although, because, when, until.* A subordinating conjunction indicates a relationship between the meaning in the dependent clause and the meaning in the independent clause. For a chart listing these relationships, see 17f.

THE SENTENCE

Dependent (Adverb) Clause	+	Independent Clause

When **the applause** stopped,   **the saxophonist** played.

| SUBORDINATING CONJUNCTION | COMPLETE SUBJECT | COMPLETE PREDICATE | | COMPLETE SUBJECT | COMPLETE PREDICATE |

Because clauses that start with subordinating conjunctions function as adverbs, they are called **adverb clauses** (or sometimes **subordinate clauses**).

They modify verbs, adjectives, other adverbs, and entire independent clauses. Adverb clauses may appear in different parts of sentences, but they always begin with a subordinating conjunction. They usually answer some question about the independent clause: *how? why? when?* or *under what conditions?*

Many Americans wait to travel to Europe **until they can get low air fares**.

If a family has relatives in another country, an international vacation can be relatively inexpensive.

The number of Americans visiting China has grown rapidly **since full diplomatic relations were established in 1979**.

♣ PUNCTUATION ALERT: When an adverb clause comes before an independent clause, separate the clauses with a comma. ♣

Since full diplomatic relations were established in 1979, the number of Americans visiting China has grown rapidly.

Other dependent clauses act as adjectives. These **adjective clauses** (also called **relative clauses**) start with relative pronouns such as *who, which,* and *that* or relative adverbs such as *when* or *where.* Adjective clauses modify nouns, pronouns, and groups of words functioning as nouns.

<table>
<tr><td colspan="3" align="center">THE SENTENCE</td></tr>
<tr><td>First Part of
Independent Clause</td><td>Dependent (Adjective)
Clause</td><td>Second Part of
Independent Clause</td></tr>
<tr><td>The talented saxophonist
↑
COMPLETE SUBJECT</td><td>who led the band
↑
RELATIVE PRONOUN</td><td>signed autographs.
↑
COMPLETE PREDICATE</td></tr>
</table>

The word starting an adjective clause refers to something specific—an antecedent—in the independent clause.

The concert hall, **which held 12,000 people**, was sold out in one day.
The tickets **that I bought** were the last ones in the balcony.

See 10f for a discussion of when to use *who, which*, or *that.* See 24e for a discussion of when to use commas with relative clauses.

Noun clauses function as subjects, objects, or complements. Noun clauses begin with many of the same words as adjective clauses: *that, who, which,* (in all their forms), as well as *when, where, whether, why,* or *how.* Noun clauses do not modify. They replace a noun or pronoun with a clause.

It depends on your generosity. [pronoun as subject]

Whether I can buy the camera depends on your generosity. [noun clause as subject]

Whoever wins the contest will appear in publicity photos. [noun clause as subject]

Because they start with similar words, it is easy to confuse noun clauses and adjective clauses. A noun clause *is* a subject, object, or complement; an adjective clause *modifies* a subject, object, or complement. The word at the start of an adjective clause has a specific antecedent elsewhere in the sentence; the word that starts a noun clause does not.

Elliptical clauses are grammatically incomplete in order to be brief and to the point. Usually the omission is limited to *that, which,* or *whom* in adjective clauses, the subject and verb in adverb clauses, or the second half of a comparison.

Lima is one of the places **[that] I want to visit this summer**. [relative pronoun omitted from adjective clause]

After [I visited] São Paolo, I decided to return to South America. [subject and verb omitted from adverb clause]

An apartment has less storage space **than a house [has]**. [second half of comparison omitted]

7p Recognizing sentence types

Sentences have four basic structures: simple, compound, complex, and compound-complex.

A **simple sentence** is composed of a single independent clause with no dependent clauses. It has one subject and one predicate. However, a simple sentence is not always short. The subject or predicate may be compound, and the sentence may contain modifying words or phrases.

The beagle is one of the world's most popular dogs.

It is a member of the hound family.

The basset and the harrier are also hounds.

A **compound sentence** is composed of two or more independent clauses joined by a coordinating conjunction or a semicolon. There are seven coordinating conjunctions: *and, but, or, nor, for, so*, and *yet*. Compound sentences operate according to principles of coordination. ♣ PUNCTUATION ALERT: Always use a comma before a coordinating conjunction that joins two independent clauses. ♣

The beagle is known for its large, velvety ears, **but** its hazel eyes are even more attractive.

The beagle is believed to be one of the oldest breeds of hounds, **and** it is still used to hunt.

A **complex sentence** is composed of one independent clause and one or more dependent clauses. ♣ PUNCTUATION ALERT: Always use a comma after a dependent clause when it occurs before an independent clause. ♣

Because it has an erect, white-tipped tail, the beagle can be seen and followed even in high grass and bushes.

Although the beagle lost some of its popularity at the beginning of this century, it has become recognized as the ideal pet for anyone **who wants a medium-sized hound.**

A **compound-complex sentence** contains two or more independent clauses and one or more dependent clauses.

The beagle gets along well with other dogs **since it is a pack animal, and** it is patient with boisterous children **who might be too rough to allow near less sturdy pets**.

Although the beagle can be a delight, it is not an easy animal to keep **because it loves to wander off hunting and investigating, so** an owner needs to be alert.

Identifying Nouns

Underline all the nouns. Write them on the lines to the right.

EXAMPLE <u>Hitting</u> a <u>baseball</u> is very difficult.   *hitting*   *baseball*

1. The baseball travels at over ninety-five miles per hour. _____ _____

2. The bat is swung at nearly two-thirds that speed. _____ _____

3. Intense concentration is required. _____ _____

4. A batter has only a tiny fraction of a second to act. _____ _____

5. If he succeeds, the ball will fly off the bat at almost one hundred miles per hour. _____ _____

6. Speed and control are critical. _____ _____

7. Bat speed is important because the faster the bat moves, the more energy it delivers to the ball. _____ _____

8. In the old days, players used heavy bats. _____ _____

9. Babe Ruth's usual bat weighed forty-two ounces. _____ _____

10. Modern batters know that weight is less important than speed. _____ _____

11. Speed can be increased by choking up on the bat. _____ _____

12. They slide their hands closer to the thick end of the bat. _____ _____

13. This makes the bat easier to control. _____ _____

14. Modern bats may be as light as twenty-eight ounces. _____ _____

15. Bats that are too thin have a problem, though. _____ _____

16. They may shatter upon impact with the ball. _____ _____

Identifying Pronouns

Underline all the pronouns. Write them on the lines to the right. If a sentence contains no pronouns, write *none* on the line.

EXAMPLE Since the 1930s, scientists have been trying to get chimpanzees to communicate with <u>them.</u>
_____them_____   _____

1. In the 1940s, one couple raised a chimpanzee named Vickie in their home.
_____   _____

2. They treated her as if she were a human child.
_____   _____

3. They tried to teach Vickie to say English words by shaping her mouth as she made sounds.
_____   _____
_____   _____

4. She learned to say only three words: *Mama*, *Papa*, and *cup*.
_____   _____

5. Even that was amazing because chimpanzees do not have the right vocal structures to produce human sounds.
_____   _____

6. Realizing this, scientists in the 1960s began teaching sign language to their chimpanzees.
_____   _____

7. Chimpanzees have their own ways of communicating among themselves.
_____   _____

8. One chimpanzee was taught over a hundred words in American Sign Language.
_____   _____

9. She also formed her own original sentences.
_____   _____
_____   _____

10. She would even hold simple conversations with anyone who knew sign language.
_____   _____

11. Other chimpanzees were trained to ask for what they wanted by pressing a series of symbols on a computer keyboard.
_____   _____

Name _____   Date _____

12. Chimpanzees are not the only   _____   _____
    animals whose trainers "talk" with
    them.
13. Gorillas, dolphins, and even parrots _____   _____
    supposedly can communicate with
    us.
14. Not everyone believes this is   _____   _____
    possible.
15. Some say members of different   _____   _____
    species can have only limited
    communication with one another.
16. What do you think about animal   _____   _____
    speech?
17. Would you want to have   _____   _____
    conversations with your pets?

Identifying Verbs

EXERCISE 7-3

(7c)

Underline all verbs, including complete verb phrases. Write them on the lines to the right.

EXAMPLE   Some people <u>define</u> karate as   ___*define*___   _____
          the art of breaking hard
          objects with parts of the
          body.

1. Competitors only appear to risk   _____   _____
   injury.
2. Karate began in the seventeenth   _____   _____
   century.
3. Its first form was called *te*, or _____   _____
   "hand."
4. It was used by the people of   _____   _____
   Okinawa.
5. Occupying troops had confiscated   _____   _____
   all of the islanders' weapons.
6. The Okinawans trained themselves   _____   _____
   to use their hands and feet against
   bamboo armor.

7. Karate can seem like magic. _____ _____

8. Actually, it follows the laws of physics. _____ _____

9. Speed, mass, and body rigidity account for karate's success. _____ _____

10. To break a board with your hand, the moment of impact must be very brief. _____ _____

11. If the impact lasts too long, the board will push back. _____ _____

12. A very sharp strike gives the board no time to recoil. _____ _____

13. To break more than four boards, greater mass is needed. _____ _____

14. A foot has a better chance of breaking multiple boards than a hand does. _____ _____

15. The foot has more mass, so it delivers more power. _____ _____

16. A rigid hand is necessary. _____ _____

17. This way less energy is absorbed by the hand, and more is transferred to the wood. _____ _____

18. Fingers do not break boards. _____ _____

19. The fleshy side of the hand does. _____ _____

20. Bones are about sixty times more pliable than a pine board. _____ _____

Identifying Forms of Verbs

Decide if each italicized word or phrase is a verb, an infinitive, a past participle, a present participle, or a gerund. Write your answers on the lines to the right.

EXAMPLE   The thermos bottle *makes* life a little nicer for many of us.

_____*verb*_____

1. The thermos *enables* hot or cold food or drink to keep its temperature.

_____

2. But how *does* it *work*?

_____

3. A thermos *slows* down the exchange of heat between its contents and the outside.

_____

4. *To do* this it has to interfere with three processes: conduction, convection, and radiation.

_____

5. The thermos, *constructed* of metal or plastic, contains a double glass bottle.

_____

6. There *is* a near vacuum between the two layers of glass.

_____

7. A vacuum is *defined* as a space from which most of the air has been taken.

_____

8. Glass is *used* because it is a poor conductor of heat.

_____

9. Cork, another poor conductor, is used for the stopper and pads *to keep* the bottle in place.

_____

10. A poor conductor is any substance that is slow at *passing* heat from molecule to molecule of a solid.

_____

11. *Having* a near vacuum between the glass layers keeps heat from escaping by convection.

_____

12. Convection *is* the movement of heat through gas or liquid.

_____

13. Where there is no gas or liquid, such as between the glass layers, there is no *changing* temperature.

_____

14. In order *to avoid* heat loss by radiation across the vacuum, the glass is treated.

_____

15. The glass is *coated* with an aluminum solution that reflects heat and does not transmit it.

_____

16. Sir James Dewar invented the thermos in 1892, *needing* a way to keep heat away from the liquid gas he used in his experiments.

_____

17. He *called* it a vacuum bottle.

_____

18. *Considering* his invention a gift to the world, Dewar never took out a patent. _____

19. However, his assistant saw the business possibilities and took out a patent in 1903, *leading* to the marketing of the thermos. _____

20. *Taking* iced tea to a picnic would not be possible without Dewar's work. _____

Identifying Adjectives

Underline all adjectives, except the articles *a*, *an*, and *the*. Write them on the lines to the right.

EXAMPLE   Jack Broughton invented the <u>boxing</u> glove.   _____*boxing*_____   _____

1. He also wrote the first set of boxing rules.   _____   _____

2. The first recorded baseball game took place in Hoboken, New Jersey, in 1846.   _____   _____

3. The distance from the pitcher's mound to home plate is sixty feet.   _____   _____

4. The first modern Olympics were held in Athens, Greece, in 1896.   _____   _____

5. The World Series began in 1903.   _____   _____

6. The Boston Red Sox beat the Pittsburgh Pirates.   _____   _____

7. The first black man to become heavyweight boxing champion was Jack Johnson in 1908.   _____   _____

8. The National Football League was founded in 1920 in Canton, Ohio.   _____   _____

9. Athlete Jim Thorpe was its first president.   _____   _____

10. The first woman to swim the English Channel was Gertrude Ederle.   _____   _____

11. She broke the men's record.   _____   _____

12. Televised sporting events began in 1931.   _____   _____

13. The first was a Japanese baseball game.

14. Cincinnati was home to the first night baseball game in 1935.

15. Sonja Henie has won more Olympic gold medals than any other female figure skater.

16. Gordie Howe holds the lifetime record for scoring goals in hockey.

17. The longest baseball game lasted over eight hours.

18. Joe Louis defended his heavyweight title twenty-five times.

19. An official baseball weighs five ounces.

20. A regulation basketball hoop hangs ten feet above the floor.

Identifying Adverbs

Underline all the adverbs and circle all the conjunctive adverbs. Remember that some phrases or clauses can function as adverbs. Write your answers on the lines to the right. If there are no adverbs, write *none* on the line.

EXAMPLE People who <u>regularly</u> watch cartoons may think the Roadrunner is a fictional animal; (however), the roadrunner is real.

regularly
adverb

however
conj. adverb

1. The roadrunner is only nine inches tall and about two feet long.

_____ _____

2. Nevertheless, it can run as fast as twenty miles an hour.

_____ _____

3. It is a distant relative of the cuckoo.

_____ _____

4. Roadrunners do not just run on highways.

_____ _____

5. They generally seek vegetation and insects.

_____ _____

6. When the roadrunner is frightened, it makes a clacking noise.

_____ _____

7. It never goes "beep."

_____ _____

8. Occasionally, the roadrunner will eat plants, but mostly it eats insects.

_____ _____

9. For variety, it will also eat other birds, snails, mice, bats, scorpions, tarantulas, and black widow spiders.

_____ _____

10. However, it is totally unharmed by their venom.

_____ _____

11. It eats many pests; therefore, farmers really love the roadrunner.

_____ _____

Identifying Prepositions and Their Objects

Underline all prepositions and circle their objects. Write them on the lines to the right.

	Prepositions	Objects
EXAMPLE Interest in (herbs) is increasing.	in	herbs

1. Herbs have always been used for seasoning.
2. People can easily grow them at home.
3. Now herbal teas are being sold in supermarkets.
4. People have a renewed interest in treating illness with herbs.
5. Herbal cosmetics are popular among some people.
6. Industrial uses exist for some herbs too.
7. The oil from the jojoba berry can be used as a lubricant.
8. Using this oil, industry can cheaply satisfy its needs without killing whales.
9. Parsley is one of the most popular herbs.
10. It was considered too sacred to eat by the ancient Greeks.
11. Rosemary, which represents eternal love, has been used as a symbol at funerals and weddings since Shakespeare's time.
12. The ancient Greeks and Romans felt the rose had a value beyond its beauty.
13. Today the rose is considered an herb by some people because it is an ingredient in perfumes.
14. Also, large amounts of vitamin C are found in roses.

Identifying Conjunctions

Underline all coordinating and subordinating conjunctions. Write them in column 1. Then indicate the type of conjunction by writing CC or SC in column 2.

	1	2
EXAMPLE Although headaches are sometimes symptoms of disease, most headaches are only temporary.	*although*	*SC*

1. Usually, headaches occur apart from other symptoms, and they leave no aftereffects. _____ _____

2. Headaches are often caused when tension puts a strain on the muscles of the head and neck. _____ _____

3. Headaches are also possible if a person gets too little or too much sleep. _____ _____

4. Being in a noisy room can also give a person a headache before she has a chance to leave. _____ _____

5. The brain tissues themselves do not ache because the brain has no feeling. _____ _____

6. The pain of a headache comes from the muscles of the head and face where feeling nerves are plentiful. _____ _____

7. The cause of a particular headache may be a mystery, but there are only two basic causes of headaches. _____ _____

8. The first kind is called a tension headache, for it is caused by strain on face, neck, and scalp muscles whenever a person is under stress. _____ _____

9. Vascular headaches, the second kind, occur when blood vessels in the head swell and press against nearby tissues. _____ _____

10. Generally, headaches are nothing to worry about unless they occur more than three times a week. _____ _____

Identifying the Parts of Speech: Review

Write the part of speech of each underscored word on the corresponding numbered line.

An avalanche <u>is</u>[1] a large mass of <u>loosened</u>[2] <u>snow</u>[3] that slides down a mountain. <u>Avalanches</u>[4] kill dozens <u>of</u>[5] people around the world each year, <u>yet</u>[6] they remain <u>mysterious</u>.[7] No one <u>knows</u>[8] exactly what causes <u>them</u>[9] <u>or</u>[10] how to control them. In an attempt <u>at</u>[11] control some places use <u>explosives</u>[12] to try to keep avalanche conditions from forming, <u>but</u>[13] <u>this</u>[14] does not <u>always</u>[15] work. In fact, snow rangers <u>had been blasting</u>[16] for four days at Alpine Meadows, <u>California</u>,[17] before a March 31, 1982, avalanche occurred. <u>Seven</u>[18] people were killed, despite warnings and evacuations. Four <u>survived</u>,[19] including one woman <u>who</u>[20] was buried <u>alive</u>[21] <u>beneath</u>[22] the snow in an air pocket <u>for</u>[23] five days. She <u>barely</u>[24] survived <u>by</u>[25] eating snow.

1. _____   9. _____   17. _____
2. _____   10. _____   18. _____
3. _____   11. _____   19. _____
4. _____   12. _____   20. _____
5. _____   13. _____   21. _____
6. _____   14. _____   22. _____
7. _____   15. _____   23. _____
8. _____   16. _____   24. _____
                                                         25. _____

Identifying Subjects and Predicates

A: Draw a line in each of these sentences to separate the complete subject from the complete predicate.

EXAMPLE   The ice in a skating rink / does not melt.

1. Warm air cannot melt the ice.
2. The temperature beneath the ice is kept very low.
3. This keeps the ice from melting even in the sun.
4. The ice at a figure-skating rink is two inches thick.
5. Ice hockey rinks have slightly thicker layers of ice.
6. The ice is on a concrete floor.
7. The concrete contains one-inch pipes located no more than two inches apart.
8. An Olympic-sized rink has about ten miles of piping.
9. A very cold liquid, like the antifreeze in cars, circulates through the pipes.
10. The liquid absorbs heat from the concrete.
11. Machinery keeps the liquid at $-5°$ to $-15°F$.
12. More and more people are enjoying an afternoon of skating at an ice rink.

B: Draw a single line under the simple subject and a double line under the verb. Be sure to underline the complete verb and all parts of compound subjects and verbs. Write them on the lines to the right.

	Subject	Verb
EXAMPLE Most Americans brush their teeth daily.	Americans	brush
1. The original toothbrushes were simply twigs with one soft, shredded end.		
2. People rubbed these "chew sticks" against their teeth.		
3. The first genuine toothbrushes originated in China 500 years ago.		
4. The bristles came from hogs.		
5. Hogs living in the cold regions of China grew stiff bristles.		
6. During this time, few Europeans brushed their teeth regularly.		

7. Horsehair toothbrushes and small sponges were used by some Europeans. _____ _____

8. Many men and women picked their teeth clean after meals. _____ _____

9. The stems of feathers or special toothpicks were employed for this. _____ _____

10. Brass or silver toothpicks were safer than animal-hair toothbrushes. _____ _____

11. Germs developed on animal bristles, leading to frequent infections. _____ _____

12. There was no solution to this problem until the 1930s. _____ _____

13. The discovery of nylon led to a big change in the toothbrush industry and made tooth care easier. _____ _____

14. Nylon was tough and resisted the growth of germs. _____ _____

15. The first nylon-bristle brushes were sold in the United States in 1938. _____ _____

16. Unfortunately, they were very hard on gums. _____ _____

17. Soft gum tissue scratched and bled easily. _____ _____

18. In the 1950s, a new, softer version of the nylon toothbrush was developed. _____ _____

19. It cost five times as much as the old, harder brushes. _____ _____

20. With this development, national dental care improved. _____ _____

21. Dentists and oral surgeons have made some suggestions for dental health. _____ _____

22. Toothbrushes should be used regularly and should be replaced every few months. _____ _____

23. Bent bristles are useless in cleaning teeth and can cut gums. _____ _____

Identifying Objects

Draw a single line under all direct objects and a double line under all indirect objects. Not all sentences have both. Write your answers on the lines to the right.

	Direct Object	Indirect Object
EXAMPLE Indian guests at the first Thanksgiving gave the <u>Pilgrims</u> <u>popcorn</u>.	_popcorn_	_Pilgrims_

1. Colonial parents served their children popcorn with cream and sugar for breakfast.

2. Earlier, West Indians had sold Columbus necklaces made of popcorn.

3. The Aztec Indians of Mexico wore strings of popcorn in their religious ceremonies.

4. By the 1880s, people could buy their friends special machines to pop corn.

5. People had to buy themselves popcorn in 25-pound sacks.

6. Stores charged customers one dollar for such a sack.

7. Americans could buy electric poppers beginning in 1907.

8. By the 1940s, most movie theaters sold their customers popcorn.

9. Another popular food has a more recent origin.

10. In Frankfurt, Germany, butchers sold people hot dogs.

11. Immigrants sold New Yorkers the first American hot dogs at Coney Island in 1871.

12. In 1904 they started giving customers buns to protect their hands.

13. Before that, it was common to lend customers gloves.

14. That must have cost the vendors a fortune.

Identifying Complements

Decide if each italicized word is a subject complement or an object complement. Indicate your answer by writing *SC* or *OC* in column 1. Then indicate if it is a noun or an adjective by writing *N* or *Adj* in column 2.

	1	2
EXAMPLE Life is *surprising*.	SC	Adj
1. A prairie dog is a *rodent*.		
2. A firefly is a *beetle*.		
3. A lead pencil is *leadless*.		
4. Its core is *graphite*.		
5. A silkworm is just a *caterpillar*.		
6. Its coccoon is *silk*.		
7. Koala bears are not *bears*.		
8. People mistakenly call them *bears*.		
9. The koala is a *marsupial*.		
10. It is *Australian*.		
11. Some people call koalas *cuddly*.		
12. The panda is a *member* of the bear family.		
13. This is new *information*.		
14. Until recently, people considered pandas *relatives* of the raccoon.		
15. I consider them *cute*.		
16. A guinea pig is not *Guinean*.		
17. It comes from South America, and it is a *rodent*.		
18. The bald eagle is not *bald*.		
19. Flat white head and neck feathers make it appear *bald*.		
20. Our ancestors considered it *majestic*.		
21. The peanut is not a *nut*.		
22. It is a *legume*.		
23. Legumes include *peas* and *beans*.		

Identifying and Using Adjectives and Adverbs

A: Decide if each italicized word is an adjective or an adverb. Write your identifications on the lines to the right.

EXAMPLE   Aspirin is the *most* [a] *frequently* [b] *used* [c] painkiller in the world.

a. *adverb*

b. *adverb*

c. *adjective*

1. It is *related* [d] to an *old* [e] folk-remedy made from the bark of the willow tree.

d. _____

e. _____

2. Aspirin was *originally* [f] made by a *French* [g] scientist.

f. _____

g. _____

3. However, the discoverer did not realize what a *truly* [h] *important* [i] medicine it was.

h. _____

i. _____

4. The formula was *ignored* [j] for *forty* [k] years.

j. _____

k. _____

5. In 1893, a *young* [l] *German* [m] chemist was looking for a cure for his father's arthritis.

l. _____

m. _____

6. *Luckily,* [n] he tried the *Frenchman's* [o] formula.

n. _____

o. _____

7. The mixture got rid of his father's pain *almost* [p] *completely.* [q]

p. _____

q. _____

8. Chemists at the Bayer Company *quickly* [r] realized this was a *key* [s] discovery.

r. _____

s. _____

9. Bayer began producing aspirin in 1899, and it *soon* [t] became the most *prescribed* [u] drug in the world.

t. _____

u. _____

10. *Every* [v] year *new* [w] discoveries are made about aspirin's benefits.

v. _____

w. _____

Name _____ Date _____

B: Fill in the blanks in each sentence with adjectives or adverbs as needed. Write your answers in column 1, and in column 2 identify each as an adjective or an adverb.

	1	2
EXAMPLE I have a (an) _____ job. I have a <u>difficult</u> job.	<u>difficult</u>	<u>adjective</u>

1. I work in very _____ conditions. _____ _____

2. The office is _____ . _____ _____

3. The breakroom is _____. _____ _____

4. Our _____ boss is _____ _____
   trying _____ hard. _____ _____

5. He _____ asks for suggestions. _____ _____

6. He has _____ tried to get _____ _____
   the _____ cleaning crew _____ _____
   to do a _____ job. _____ _____

7. He has encouraged us to bring _____ _____
   in _____ pictures and plants.

8. He wants to make the _____ _____
   office _____ _____ _____
   _____.

9. What we _____ need is _____ _____
   a _____ raise. _____ _____

10. _____ workers would _____ _____
    also improve the _____ _____ _____
    situation here.

99

Identifying Appositives

Appositives in these sentences have been italicized. On the lines to the right, write the words or phrases modified by the appositives.

EXAMPLE   Clarence A. Crane, a *candy maker* from   *Clarence A. Crane*
Cleveland, Ohio, invented Life Savers.

1. He was also the father of poet *Hart Crane.*[a]   a. _____

2. Tupperware, *the famous line of plastic containers,*[b] was   b. _____
founded by Earl W. Tupper in 1945.

3. The symbol of Camels, *the first blended cigarettes,*[c] was   c. _____
Old Joe, *a camel from the 1913 Barnum and Bailey*   d. _____
Circus.[d]

4. The original Chef-Boy-Ar-Dee, *Hector Boiardi,*[e] began   e. _____
working in restaurants when he was only nine.

5. Ivory Soap, *the soap that floats,*[f] was discovered by   f. _____
accident when workers let a vat of soap mix too long,
absorbing air.

6. Sanka brand coffee takes its name from the French   g. _____
phrase *sans caffeine.*[g]

7. Log Cabin Syrup is named after its inventor's favorite   h. _____
president, *Lincoln,*[h] *the president who grew up in a log*   i. _____
cabin.[i]

8. One famous soft drink is named after the father of its   j. _____
inventor's girlfriend, *Dr. Pepper.*[j]

9. The Sun Maid Raisin symbol, *a little girl holding an*   k. _____
armful of raisins,[k] was a real person, *Lorraine Collette*   l. _____
Petersen.[l]

10. The original Animal Crackers, *that favorite of generations*   m. _____
of children,[m] had a string on top so the boxes could be
hung on Christmas trees.

11. H. E. Hires, *a Philadelphia druggist,*[n] mixed together   n. _____
roots, bark, and berries trying to duplicate an herb tea he
had once tasted.

12. Hires Root Beer, *the original behind many imitators,*[o]   o. _____
was the result.

13. The Reverend Sylvester W. Graham, *a health food*   p. _____
activist,[p] popularized graham crackers.

14. M&M's, *the candy that melts in your mouth and not in*   q. _____
your hands,[q] were introduced in the 1940s and became
popular with the Army because soldiers could eat them
without getting goo on their guns.

Identifying Phrases

A: Identify the italicized phrases, and write on the lines to the right *NP* for a noun phrase, *VP* for a verb phrase, *PP* for a prepositional phrase, and *AP* for an absolute phrase.

EXAMPLE   Many people live in fear *of going bald.*   _____*PP*_____

1. Going bald is *something one has little control over.*   _____

2. Some people *have tried* hair transplants or toupees.   _____

3. *A few people* just shave their heads completely.   _____

4. Most of us associate baldness *with men.*   _____

5. *Their hair loss usually occurring only at the top of their heads,* women are less likely to appear dramatically bald.   _____

6. *The most common form of balding* is "male pattern baldness."   _____

7. In this condition, hair *is lost* from the top and front of the scalp.   _____

8. *With people normally losing up to 125 hairs per day,* finding a few hairs in our combs should be no cause for concern.   _____

9. New hair *is developing* constantly.   _____

10. Usually, a new hair replaces *each lost hair.*   _____

11. However, *in male pattern baldness* no replacement hairs develop.   _____

12. Male pattern baldness was once considered to be inherited *from the mother's side of the family.*   _____

13. *Dermatologists not believing this any longer,* bald men cannot blame their mothers.   _____

14. Instead, many factors *appear to be involved.*

B: Identify the italicized verbal phrases, and write on the lines to the right *inf* for an infinitive phrase, *part* for a participial phrase, and *ger* for a gerund phrase.

EXAMPLE   *Understanding alcohol's effects* on the body is important.   _____*ger*_____

1. *Believing myths about drinking*, many people do not have an accurate idea of alcohol's impact.   _____

2. Some people say they drink *to relax*.   _____

3. *Drinking large amounts of beer*, other people deny they have a problem because "It's only beer."   _____

4. *Having a cup of coffee*, some claim, will make them sober enough to drive.   _____

5. *Putting faith* in these myths can be dangerous.   _____

6. Alcohol works *to weaken* many parts of the body.   _____

7. Drinkable alcohol, *called ethanol*, is made up of very small particles.   _____

8. *Travelling throughout the body*, these particles can quickly enter every organ.   _____

9. *Burning in the throat* is the first sign of damage.   _____

10. *To slow down absorption of alcohol*, avoid carbonated drinks.   _____

11. *Speeding passage of alcohol into the small intestines*, carbonated mixers may accelerate the impact of even small amounts of alcohol.   _____

12. *Eating before or during drinking* can slow down absorption.   _____

13. Milk products are very likely *to have* such an effect.   _____

14. *Drinking alcohol* also results in a false sense of warmth, which can be fatal to those who then fail to dress properly in cold weather.   _____

EXERCISE **7-16**

Identifying Dependent Clauses
(7o-2)

Underline all dependent clauses. Write the first and last words of each dependent clause on the lines to the right.

EXAMPLE   Most people are unaware <u>that the potato is originally from Peru</u>.   *that . . . Peru*

1. Spanish explorers who came to the New World seeking   _____
    gold discovered the potato.

2. Because it is such a nutritious food, the potato is now   _____
    grown in at least 130 countries.

3. A pound of potatoes, which is more than most people   _____
    eat at one time, has only about 360 calories, about 110
    per potato.

4. If a potato is eaten without butter, it is 99.9 percent fat   _____
    free.

5. Since an acre of potatoes produces twice as much food   _____
    as two acres of grain, it is an efficient crop.

6. The average annual world crop is 291 million tons   _____
    although about half is fed to farm animals.

7. The potato produces more nutritious food more quickly   _____
    on less land under poorer conditions than any other
    major food crop does.

8. The potato can survive almost wherever humans can.   _____

9. The jungles, where humidity causes diseases deadly to   _____
    the potato, are the only parts of the world where it
    cannot grow.

10. When gasoline still cost only pennies a gallon,   _____
    automaker Henry Ford predicted that potatoes would be
    used to make fuel.

11. Researchers have discovered that one acre of potatoes   _____
    can produce 1,200 gallons of fuel a year.

12. Currently, the former Soviet Union produces one-third of   _____
    the world's potatoes while the United States produces
    just five percent.

Using Subordination

Using the subordinating conjunction or relative pronoun given in parentheses, join each of these pairs of sentences. You may sometimes need to omit a word, but no major rewordings are required.

EXAMPLE   Eight different species of potatoes are grown.
Most North Americans know only one kind of potato.   (although)
Although most North Americans know only one kind of potato, eight different species are grown.

1. Potatoes grown from seed may not inherit the parent plant's characteristics.
   Potatoes are usually grown from the eye of a planted piece of potato.   (since)

   _____

2. Potato blossoms look like those of the poisonous nightshade plant.
   Centuries ago, Europeans were afraid to eat potatoes.   (because)

   _____

3. Tomatoes, tobacco, and eggplant are all relatives of the potato.
   They do not look alike.   (although)

   _____

4. The sweet potato is not related to the potato.
   Its Indian name, *batata*, was mistakenly taken to mean "potato" by its European "discoverers."   (even though)

   _____

5. The potato skin is a good source of dietary fiber.
   Most people throw it away.   (which)

   _____

6. Thirty-two percent of the U.S. potato crop is eaten fresh.
   Twenty-seven percent is made into frozen products, such as french fries.   (while)

   _____

7. Would you believe something?
   Twelve percent of the U.S. crop is made into potato chips.   (that)

   _____

8. There are misinformed people.
   They believe the potato is only a poor person's food.   (who)

   _____

9. They overlook something.
   Potatoes have nourished the people of Europe since the eighteenth
   century.   (that)

   _____

10. Nutritious potatoes allowed the population to expand until 1845.
    Europe—especially Ireland—was almost destroyed by a disease that killed
    the potato crop.   (when)

    _____

11. Potato chips were created in New England.
    A hotel chef became angry with a fussy customer.   (because)

    _____

12. The customer sent back his french fries twice, saying they were not crisp
    enough.
    No one else had ever complained.   (although)

    _____

13. The chef apparently had a bad temper.
    He decided to teach the man a lesson.   (who)

    _____

14. He cut the potatoes paper-thin and fried them.
    They were too crispy to pick up with a fork.   (until)

    _____

15. The customer tasted these potatoes.
    He was delighted.   (once)

    _____

16. The chef never got his revenge, but he did get his own restaurant.
    These "chips" became very popular.   (so that)

    _____

6. Repression occurs in the mentally ill.
   It occurs also in mentally healthy people.   (compound)

   _____

   _____

7. A certain kind of learning atmosphere leads to better memory.
   This kind of learning atmosphere is the kind where people can
   relax.   (complex)

   _____

   _____

8. Any student knows this.
   So does any teacher.   (compound)

   _____

   _____

9. People are often distracted in stressful situations.
   They simply do not see everything.
   Therefore, they cannot remember everything.   (compound-complex)

   _____

   _____

10. This may explain something.
    Accident victims often do not recall details of their experiences.   (complex)

    _____

    _____

11. Many people do not remember much from their childhoods.
    This does not mean that they are repressing bad memories.   (compound)

    _____

    _____

12. They may have been too interested in some events to notice any others.
    These other events were happening at the same time.
    Maybe their childhoods were simply too boring to remember.   (compound-complex)

    _____

    _____

Name _____ Date _____

B: Using independent and dependent clauses, expand each of these simple sentences, making a compound, then a complex, and finally a compound-complex sentence.

Example   He is always late.
(compound) _He is always late, and his brother is always early._
(complex) _He is always late because he oversleeps._
(compound-complex) _He is always late when there is a test, so the_ teacher is moving him to a later class.

1. Fast food is not cheap.

(compound) _____

(complex) _____

(compound-complex) _____

_____

2. The movie theater was crowded.

(compound) _____

(complex) _____

(compound-complex) _____

_____

3. Read contracts before you sign them.

(compound) _____

(complex) _____

(compound-complex) _____

_____

4. Ice cream is a popular dessert.

(compound) _____

(complex) _____

(compound-complex) _____

_____

5. Grocery stores should be open twenty-four hours a day.

(compound) _____

(complex) _____

(compound-complex) _____

C: Write complete sentences by adding one or more independent clauses to each of these subordinate clauses.

EXAMPLE if I have a chance
   If I have a chance, I'll learn to draw.

1. because she has a pet snake

 _____

2. whoever has the flu

 _____

3. before the union votes on the contract

 _____

4. even though they paid the electric bill

 _____

5. where the keys are

 _____

6. that cost a dollar

 _____

7. who has the prize-winning ticket

 _____

8. since she learned to drive

 _____

9. whether the bus stops on that corner

 _____

10. if the milk is sour

 _____

8 | *Verbs*

8a Understanding verbs

Verbs convey information about what is happening, what has happened, and what will happen. In English, a verb tells of an action (*move, juggle, race*), an occurrence (*become, change, happen*), or a state of being (*be, seem, feel, exist*).

Americans **enjoy** sports. [action]
Football **becomes** more popular every year. [occurrence]
Soccer **is** a new favorite of many people. [state of being]

Verbs convey information through their person, number, tense, mood, and voice. Three types of verbs are main verbs, linking verbs, and auxiliary verbs.

VERB FORMS

8b Recognizing the forms of main verbs

Every main verb has five forms. The **simple form** is also known as the **dictionary form** or the **base form**. The simple form shows action (or occurrence or state of being) taking place in the present for *I, you, we,* and *they: I travel, they explore.*

The **past-tense** form indicates an action or occurrence or state of being completed in the past. The past tense of all regular verbs adds final *-ed* or *-d* to the simple form. Many verbs, however, are irregular. That is, their past-tense forms, and often their past participles as well, either change in spelling or use different words instead of adding *-ed* or *-d: ring, rang, rung; fly, flew, flown.* The principal parts of common irregular verbs are listed in 8d–2. Except for the past tense of *be* (8e), the past tense form of each verb is the same for all persons and numbers.

The **past participle** is the third form. In regular verbs, the past participle has the same form as the past tense. However, for many irregular verbs these forms differ and must be memorized (see 8d–2).

To function as a verb, a past participle must combine with an auxiliary verb (8e) in a **verb phrase**. Verb phrases formed with past participles make the **perfect** tenses (8i) and **passive** constructions (8n): *I have succeeded; they are shocked.* For a discussion of other uses of the past participle, see 7d.

The present participle adds *-ing* to the simple form. To function as a verb, a present participle combines with a subject and one or more auxiliary verbs. Otherwise, present participles function as adjectives.

The infinitive uses the simple form, usually but not always following *to*. The infinitive functions as a noun, adjective, or adverb, not a verb.

8c Using the *-s* form of verbs

Except for *be* and *have* (8e), all verbs in the present tense add an *-s* or *-es* ending to the simple form when the subject is third person singular: *Everybody likes candy*.

Be and *have*—irregular verbs—do not use their simple forms in the third person singular of the present tense. Instead, *be* uses *is* and *have* uses *has*:

Candy **is** fattening; it **has** a lot of calories.

Some dialects of English use forms such as *candy be* and *it have* for third person singular in the present tense. Academic writing requires *is* and *has*.

Also, if you drop the *-s* or *-es* ending when you speak, you may forget to use it when you write. Be sure to proofread your writing to make sure you have used the *-s* form correctly.

8d Using regular and irregular verbs

1 Forming the past tense and past participle of a regular verb by adding *-ed* or *-d*

A **regular verb** is one that forms its simple past and past participle by adding *-ed* or *-d* to the simple form. Most verbs in English are regular: *walk, walked, walked; bake, baked, baked*. Some regular verbs, however, require spelling changes at the end of the simple form: *deny, denied*. (See 22e.)

Some speakers omit the *-ed* sound in the past tense. If you are unused to hearing or pronouncing this sound, particularly before a word beginning with a *t* or *d*, you may forget to add it when you write the past tense or past participle. Nevertheless, written English requires the *-ed* ending.

2 Memorizing the principal parts of irregular verbs

About two hundred of the most common verbs in English are **irregular**: They do not add the *-ed* or *-d* to form the past tense or past participle. They form the past tense and past participle in different ways. Some irregular verbs change an internal vowel in the simple form to make the past tense and past participle: *ring, rang, rung*. Some change an internal vowel and add an ending other than *-ed* or *-d: rise, rose, risen*. Some use the simple form throughout: *cost, cost, cost*.

Unfortunately, a verb's simple form does not indicate whether the verb is irregular or regular. If you do not know the principal parts of a verb you are using, you need to find them in a college dictionary.

Common irregular verbs

SIMPLE FORM	PAST TENSE	PAST PARTICIPLE
arise	arose	arisen
awake	awoke *or* awaked	awaked *or* awoken
be (is, am, are)	was, were	been
beat	beat	beaten
become	became	become
begin	began	begun
bend	bent	bent
bite	bit	bitten *or* bit
blow	blew	blown
break	broke	broken
bring	brought	brought
build	built	built
buy	bought	bought
catch	caught	caught
choose	chose	chosen
come	came	come
cost	cost	cost
creep	crept	crept
cut	cut	cut
deal	dealt	dealt
dig	dug	dug
dive	dived *or* dove	dived
do	did	done
draw	drew	drawn
drink	drank	drunk
drive	drove	driven
eat	ate	eaten
fall	fell	fallen
feel	felt	felt
fight	fought	fought
find	found	found
flee	fled	fled
fly	flew	flown
forbid	forbade *or* forbad	forbidden
forget	forgot	forgotten *or* forgot
freeze	froze	frozen
get	got	got *or* gotten
give	gave	given
go	went	gone
have	had	had
hear	heard	heard
hide	hid	hidden
hit	hit	hit
hold	held	held
hurt	hurt	hurt

➜

Common irregular verbs (continued)

SIMPLE FORM	PAST TENSE	PAST PARTICIPLE
keep	kept	kept
know	knew	known
lay	laid	laid
lead	led	led
leave	left	left
lend	lent	lent
let	let	let
lie	lay	lain
lose	lost	lost
make	made	made
mean	meant	meant
meet	met	met
pay	paid	paid
quit	quit	quit
read	read	read
ride	rode	ridden
ring	rang	rung
rise	rose	risen
run	ran	run
say	said	said
see	saw	seen
seek	sought	sought
send	sent	sent
set	set	set
shake	shook	shaken
shoot	shot	shot
sing	sang	sung
sit	sat	sat
sleep	slept	slept
speak	spoke	spoken
spend	spent	spent
spring	sprang *or* sprung	sprung
stand	stood	stood
strike	struck	struck
swim	swam	swum
swing	swung	swung
take	took	taken
teach	taught	taught
tear	tore	torn
tell	told	told
think	thought	thought
throw	threw	thrown
wear	wore	worn
write	wrote	written

8e Using auxiliary verbs to form verb phrases

The verbs *be, do,* and *have* function both as main verbs and as auxiliary (or helping) verbs. *Be,* the most common verb in English, is the most irregular as well.

THE FORMS OF *BE*

Simple Form	be	
Past Tense	was, were	
Past Participle	been	
***-s* Form**	is	
Present Participle	being	

PERSON	PRESENT TENSE	PAST TENSE
I	am	was
you (singular)	are	were
he, she, it	is	was
we	are	were
you (plural)	are	were
they	are	were

Do and *have* are not as irregular as *be.*

THE FORMS OF *DO* AND *HAVE*

Simple Form	do	**Simple Form**	have
Past Tense	did	**Past Tense**	had
Past Participle	done	**Past Participle**	had
***-s* Form**	does	***-s* Form**	has
Present Participle	doing	**Present Participle**	having

When used as main verbs, forms of *be* are **linking verbs**. They join a subject to a **subject complement** (7m−1), a word or group of words that renames or describes the subject.

> Water pollution **is** a danger to many communities. [*is* = linking verb, *water pollution* = subject, *a danger to many communities* = subject complement]

> Underground streams **are** sources of well water. [*are* = linking verb, *underground streams* = subject, *sources of well water* = subject complement]

When used alone as main verbs, *have* is transitive and *do* can be transitive. Transitive verbs must be followed by a direct object (see 8f).

Combined with participles of main verbs, forms of *be* and *have* are **auxiliary verbs**, or **helping verbs**, that help the participles to show tense (8i, j) and mood (8l).

> I **am waiting**. [auxiliary verb *am* + present participle *waiting* = present progressive tense]
>
> The news **has been expected** for days. [auxiliary verb *has* + auxiliary verb *been* + past participle *expected* = present perfect tense in the passive voice]

The auxiliary verbs *will* and *shall* help to create two tenses: the future (*I shall try, you will pass*) and, with *have* and past participles of main verbs, the future perfect (*I shall have tried, you will have passed*). *Will* and *shall* never change form. Formal writing reserves *shall* for the first person (*I, we*) and *will* for all other persons (*you, he, she, it, they*).

The verbs *can, could, may, might, should, would, must*, and *ought to* are called **modal auxiliary verbs**. Modal auxiliary verbs have only one form; they do not change, no matter what constructions they appear in.

Modal auxiliaries add to the main verb a sense of needing, wanting, or having to do something, or a sense of possibility, permission, or ability.

> The ant **can carry** many times its own weight. [ability]
>
> Ants **may be observed** gathering around crumbs on the sidewalk. [possibility]
>
> We **must sweep** up dropped food or we **might attract** ants in our homes. [necessity, possibility]

Always use the simple form of the verb after a modal auxiliary.

8f Using intransitive and transitive verbs, especially *sit* and *set, lie* and *lay, rise* and *raise*

The difference between *I see clearly* and *I see a fire* is that the first sentence tells *how* the subject does something while the second points to *what* the subject does. In the first sentence, the verb is **intransitive**—it stops with the action. In the second sentence, the verb is **transitive**—the action of the verb carries over to whatever is named in the **direct object**. Many verbs in English can be both intransitive and transitive depending upon how they are used in particular sentences.

INTRANSITIVE (NO OBJECT)	**TRANSITIVE (WITH AN OBJECT)**
The trees **shook** in the wind.	The boys **shook** the apple tree.
The train **leaves** tonight.	The train **leaves** the station.

Three important pairs of verbs are not this flexible. In these pairs—*sit* and *set, lie* and *lay, rise* and *raise*—one verb is intransitive, the other transitive.

SUMMARY OF FORMS FOR *SIT, LIE, RISE,* AND *SET, LAY, RAISE*

INTRANSITIVE (NO OBJECT)

Simple Form	Past Tense	Past Participle	-s Form	Present Participle
sit	sat	sat	sits	sitting
lie	lay	lain	lies	lying
rise	rose	risen	rises	rising

TRANSITIVE (WITH AN OBJECT)

Simple Form	Past Tense	Past Participle	-s Form	Present Participle
set	set	set	sets	setting
lay	laid	laid	lays	laying
raise	raised	raised	raises	raising

To *sit* means to seat oneself; to *set* means to place something else down.

INTRANSITIVE	I **sit** down. I **sat** down. [*down* = modifier]
TRANSITIVE	I **set** the stapler on the desk. [*stapler* = direct object]

To *lie* means to place oneself down or to recline; to *lay* means to place something else down.

INTRANSITIVE	Oscar **lies** on the couch. Oscar **lay** on the coach. [*on the couch* = modifier]
TRANSITIVE	Oscar **lays** bricks for a living. Oscar **laid** bricks for a living. [*bricks* = direct object]

To *rise* means to stand up, to get up out of bed, or to elevate oneself in some other way; to *raise* is to lift up or elevate someone or something else.

INTRANSITIVE	Wendy **rises** every morning at 6:30. Wendy **rose** every morning at 6:30. [*every morning at 6:30* = modifier]
TRANSITIVE	Wendy **raises** the rent. Wendy **raised** the rent. [*the rent* = direct object]

VERB TENSE

8g Understanding verb tense

The **tense** of a verb indicates *when* the action, occurrence, or state of being it expresses takes place. Verbs are the only words that change form to express time.

English verb tenses are divided into two general groups: simple and perfect.

The three **simple tenses** divide time into present, past, and future. The **present** tense describes what is happening, what is true at the moment, and what is always true. It uses the simple form (8b) and the *-s* form (8c).

> I **study** Italian at the university.
> Joe **studies** hard all the time.

The **past tense** tells of a completed action or a condition that has ended. It uses the past tense form (8b, 8d).

> We **joined** the Italian conversation group.
> We **hoped** to practice speaking.

The **future tense** indicates action not yet taken. This tense uses the auxiliary verbs *will* or *shall* and the simple form (8b).

> We **shall see** an Italian movie at the next meeting.

The second group of tenses are the **perfect tenses**. They also divide time into present, past, and future (8i).

All six tenses also have **progressive forms**, made from the *-ing* form and the verb *to be* (8j).

8h Using the simple present tense

The **simple present tense** describes what is happening or what is true at the moment. It also has special functions, summarized below.

SUMMARY OF USES FOR THE SIMPLE PRESENT TENSE

DESCRIBING WHAT IS HAPPENING NOW, IN THE PRESENT

You **work** efficiently.
The gale **rattles** the windows.

DESCRIBING A HABITUAL OR REGULARLY OCCURRING ACTION

My accounting class **meets** at 10:00 on Tuesdays.
Horror movies **give** him nightmares.

EXPRESSING A GENERAL TRUTH OR WIDELY HELD OPINION

A kilogram **is** roughly 2.2 pounds.
Good fences **make** good neighbors.

DESCRIBING A FIXED-TIME FUTURE EVENT

The semester **ends** on May 30.

SUMMARY OF USES FOR THE SIMPLE PRESENT TENSE *(continued)*

The ship **leaves** port at midnight.
His birthday **falls** on a Sunday this year.

DISCUSSING "TIMELESS" EVENTS AND ACTIVITIES AND INTENTIONS OF THOSE WHO CREATE THEM

Jay Gatsby **wants** it all.
Luke Skywalker and Hans Solo repeatedly **save** Princess Leia.
Einstein **speaks** of matter as something that is interchangeable with energy.

8i Forming and using the perfect tenses

The perfect tenses usually describe actions or occurrences that have **already** been completed or that will be completed before another point in time.

The **present perfect tense** shows that an action begun in the past continues into the present, or that an action completed in the past affects the present.

Betty **has applied** for a summer job.
We **have** always **tried** to do our best.

The **past perfect tense** indicates that an action was completed before another one took place.

The blizzard **had trapped** the climbers before they could get down the mountain.

The **future perfect tense** indicates that an action will be complete before some specified or predictable time.

The space craft **will have sent** back pictures of the outer planets before it flies out of the solar system.

8j Forming and using the progressive forms

The **progressive form** uses the present participle along with the various forms of *be* and other auxiliary verbs. It shows that an action or condition is ongoing. (Another name for progressive forms is *continuous forms*.)

The **present progressive** indicates something taking place at the time it is written or spoken about.

Rents **are rising**.

The **past progressive** shows the continuing nature of a past action.

The fire **was spreading** rapidly when the firefighters arrived.

The **future progressive** shows that a future action will continue for some time.

After vacation, **we shall be returning** to our study of verb tenses.

The **present perfect progressive** describes something that began in the past and is likely to continue in the future.

The kitchen tap **has been dripping** for weeks.

The **past perfect progressive** describes an ongoing condition in the past that has been ended by something stated in the sentence.

The stereo **had been playing** well until the movers dropped it.

The **future perfect progressive** describes an action or condition continuing until some specific future time.

On November 11, **we shall have been going** together for two years.

SUMMARY OF TENSES INCLUDING PROGRESSIVE FORMS

SIMPLE TENSES

	REGULAR VERB	IRREGULAR VERB	PROGRESSIVE FORM
Present	I talk	I eat	I am talking, I am eating
Past	I talked	I ate	I was talking, I was eating
Future	I will talk	I will eat	I will be talking, I will be eating
PERFECT TENSES			
Present Perfect	I have talked	I have eaten	I have been talking, I have been eating
Past Perfect	I had talked	I had eaten	I had been talking, I had been eating
Future Perfect	I will have talked	I will have eaten	I will have been talking, I will have been eating

8k Using accurate tense sequence

Sentences often have more than one verb, and these verbs often refer to actions taking place at different times. Showing the right time relationships—that is, using accurate tense sequences—is necessary to avoid confusion. The tense of the verb in an independent clause determines the possibilities for verb tense in that sentence's dependent clauses.

SUMMARY OF SEQUENCE OF TENSES

WHEN INDEPENDENT-CLAUSE VERB IS IN THE SIMPLE PRESENT TENSE, FOR THE DEPENDENT-CLAUSE VERB:

Use the present tense to show same-time action.

> The director **says** that the movie **is** a tribute to factory workers.
> I **avoid** shellfish because I **am** allergic to it.

Use the past tense to show earlier action.

> I **am** sure that I **deposited** the check.

Use the present perfect tense to show a period of time extending from some point in the past to the present.

> They **claim** that they **have visited** the planet Venus.

Use the future tense for action to come.

> The book **is** open because I **will be reading** it later.

WHEN INDEPENDENT-CLAUSE VERB IS IN THE PAST TENSE, FOR THE DEPENDENT-CLAUSE VERB:

Use the past tense to show earlier action.

> I **ate** dinner before you **offered** to take me out for pizza.

Use the past perfect tense to emphasize earlier action.

> The sprinter **knew** she **had broken** the record.

Use the present tense to state a general truth.

> Christopher Columbus **discovered** that the world **is** round.

WHEN INDEPENDENT-CLAUSE VERB IS IN THE PRESENT PERFECT OR PAST PERFECT TENSE, FOR THE DEPENDENT-CLAUSE VERB:

Use the past tense.

> The milk **has become** sour since I **bought** it last week.
> The price of sugar **had** already **declined** when artificial sweeteners first **appeared**.

WHEN INDEPENDENT-CLAUSE VERB IS IN THE FUTURE TENSE, FOR THE DEPENDENT-CLAUSE VERB:

Use the present tense to show action happening at the same time.

> You **will be** rich if you **win** the prize.

SUMMARY OF SEQUENCE OF TENSES *(continued)*

Use the past tense to show earlier action.

> You **will** surely **win** the prize if you **remembered** to mail the entry form.

Use the present perfect tense to show future action earlier than the action of the independent-clause verb.

> The river **will flood** again next year unless we **have built** a better dam by then.

WHEN THE INDEPENDENT-CLAUSE VERB IS IN THE FUTURE PERFECT TENSE, FOR THE DEPENDENT-CLAUSE VERB:

Use either the present tense or the present perfect tense.

> Dr. Chang **will have delivered** 5,000 babies by the time she **retires**.
> Dr. Chang **will have delivered** 5,000 babies by the time she **has retired**.

MOOD

8l Understanding mood

The **mood** of a verb conveys a writer's attitude toward a statement. The most common mood in English is the **indicative mood**. It is used for statements about real things, or highly likely ones, and for questions about fact: *The car started; how much does that jacket cost?* Most statements are in the indicative mood.

The **imperative mood**, which always uses the simple form of the verb, expresses commands and direct requests. The subject is often omitted in an imperative sentence. It is assumed to be *you: Sit down! Please do not smoke in here.*

The **subjunctive mood** expresses conditions including wishes, recommendations, indirect requests, and speculations (see 8m). The subjunctive mood in English is rare. Therefore, its forms are less familiar than those of the indicative mood and the imperative mood.

8m Using correct subjunctive forms

The **present subjunctive** of all verbs except *be* uses the simple form of the verb for all persons and numbers. The present subjunctive of *be* is *be* for all persons and numbers.

> It is important that the vandals **be** [not *are*] found
> I am demanding that he **pay** [not *pays*] his bill.

The **past subjunctive** uses the same form as the past indicative. The past subjunctive of *be* for all persons and numbers is the same as the past plural indicative, *were*.

He wishes he **were** [not *was*] richer.

Although the subjunctive is not as common as it once was, it is still used in four situations:

1. Use the subjunctive in *if* clauses and some *unless* clauses for speculations or conditions contrary to fact.

   Unless a meltdown **were** [not *was*] to take place, the risks from a nuclear power plant are small.

2. Use the subjunctive for judgments introduced by *as if* or *as though*.

   The runner looks as though he **were** [not *was*] about to collapse.

3. Use the subjunctive in *that* clauses for wishes, indirect requests, recommendations, and demands.

   I wish that this building **were** [not *was*] air-conditioned.
   Her mechanic recommended that she **look** [not *looked*] for a new car.

4. Use the subjunctive in certain standard expressions.

Please let me **be**.	**Come** what may
Be that as it may....	Far **be** it from me....

Modal auxiliary verbs like *would, could, might,* and *should* can convey speculations and conditions contrary to fact and are often used with the subjunctive:

If my father **were** [not *was*] here, he **would** gladly cook the fish.

When the independent clause expresses a conditional statement with a modal auxiliary, be sure to use the appropriate subjunctive form, not another modal auxiliary, in the dependent clause.

No	If I **would have studied** for the final, I **might have improved** my grade.
Yes	If I **had studied** for the final, I **might have improved** my grade.

VOICE

8n Understanding voice

The **voice** of a verb indicates whether a subject does or receives the action named by the verb. English has two voices: active and passive.
In the **active voice**, the subject performs the action.

Roaches **infest** most cities.

In the **passive voice**, the subject is acted upon, and the person or thing doing the action often appears as the object of the preposition *by*.

Roaches **are considered** a nuisance by many people.

The passive voice uses verb phrases. A past participle indicates the action, and a form of *be* specifies person, number, and tense: *is seen, were seen, have been seen.*

---

80 Writing in the active voice, not the passive voice, except to convey special types of emphasis

The active voice emphasizes the doer of the action, so active constructions have a more direct and dramatic effect. Active constructions also use fewer words than passive constructions. Therefore, use the active voice wherever you can. Most sentences in the passive voice can easily be converted to the active voice.

PASSIVE   Bicycling tours of Canada **are often taken by young travelers**.
ACTIVE   **Young travelers often take** bicycling tours of Canada.

However, the passive voice is useful in two special situations.

1. You should use the passive voice when the doer of the action is unknown or unimportant.

    The painting **was stolen** some time after midnight. [Who stole the painting is unknown.]

2. You can also use the passive voice to focus attention on the action rather than the doer of the action. For example, in a passage about important contributions to the history of biology, you might want to emphasize a doer by using the active voice.

    William Harvey **studied** the human circulatory system.

    However, in a passage summarizing what scientists know about circulation, you might want to emphasize what was done.

    The human circulatory system **was studied** by William Harvey.

Writing Present-Tense Verbs

(8c)

Fill in the blanks with the third person singular, present tense of the verbs in parentheses.

EXAMPLE   Every patient (to want) _____*wants*_____ a good doctor.

1. Proper training (to provide) _____ a doctor with the necessary knowledge.

2. Feeling for people (to help) _____ the doctor apply that knowledge.

3. Each patient (to prefer) _____ a slightly different combination of characteristics in a doctor.

4. One patient (to insist) _____ on seeing a doctor who is older than he is.

5. Another patient (to desire) _____ a doctor about her own age.

6. A third patient (to feel) _____ more comfortable with a doctor of the same sex.

7. A patient often (to require) _____ a doctor who is warm and friendly, but not everyone (to think) _____ this is essential.

8. Others believe that a doctor's technical knowledge alone (to determine) _____ how good the medical care will be.

9. Each local hospital (to offer) _____ a list of doctors and their specialties.

10. This list (to aid) _____ people who are looking for a new doctor.

11. A person (to call) _____ the local hospital's physician referral service to get the list.

12. Another source of information (to exist) _____ even closer to home.

13. A neighbor (to know) _____ the reputation of local doctors.

14. A doctor's reputation (to indicate) _____ if others have been happy with her.

15. A good hospital (to keep) _____ the best doctors it can get.

16. Therefore, the careful new patient (to find) _____ out which hospitals the doctor is connected with.

17. The best way to decide if a doctor is the right one (to continue) _____ to be to see how the doctor-patient relationship (to develop) _____ after a few visits.

18. A well-organized office (to enable) _____ the doctor to follow up on treatments, keep waiting time down, and spend enough time with each patient.

19. A good doctor (to set) _____ up a system for handling weekend and after-hours emergencies.

20. She also (to leave) _____ time to see emergency patients who do not have appointments.

21. The good doctor (to spend) _____ enough time with a patient to get all the necessary information and to answer all questions completely.

22. The patient (to deserve) _____ an explanation of every test that the doctor (to conduct) _____ and every medication she (to prescribe) _____ .

23. A good doctor willingly (to consult) _____ with specialists when a patient's problem is outside her own area.

24. She also (to discuss) _____ possible treatments with the patient when there are choices to be made.

25. This way, the patient (to decide) _____ after knowing the advantages and disadvantages of each possibility.

Writing Past Tense Verbs

Fill in the blanks with the past tense forms of the verbs in parentheses.

EXAMPLE   Have you ever (to wonder) ___wondered___ why people fly kites?

1. Malayans (to start) _____ to use kites for ceremonial purposes at least 3000 years ago.

2. In ancient hieroglyphics, Egyptians (to record) _____ legends about kites.

3. Yet kites probably (to develop) _____ first in China.

4. In the Han Dynasty, the emperor (to use) _____ kites to intimidate invaders.

5. He (to insert) _____ bamboo pipes into the kites.

6. When flown above the invaders' camp, the kites (to issue) _____ moaning sounds that (to startle) _____ the men below.

7. Because the night was dark, the men (to perceive) _____ nothing in the sky above them.

8. It is not surprising that they (to jerk) _____ up their tents and immediately (to head) _____ for home.

9. More recently, Benjamin Franklin (to employ) _____ a kite for his experiments with electricity.

10. An Englishman, George Pocock, (to pull) _____ a carriage and passengers with two eight-foot kites.

11. The Wright brothers (to experiment) _____ with kites even after their success with the airplane.

12. And you (to imagine) _____ that people flew kites just for fun!

Writing Irregular Past-Tense Verbs

Fill in the blanks with the correct past-tense forms of the irregular verbs in parentheses.

EXAMPLE   The first correspondents (to write) ____*wrote*____ on clay, parchment, or papyrus.

1. Once couriers (to run) _____ from one person to another with memorized messages.

2. What we consider the postal system (to arise) _____ from such beginnings.

3. Augustus Caesar (to build) _____ fine roads to accommodate his messengers.

4. When the Roman Empire (to fall) _____ , it (to bring) _____ an end to the Roman postal system.

5. However, by the thirteenth century the China of Kublai Khan (to have) _____ a system of messengers and horses.

6. At about the same time, the Aztecs (to find) _____ a method to disperse packages of fish among their villages.

7. During the 1400s, England's Edward IV (to set) _____ up post houses for carrying both official and private mail.

8. Henry VIII (to make) _____ Sir Brian Tuke the first Master of the Posts.

9. In 1683, Charles II (to begin) _____ the London Penny Post.

10. It (to cost) _____ just one cent to mail a letter anywhere in London.

11. In 1639, the colony of Massachusetts (to give) _____ Richard Fairbanks the right to handle mail arriving by ship.

12. The Second Continental Congress (to choose) _____ Benjamin Franklin as the first American postmaster general in 1775.

13. George Washington personally (to oversee) _____ the surveying of post routes in the new republic.

14. When the Continental Congress (to forbid) _____ postal workers to open private letters, the mail service (to become) _____ a symbol of freedom.

15. As the new nation (to grow) _____ , the government (to bear) _____ the cost of building new post offices.

16. After 1900, however, improved highways (to mean) _____ fewer post offices (to be) _____ necessary.

17. By midcentury, the United States (to lead) _____ the world in the number of pieces of mail handled daily.

EXERCISE 8-4

Conjugating be

(8e)

The verb *be* has many irregular forms. Fill in the chart with all of its forms. Then check yourself by looking at the chart in 8e.

	Person	Present Tense	Past Tense
Singular	First	_____	_____
	Second	_____	_____
	Third	_____	_____
Plural	First	_____	_____
	Second	_____	_____
	Third	_____	_____

Present Participle _____   Past Participle _____

Name _____ Date _____

Using the Verb be

Fill in the blanks with appropriate forms of the verb *be*.

For some people a garden _____ a hobby. For others it _____ a necessity. In either case, _____ a gardener is hard work.

The first thing you must do each spring _____ prepare the garden plot with spade, plow, or rototiller. Your muscles _____ sure to ache after a day of turning the soil. Planting and mulching _____ next. I _____ always excited to see new plants coming up. You will _____ too. However, weeds _____ apt to grow faster than the seeds you planted.

Unless your idea of an aerobic workout _____ thirty minutes with a hoe, you should _____ enthusiastic about mulch. Mulch can _____ straw mounded around plants or plastic sheets covering the ground between rows. If you _____ using plastic, _____ sure you have the kind that can breathe. Otherwise, there will _____ inadequate moisture for your plants.

A garden _____ guaranteed to cultivate your patience while you _____ cultivating it. It cannot _____ rushed. If you hope _____ a successful gardener, you must _____ willing to work at it.

Using Helping Verbs

Fill in the blanks with helping verbs from this list. Some sentences have several possible answers, but be sure to use each helping verb at least once.

are	do	is	was
be	does	may	were
can	has	seem	will
could	have	should	would

EXAMPLE A professional boxer _____*can*_____ deliver a punch having about 1,000 pounds of force.

1. Since 1945, boxing _____ killed about 350 men.

2. About a dozen _____ died since the early 1970s.

3. The statistics _____ to be getting better, but boxing remains a dangerous sport.

4. For example, in 1982 Duk Koo Kim died when he _____ hit over forty times by Ray "Boom Boom" Mancini.

5. The last punch _____ have killed him all by itself.

6. A killer punch _____ described by experts as a combination of force and placement.

7. Any blow that makes the head tilt violently to the side _____ produce brain damage.

8. When the head twists in this way, the brain _____ be slapped against the inside of the skull.

9. Nerve tissue can _____ damaged.

10. Blood vessels _____ rupture and bleed into the skull.

11. If bleeding is severe enough, pressure _____ build up, destroying nerves and cutting off oxygen to the brain.

12. When this _____ happen, the boxer's breathing and heartbeat can be affected.

13. Other difficulties, such as slurred speech, _____ show up years later as a result of constant small injuries to the brain.

14. Before formal rules for boxing _____ established, prizefighters fought bare-handed.

15. Just a century ago, John L. Sullivan, world boxing champion, _____ frequently fight without gloves.

16. Today some people _____ calling for a ban on boxing.

17. Others say that the sport _____ become safer over the years and that helmets _____ prevent most serious injuries.

18. Do you think boxing _____ be banned?

Identifying Transitive, Intransitive, and Linking Verbs

Identify each italicized verb by writing *transitive, intransitive,* or *linking* on the lines to the right.

EXAMPLE   The platypus of Australia *is* an unusual animal.   _____*linking*_____

1. Europeans first *saw* the platypus in 1796.   _____
2. The platypus *is* nocturnal.   _____
3. Usually it *stays* out of sight.   _____
4. The Europeans *could* hardly *believe* their eyes.   _____
5. The platypus *has* a bizarre appearance.   _____
6. Its bill *resembles* that of a duck.   _____
7. However, the bill *is* really a soft snout.   _____
8. With the bill the platypus *probes* in the mud for food.   _____
9. The platypus *has* a tail and fur like a beaver.   _____
10. With its webbed feet it *swims* well.   _____
11. Nevertheless, the feet *have* claws for digging in river banks.   _____
12. The platypus *is* a mammal.   _____
13. Yet it *lays* eggs.   _____
14. After hatching, the young *nurse*.   _____
15. No wonder one scientist *named* the platypus paradoxus.   _____
16. It *is* indeed a paradox.   _____

Writing Sentences with
Transitive and Intransitive Verbs

Write two sentences for each of the following verbs, one in which it is transitive and one in which it is intransitive.

EXAMPLE swim

The champion swims quickly.

The champion swims the mile in record time.

1. operate

    intransitive: _____

    transitive: _____

2. multiply

    intransitive: _____

    transitive: _____

3. meet

    intransitive: _____

    transitive: _____

4. lift

    intransitive: _____

    transitive: _____

5. evaporate

    intransitive: _____

    transitive: _____

Distinguishing the Forms of
lie/lay, sit/set, *and* rise/raise

EXERCISE 8-9

(8f)

A: The forms of *lie* and *lay,* *sit* and *set,* and *rise* and *raise* are easily confused. Fill in their forms below. Then check yourself by looking at the chart in 8f.

	-s Form	**Past Tense**	**Past Participle**	**Present Participle**
lie	_____	_____	_____	_____
lay	_____	_____	_____	_____
sit	_____	_____	_____	_____
set	_____	_____	_____	_____
rise	_____	_____	_____	_____
raise	_____	_____	_____	_____

B: Fill in the blanks with the verb in parentheses that best suits the meaning of each sentence.

EXAMPLE Columbus (set, sat) _____*set*_____ sail in 1492.

1. The New World (lay, laid) _____ to the west of Europe.

2. Columbus could keep a reasonably straight course by seeing where the sun (rose, raised) _____ each morning and where it (sat, set) _____ at night.

3. As long as the sun kept (setting, sitting) _____ in front of them, the crew knew they were on course.

4. This course had not been (laid, lain) _____ with precision.

5. Because European sailors did not know about hammocks yet, they all (laid, lay) _____ on the floor to sleep.

6. There probably was not much to do after work or much room to do it in, so the crew spent a lot of time just (laying, lying) _____ around.

7. The work was either hard, such as (sitting, setting) _____ the sails, or boring, such as (sitting, setting) _____ in the crow's nest looking for land.

8. When Columbus finally landed in Hispañola, he (laid, lay) _____ claim to the area for Spain.

9. Little did he realize the great cities that would one day (rise, raise) _____ in the New World.

10. He also didn't realize that the riches (lying, laying) _____ in his ships' holds would be the cause of centuries of war over power and trade.

Using the Perfect and Progressive Tenses

Fill in the blanks with the verb forms described in parentheses. Be prepared to discuss why each verb is appropriate in its sentence.

EXAMPLE   Many people who (to suffer: present perfect) _have suffered_ depression every winter of their lives are now getting help.

1. Some people (to report: present perfect) _____ that they feel sadder and sadder as winter days get shorter.

2. At the end of winter, when days (to begin: present progressive) _____ to get longer, the feelings of sadness go away.

3. Scientists (to begin: present perfect) _____ to call severe cases of this kind of sadness Seasonal Affective Disorder.

4. Newspapers (to use: present progressive) _____ the disorder's initials to form a useful nickname.

5. They (to call: present progressive) _____ the disorder SAD.

6. In the past, SAD sufferers (to say: past perfect) _____ that the only way they could feel better in the winter was to go south.

7. Scientists (to know: past perfect) _____ about this cure for winter depression, but they did not understand why it worked.

8. A new theory (to develop: present progressive) _____ .

9. Research indicates that the lack of sunlight in the winter (to cause: present perfect progressive) _____ the trouble.

10. People who (to spend: present perfect progressive) _____ winters in the south (to get: present perfect progressive) _____ more hours of bright sunlight.

11. This discovery (to lead: present perfect) _____ to the use of special, very bright lights for several hours a day as a treatment for the winter blues.

12. People who (to say: past perfect progressive) _____ that they felt better when they spent the winter in Florida or Arizona (to discover: past perfect) _____ an important scientific fact.

13. Scientists are not certain why increasing the number of hours of sunlight helps, but recent experiments (to provide: present perfect) _____ some clues.

14. After years of investigation, researchers (to connect: present perfect) _____ these winter mood changes to the pineal gland.

15. Scientists (to know: present perfect) _____ about the pineal gland for years.

Identifying Active and Passive Verbs

Underline the entire main verb in each sentence, and then identify it as *active* or *passive* on the lines to the right.

EXAMPLE   The Louvre ____*contains*____ some of the   ____*active*____
world's most famous art work.

1. The Louvre in Paris was not built as an art museum.   _____
2. The original Louvre was constructed in the twelfth   _____
century as a fortress.
3. Francis I erected the present building as a residence.   _____
4. A gallery connecting it with the Tuileries Palace was   _____
started by Henry IV and completed by Louis XIV.
5. A second gallery, begun by Napoleon, would have   _____
enclosed a great square.
6. However, it was not finished until after his abdication.   _____
7. Revolutionaries overthrew the Bastille on July 14, 1789.   _____
8. Just four years later, the art collection of the Louvre was   _____
opened to the public.
9. The collection can be traced back to Francis I.   _____
10. Francis, an ardent collector, invited Leonardo da Vinci to   _____
France in 1515.
11. Leonardo brought the *Mona Lisa* with him from Italy.   _____
12. Nevertheless, the royal art collection may have been   _____
expanded more by ministers than by kings.
13. Cardinals Richelieu and Mazarin can take credit for many   _____
important acquisitions.
14. Today the Louvre has a new entrance.   _____
15. A glass pyramid in the courtyard was designed by   _____
I. M. Pei.
16. Pei's name can be added to a distinguished list of   _____
Louvre architects.

Revising for the Active Voice

A: Change each of the passive sentences you identified in Exercise 8-11 into the active voice. You may need to add words to act as subjects of your new sentences. Use your own paper.

B: On the lines to the right, identify each sentence as *active* or *passive*. Then rewrite each passive sentence into the active voice. However, if you think a sentence is better left passive, write your reason on the line instead.

EXAMPLE   Today's country of Zimbabwe was named after important ruins.

passive

Patriots named today's country of Zimbabwe after important ruins.

1. The ruins were not known by people outside Africa until 1868.

2. The largest of the ruins, Great Zimbabwe, has two main structures.

3. The building on the hill was constructed primarily for defense.

4. Its stones are fitted together without mortar.

5. A lower, elliptical building is encircled by a thirty-foot wall.

6. An inner wall forms a passage to a sacred enclosure.

7. Majestic soapstone sculptures were discovered there.

8. The enclosure contains towers forty feet high.

136

9. Ancestors of the Shona-speaking people maintained   _____
Great Zimbabwe as a trade center from the 12th
through the 15th centuries.

_____

10. Tools for working with gold have been found in the   _____
ruins.

_____

11. The Shona traded gold and ivory with Arab merchants.   _____

_____

9 | *Case of Nouns and Pronouns*

9a Understanding case

The **case** (form) of a noun or pronoun shows how that word relates to other words in a sentence. For example, *we, us* and *our* are three different cases of the first-person-plural pronoun:

As **we** walked through the park, a crowd gathered around **us** to see **our** pet alligator.

English has three cases: **subjective, objective**, and **possessive**. Nouns use one form for the subjective and objective cases and have a separate possessive form, made with the apostrophe. Many pronouns, however, have three distinct forms for the three cases. **Personal pronouns**, the most common type of pronouns, have a full range of forms (cases) that show changes in **person** (first, second, and third person) and **number** (singular and plural). (For an explanation of *person*, see 11a).

CASES OF PERSONAL PRONOUNS					
	SUBJECTIVE		**OBJECTIVE**		**POSSESSIVE**
	Singular/Plural		Singular/Plural		Singular/Plural
First person	I	we	me	us	my/mine · our/ours
Second person	you	you	you	you	your/yours · your/yours
Third person	he she it	they	him her it	them	his · their/theirs · her/hers · its

The plural of *you* is simply *you*. Avoid the nonstandard plural *yous*.

A pronoun in the **subjective case** functions as a subject of a sentence or clause.

We needed an apartment. [*We* is the subject.]

A pronoun in the **objective case** functions as a direct object or an indirect object.

A friend called **us** one night. [*Us* is the direct object.]
He told **us** a secret. [*Us* is the indirect object.]
He had a surprise for **us**. [*Us* is the object of a preposition.]

A pronoun in the **possessive case** indicates possession or ownership.

♣ PUNCTUATION ALERT: Do not use an apostrophe for a personal pronoun in the possessive case. ♣

He said that **his** neighbor was moving next month.
We called the neighbor and agreed to sublet **her** apartment.
Its windows look out over a park.

9b Using the same cases for pronouns in compound constructions as in single constructions

A compound construction contains more than one subject or object (see 7k–1, 7l). This compounding has no effect on the choice of a pronoun case.

He and **I** saw the eclipse of the sun. [compound subject.]
The beauty of the eclipse astounded both **him** and **me**. [compound object.]

If you are unsure which case to use, try this "drop test." Temporarily *drop all of the compound element except the pronoun in question*, and then you will be able to tell which pronoun case is needed. Here is how the method works for compound subjects.

EXAMPLE **Janet and (me, I)** read that the moon has one-eightieth the mass of the earth.

STEP 1 Drop *Janet and*.

STEP 2 Which reads correctly: "**Me** read that the moon has one-eightieth the mass of the earth" or "**I** read that the moon has one-eightieth the mass of the earth"?

STEP 3 Answer: Janet and **I** read that the moon has one-eightieth the mass of the earth.

The same test works for compound objects:

EXAMPLE The instructor told **Janet and (I, me)** that the moon has one-fiftieth the volume of the earth.

STEP 1 Drop *Janet and*.

STEP 2 Which reads correctly: "The instructor told **I** that the moon has one-fiftieth the volume of the earth" or "The instructor told **me** that the moon has one-fiftieth the volume of the earth"?

9d

Step 3   **Answer:** The instructor told Janet and **me** that the moon has one-fiftieth the volume of the earth.

When pronouns in a **prepositional phrase** (7n) occur in compound constructions (*The book was about* **him** *and* **me**), the pronouns often appear in the wrong case. You may hear people say "with he and I" or "between you and I," but this usage is incorrect. A prepositional phrase always includes an object, so any pronouns that follow words such as *with, to, from, for, after,* or *between* must be in the objective case. See 7g for a complete list of prepositions.

No   The reward will be divided **between you and I**. [*I* is in the subjective case and cannot follow a preposition.]

Yes   The reward will be divided **between you and me**. [*Me* is in the objective case, so it is correct.]

9c Matching noun and pronoun cases in appositives

When one or more pronouns occur in an **appositive** (7m–3)—a word or group of words that renames the noun or noun phrase next to it—the pronoun takes the same case as the noun replaced.

No   **Us** working women lead productive lives. [*Working women* is the subject, so *us*, an objective pronoun, is incorrect.]

Yes   **We** working women lead productive lives. [*We* is a subjective pronoun: correct.]

No   Someone ought to give working mothers, **she** and **I**, better job opportunities. [*Working mothers* is the object, so *she* and *I*, subjective pronouns, are incorrect.]

Yes   Someone ought to give working mothers, **her** and **me**, better job opportunities. [*Her* and *me* are objective pronouns: correct.]

9d Avoiding the objective case after linking verbs

A **linking verb** connects the subject to a word that renames it. Such a renaming word is called a **complement**. Because a pronoun coming after a linking verb renames the subject, that pronoun must be in the subjective case.

Is Lee at home? This is **he**. [*He* renames *this*, the subject, so the subjective case is required.]

Who is there? It is **I**. [*I* renames *it*, the subject, so the subjective case is required.]

The winner of the speed skating event was **she**. [*She* renames *the winner*, the subject, so the subjective case is required.]

In speech and informal writing the objective case is often used in these situations, but academic writing is more formal and requires the subjective case.

9e Using *who, whoever, whom,* and *whomever*

Who and *whoever*, which function as both **relative** and **interrogative pronouns** (7b), change forms in the different cases. Within each case, however, they remain the same for all persons and for singular and plural.

CASES OF RELATIVE AND INTERROGATIVE PRONOUNS		
SUBJECTIVE	**OBJECTIVE**	**POSSESSIVE**
who	whom	whose
whoever	whomever	——

To determine whether *who, whom, whoever,* or *whomever* is correct in a dependent clause (7o–2), temporarily drop everything in the sentence up to the pronoun in question, and then make substitutions—remembering that *he, she, they, who,* and *whoever* are subjects, and *him, her, them, whom,* and *whomever* are objects.

STEP 1   I asked (**who, whom**) attended the World Series.

STEP 2   Omit *I asked.*

STEP 3   Test what other pronoun would make a sensible sentence: "**He** attended the World Series" or "**Him** attended the World Series."

STEP 4   Answer: "**He** attended the World Series."

STEP 5   Therefore, because *he* is subjective, *who,* which is also subjective, is correct: "I asked **who** attended the World Series."

The subjective case is called for even when expressions such as *I think* and *he says* come between the subject and the verb. Ignore these expressions when determining the correct pronoun.

He is the pitcher **who** [I think] will be elected Most Valuable Player.

This process also works for the objective case (*whom*), as well as for *whoever* and *whomever.*

At the beginning of questions, use *who* if the question is about the subject and *whom* if the question is about the object. If you are unsure, reword the question as a statement.

Who repaired the radio? ["*I* repaired the radio" uses the subjective pronoun *I,* so *who* is correct.]

Jacques admires **whom**? ["Jacques admires *him*" uses the objective pronoun *him,* so *whom* is correct.]

To **whom** does Jacques speak about becoming an electrician? ["Jacques speaks to *me* about becoming an electrician" uses the objective pronoun *me,* so *whom* is correct.]

In speech and informal writing, *who* is often used for both subjects and objects

(*Who does Jacques ask?*), but such practice is nonstandard and should be avoided in academic writing.

9f Using the pronoun case after *than* or *as*

When a pronoun follows *than* or *as*, the pronoun case carries essential information about what is being said. For example, the following two sentences convey two very different messages, simply because of the choice between the words *me* and *I* after *than*.

1. My sister photographs landscapes more **than** *me*.
2. My sister photographs landscapes more **than** *I*.

Sentence 1 means "My sister photographs landscapes more *than she photographs me*." On the other hand, sentence 2 means "My sister photographs landscapes more *than I photograph landscapes*." To make sure that any sentence of comparison is clear, either include all the words in the second half or mentally fill in the words to check whether you have chosen the correct pronoun case.

9g Using pronouns with infinitives

Objective pronouns occur as both subjects and objects of infinitives (7d).

His nephew wanted **him** to challenge *me* to a raft race. [*Him* is the subject of the infinitive *to challenge*; *me* is the object of the infinitive; both are in the objective case.]

9h Using pronouns with *-ing* words

A **gerund** is the *-ing* form of a verb that functions as a noun: ***Singing in the shower*** *is a common pastime.* When a noun or pronoun precedes a gerund, the possessive case is called for.

Igor's singing annoyed the neighbors.
His singing annoyed the neighbors.

In contrast, the **present participle** is the *-ing* form that functions as an adjective. It does not take the possessive case.

Igor, **singing in the shower**, annoyed the neighbors.

9i Using *-self* pronouns

Reflexive pronouns reflect back on the subject or object.

The diver prepared **herself** for the finals.
She had to force **herself** to relax.

Reflexive pronouns should not be used as substitutes for subjects or objects.

The diver and **I** [not *myself*] wished the sportscasters would go away.
They bothered her and **me** [not *myself*] for interviews.

Intensive pronouns provide emphasis.

The diver felt that competing **itself** was stressful enough without giving interviews.
The sportscasters acted as though they **themselves** were the only reason for the event.

Avoid the following nonstandard forms of reflexive and intensive pronouns in academic writing: *hisself*, nonstandard for *himself*; *theirself, theirselves, themself,* and *themselfs*, nonstandard for *themselves*.

Knowing the Personal Pronouns

The personal pronouns change form to show whether they are being used as subjects, objects, or possessives and to match the person and number of their antecedents. Fill in this chart with the appropriate forms of the personal pronouns. Then check yourself by looking at the chart at the beginning of this chapter.

	Person	Subjective Case	Objective Case	Possessive Case
Singular	First	_____	_____	_____
	Second	_____	_____	_____
	Third	_____	_____	_____
Plural	First	_____	_____	_____
	Second	_____	_____	_____
	Third	_____	_____	_____

Identifying Pronoun Case

Underline the personal pronouns. Then on the lines to the right indicate their cases.

EXAMPLE <u>I</u> recently read an article about <u>my</u> least favorite animal.

	subjective	possessive

1. Just thinking about cockroaches makes me uncomfortable.

2. How do they affect you?

3. The author of the article says that the cockroach is his enemy.

4. He is a pest-control specialist.

5. According to him, cockroaches have been around since before the dinosaurs.

6. Roaches have lasted this long because their bodies are perfect for what they do.

7. They can eat almost anything and can survive on very little.

8. A dozen of them can live for a week on the glue of one postage stamp.

9. One variety can live for a month without food as long as it has water.

10. They reproduce very quickly, 100,000 offspring a year from a single pair.

11. A scientist who has spent ten years studying roaches says each one has its own personality.

12. She learned this by studying their nighttime behavior.

13. Research shows that they learn from experience and change their behavior to escape danger.

14. No place is free from them—even submarines.

15. One roach destroyed a $975,000 computer by getting inside it and eating its wires.

16. Roaches can also harm us because   _____   _____
    they may carry dangerous bacteria.   _____   _____
17. Our best defense against roaches   _____   _____
    may be new chemicals that stop
    them from reproducing.   _____   _____
18. In the meantime, we may have to   _____   _____
    continue sharing our planet with
    them.   _____   _____

EXERCISE 9-3

Using Personal Pronouns

(9a)

Select the correct pronoun from the choice in parentheses. Write your answers on the lines to the right. If two choices are needed, use a comma to separate them on the answer line.

EXAMPLE   My friend and (I, me) visited Washington, D.C., last   _____
          spring.

1. Other tourists and (we, us) were delighted by what (we,   _____
   us) saw.   _____

2. (It, Its) is a beautiful city.   _____
3. By the end of the week, each of (us, ours) had a favorite   _____
   place.
4. My little brother was impressed by what (he, his) saw at   _____
   the Bureau of Engraving and Printing.
5. (He, Him) and (I, me) took a tour of the Bureau.   _____
                                                               _____

6. We could not believe (our, ours) eyes when we saw   _____
   people actually making money.
7. As (I, me) and (he, him) watched people printing paper   _____
   money, my brother said it was a great job because the   _____
   people could keep some money for (them, themselves).   _____
8. I told (he, him) that he was kidding (him, himself) if he   _____
   really believed that.   _____
9. Employees have security people watching (them,   _____
   themselves) and the money (it, itself) is counted and   _____
   recounted to prevent theft.
10. I wondered if (them, their) working around money all day   _____
    might make money less exciting to these people after a
    while.

11. Still, it was fascinating for (we, us) to watch all that
    money being printed.   _____

12. The Lincoln Memorial was (me, my) favorite place.   _____

13. The Memorial is a simple statue of Abraham Lincoln   _____
    (hisself, himself), seated looking out over the capital.

14. Standing near that huge statue made my sister and (I,   _____
    me) feel very calm, as if Lincoln were watching out for   _____
    (us, ourselves).

15. My sister said that the most exciting place for (she, her)   _____
    was the National Air and Space Museum.

16. This is probably because of (her, hers) desire to be an   _____
    astronaut.

17. If (you, yous) go to Washington, D.C., visit the National   _____
    Air and Space Museum even if (you, your) are not   _____
    planning to be a pilot or an astronaut.

18. Children will especially enjoy the chance the Museum   _____
    gives (they, them) to see and sometimes touch famous
    old airplanes.

19. While there, they can also see for (theirselfs,   _____
    themselves) copies of space vehicles.

20. Now that I have told you about my family's favorite   _____
    places in Washington, D.C., will you tell me about (your,
    yours)?

Identifying and Using Personal Pronouns as Appositives and Complements

A: Underline all personal pronouns used as appositives or complements. Then draw an arrow connecting each to its antecedent. Be prepared to explain why each pronoun takes the case it does.

EXAMPLE   The winner is *I*.

1. The partners, he and she, have been together for years.

2. A legend in his own time is he.

3. The judges selected the best cheesecake, ours.

4. The first ones in the group to marry were they.

5. The letter finally reached the addressee, me, six years later.

B: Select the correct pronoun for formal situations from the choices in parentheses. Write your answers on the lines to the right.

EXAMPLE   The smartest couple, you and (I, me) _____, _____*I*_____
             will be on the cover of the yearbook.

1. If anyone deserves a medal, it is (she, her) _____.   _____

2. Our travel agent has booked a vacation tour for us, just   _____
   you and (I, me) _____ .

3. The recipient of the donated heart was (he, him) _____.   _____

4. I saw the thieves, (he, him) _____ and his   _____
   brother.

5. Altos, (I, me) _____ for one, don't get to sing   _____
   any of the great opera roles.

Using who *and* whom

Select the correct relative or interrogative pronoun (*who, whom, whoever,* or *whomever*) from the choices in parentheses. Write your answers on the lines to the right.

EXAMPLE   The number of children (who, whom) are in a
family may affect the intelligence of all the children.   _____who_____

1. Researchers (who, whom) studied over 350,000 men in the 1940s found that IQ fell as family size increased.   _____

2. Children (who, whom) were born into a family later tended to have lower IQ's.   _____

3. Recent research supports the theory that (whoever, whomever) is born first has an advantage.   _____

4. Children (who, whom) researchers checked for IQ and school performance did better if they were the oldest in small families.   _____

5. (Whoever, Whomever) was an only child, however, scored like a younger child.   _____

6. (Who, Whom) can be sure why these trends occur?   _____

7. It may be that younger children receive less mental stimulation because their brothers and sisters (who, whom) teach them are immature.   _____

8. Only children, (who, whom) are usually considered lucky, may miss out because they never have a chance to grow by teaching their own younger brothers and sisters.   _____

9. Perhaps parents' attention, no matter to (who, whom) it is given, is limited, so there is simply more of it per child in smaller families.   _____

10. Of course, there are highly intelligent and successful people (who, whom) are born into large families.   _____

11. Teachers and parents of young children should be careful about (who, whom) they make judgments.   _____

12. We cannot use these studies to predict the future of (whoever, whomever) we please, because in the end success depends on a lot more than birth order and family size.   _____

13. Few successful people (who, whom) have been asked the secret of their success talk about birth order.   _____

14. Often, successful people give credit to their drive to achieve something and to the people (who, whom) supported them.   _____

15. For example, listen to the speeches at any awards   _____
    ceremony and you will hear people thanking the parents,
    teachers, and friends without (who, whom) they could
    not have succeeded.

16. (Who, Whom) would you thank if you were giving such   _____
    a speech?

Choosing Pronoun Cases Carefully

EXERCISE **9-6**

(9f-i)

Select the correct pronoun from the choices in parentheses. Write your answers on the lines to the right.

EXAMPLE   J. Edgar Hoover changed the way FBI agents   ___*them*___
           worked from the moment he was appointed to
           lead (they, them) in 1924.

1. After he proved (him, himself) as a special assistant to   _____
   the U.S. Attorney General, Hoover was named director
   of the Bureau of Investigation.

2. The government wanted (he, him) to reorganize the   _____
   Bureau, which had been filled with scandal.

3. As head of the Bureau, Hoover set new standards for (it,   _____
   its) recruiting and training of agents.

4. Some nations were reorganizing their police files to keep   _____
   better track of criminals; Hoover established a
   fingerprint file that was bigger than any of (them, theirs).

5. He set up a scientific crime lab to help (he, him) and his   _____
   agents analyze evidence.

6. One of his greatest contributions was (him, his) opening   _____
   of the FBI National Academy, to which law officers from
   all over the country are still sent for training.

7. In those early years, the FBI concentrated on fighting   _____
   organized crime, but to many people the gangsters
   (they, themselves) were romantic figures.

8. Hoover responded by setting up a publicity campaign for   _____
   the agents to make (they, them) glamorous in the
   public's eyes.

9. (Him, His) heading the FBI made Hoover a world figure.   _____

10. People, in comparing his agency to other crime-fighting units, said the others were not as free of political control as (he, his) was.

    _____

11. Unfortunately, in his later years as director, he and the Bureau (it, itself) came under attack for suspicious actions.

    _____

12. Some even said that presidents agreed to keep (he, him) in power because of the files he had on them.

    _____

13. However, these charges against Hoover were not proven, and (him, his) dying in office in 1972 closed a long and eventful career.

    _____

14. Several people have served as FBI directors since Hoover's death, but none has been as powerful as (he, him).

    _____

15. The FBI continues to protect (we, us) Americans, but in a less dramatic way than when Hoover was its leader.

    _____

10 | *Pronoun Reference*

The meaning of a pronoun comes from its **antecedent**, the noun or pronoun to which the pronoun refers. In order for your writing to communicate its message clearly, each pronoun must relate directly to an antecedent. You can accomplish this by following a few simple rules.

10a Making a pronoun refer clearly to a single antecedent

To be understood, a pronoun must refer to a specific single (or compound) antecedent.

> Daniel Boone was born near Reading, Pennsylvania, in 1734, but as a youngster **he** moved to the North Carolina frontier with **his** family.

Often the same pronoun fits more than one possible antecedent. This situation can be confusing.

> Boone is often confused with Davy Crockett. **He** was born in eastern Tennessee in 1786. **His** family was just as poor as **his**; both had little formal education. **He** became a member of the Tennessee legislature in 1821 and eventually died at the Alamo in 1836. **He** became famous for opening up Kentucky to settlers, and **he** died in 1820—long before the Battle of the Alamo.

A writer can clarify such a passage by replacing some pronouns with nouns so that each remaining pronoun clearly refers to a single antecedent.

> **Boone** is often confused with **Davy Crockett. Crockett** was born in eastern Tennessee in 1786. **His** family was just as poor as **Boone's**; both had little formal education. **Crockett** became a member of the Tennessee legislature in 1821 and eventually died at the Alamo in 1836. **Boone** became famous for opening up Kentucky to settlers, and **he** died in 1820—long before the Battle of the Alamo.

Using *said* and *told* with pronouns that appear to refer to more than one person is especially likely to create confusion. Use quotation marks and slightly reword the sentence to make the meaning clearer.

No	Her aunt told her she was returning to school.
Yes	Her aunt told her, "You are returning to school."
Yes	Her aunt told her, "I am returning to school."

10b Placing pronouns close to their antecedents for clarity

If too much material comes between a pronoun and its antecedent, unclear pronoun reference results. Readers lose track of the meaning of a passage if they have to trace too far back to find the antecedent of a pronoun.

> **No**   **Patrick Henry**, who said "Give me liberty, or give me death," turned down many important political positions: a seat in the Senate, ambassadorships to Spain and France, Secretary of State, and Chief Justice of the Supreme Court. **He** did, however, serve as Governor of Virginia for five terms. **He** was elected to a sixth, but refused to serve. [Although *he* can refer only to *Patrick Henry*, too much material comes between the first pronoun and its antecedent.]

> **Yes**   **Patrick Henry**, who said "Give me liberty, or give me death," turned down many important political positions: a seat in the Senate, ambassadorships to Spain and France, Secretary of State, and Chief Justice of the Supreme Court. **Henry** did, however, serve as Governor of Virginia for five terms. **He** was elected to a sixth, but refused to serve.

10c Making a pronoun refer to a definite antecedent

A noun in its possessive form (*the car's exhaust*) cannot also serve as the subject (*The car stalled*) or object (*I sold the car*) of its sentence. Thus a pronoun cannot refer back to a noun in its possessive form.

> **No**   **Galen's** formula for cold cream has not changed much since **he** invented it 1,700 years ago. [*He* cannot refer to the possessive *Galen's*.]

> **Yes**   **Galen's** formula for cold cream has not changed much since **the Roman physician** invented it 1,700 years ago.

An adjective serves as a modifier, not as a subject or object. Thus a pronoun cannot refer back to an adjective.

> **No**   Janet works at the **cosmetics** counter. **They** are inexpensive. [*They* cannot refer to the adjective *cosmetics*.]

> **Yes**   Janet works at the cosmetics counter. **The products** are inexpensive.

> **No**   **Pink** lipstick is always popular. **It** is Janet's favorite color.

> **Yes**   **Pink** lipstick is always popular. Janet's favorite color is **pink**.

Pronouns such as *it, that, this,* and *which* are particularly prone to unclear reference. As you write and revise, check carefully to see that each of these pronouns refers to only one antecedent that can be determined easily by your readers. When necessary, replace the confusing pronoun with a noun.

> **No**   Annie Taylor, a 43-year-old widow, was the first person to go over Niagara

Falls in a barrel. **This** was fantastic. [What does *this* refer to? Her age? Her being a widow? A female being the first person to go over the Falls?]

Yes   Annie Taylor, a 43-year-old widow, was the first person to go over Niagara Falls in a barrel. **That anyone would want to do this** was fantastic.

No   After going over the Falls, Taylor admitted she could not swim. **It was very dangerous.** [What does *it* refer to?]

Yes   After going over the Falls, Taylor admitted she could not swim. **Her stunt** was very dangerous.

In speech, such statements as *it said in the papers* and *at the United Nations they say* are common. Such expressions are inexact, however, and should be avoided.

The newspapers report [not *It said in the newspapers*] that many United Nations officials receive high salaries.

A United Nations spokesperson says [not *At the United Nations they say*] **that the** high salaries are rewards for doing difficult jobs well.

A piece of writing has to stand on its own, so when you are referring to a title, be sure to repeat or reword whatever part of the title you want to use. Do not use a pronoun in the first sentence of an essay to refer to the essay's title.

Title   *Airport Security Must Be Strict*

No   Yes, I agree with this.

Yes   Because of the dangerous state of world affairs, airport security must be strict.

10d Not overusing *it*

It has three different uses in English.

1. *It* is a personal pronoun: *Rachel decided which VCR she wants, but she doesn't have enough money to buy **it** yet.*
2. *It* is an expletive, a word that postpones the subject: *It is lucky that the price of VCR's is falling.*
3. *It* is part of idiomatic expressions of weather, time, or distance: *It is raining.*

All of these uses are acceptable, but combining them in the same sentence can create confusion.

No   **It** was fortunate that I tried the new restaurant on the day that **it** opened an outdoor cafe section, because **it** was a sunny day.

Yes   I was fortunate to try the new restaurant on the day that the outdoor cafe section opened, because **it** was a sunny day.

10e Using *you* only for direct address

You is used frequently in speech and informal writing to refer to general groups of people (*You can never tell what fashions will be popular*). In academic writing, however, *you* is acceptable only if the writer is directly addressing the reader. For example, *you* is used in this workbook because we, the authors, are directly addressing you, our reader. Similarly, your instructor might write on one of your essays: "Your introduction makes me want to read on."

You should not be used in academic writing to refer to people in general, however.

No	At many libraries, **you** can check books out for two weeks. [Does this mean that libraries have a special circulation period just for the reader?]
YES	At many libraries, **borrowers** can check books out for two weeks.

10f Using *who, which,* and *that*

Who refers to people or to animals with names or special talents.

The Pied Piper was a real man, **who** led all the plague-carrying rats out of Hamlin, Germany, on July 22, 1376.

The movie *Willard* featured a rat named Ben, **who** was the hero's friend.

Which and *that* refer to animals, things, and sometimes anonymous or collective groups of people. The choice between *which* and *that* depends on whether the clause introduced by the pronoun is restrictive (essential) or nonrestrictive (nonessential). Use *that* with restrictive clauses and *which* with nonrestrictive clauses. Use *who* for people in both kinds of clauses. ♣ COMMA CAUTION: Set off nonrestrictive clauses with commas. For a fuller explanation, see 24e. ♣

Rats, **which** often carry disease-bearing fleas, are health problems.

Garbage, **which** rats love, must be cleaned up before the rats can be driven out.

Rats **that** have been inbred for generations are the ideal lab animals.

All traits **that** might interfere with experiments have been eliminated.

Lab workers **that** handle rats every day probably are not repelled by them.

Using Pronouns to Refer to a Single Nearby Antecedent

Underline the pronouns in these passages. Then, if the antecedents are clear and close enough to their pronouns, copy the sentences onto the lines. If the antecedents are unclear or too far away, use the lines to revise the sentences.

EXAMPLE   Henry C. Wallace and his son Henry A. Wallace held the same cabinet post. He was the Secretary of Agriculture under Harding and Coolidge, and he was Secretary of Agriculture under Franklin Roosevelt.

Henry C. Wallace and his son Henry A. Wallace held the same cabinet post. Henry C. Wallace was the Secretary of Agriculture under Harding and Coolidge, and Henry A. Wallace was the Secretary of Agriculture under Franklin Roosevelt.

1. House of Representative and Senate members work with young people called pages. They run errands for them.

   _____

2. The longest filibuster in the U.S. Senate was delivered by Senator Wayne Morse of Oregon. However, Texas State Senator Mike McKool spoke far longer. He spoke for 42 hours and 33 minutes.

   _____

   _____

3. For religious reasons, Zachary Taylor refused to take the presidential oath of office on a Sunday, so David Rice Atchison (president of the Senate) was president for a day. He spent the day appointing his temporary cabinet.

   _____

   _____

4. Calvin Coolidge was sworn into office by his own father.

   _____

5. An American Indian, Charles Curtis, became vice-president when Herbert Hoover was elected president in 1928. He was one-half Kaw.

   _____

   _____

6. William DeVance King, vice-president under Franklin Pierce, was in Cuba during the election and had to be sworn in by an act of Congress, never bothering to return to Washington. A month later, never having carried out any official duties, he died.

_____

_____

7. The Republicans got their elephant and the Democrats got their donkey as symbols from political cartoonist Thomas Nast.

_____

_____

8. The first woman presidential candidate was Victoria Woodhull. Years before Geraldine Ferraro ran for vice-president, she was on the Equal Rights Party ticket—in 1872.

_____

_____

9. President Grover Cleveland installed the first telephone in the White House in the late 1880s. Whenever it rang, he answered it himself.

_____

_____

10. As a child, president-to-be Andrew Johnson was sold as an indentured servant to a tailor. He was supposed to work for seven years, but he ran away.

_____

_____

11. President William McKinley had a pet parrot. Whenever he whistled the beginning of "Yankee Doodle," it would complete it.

_____

_____

Using Pronouns to Refer
to Definite Antecedents

Revise these vague passages so that all pronouns have definite antecedents. Be alert for implied antecedents and the misuse of *it, they,* and *you.*

EXAMPLE   It says in the Census Report that 84 percent of Americans get to work by car, truck, or van.

The Census Report says that 84 percent of Americans get to work by car, truck, or van.

1. In 1981, over 27 percent of the cars bought in the United States were imports, compared with 6.4 percent twenty years earlier. It explains why American automobile plants had so many layoffs.

   _____

   _____

2. Eighteen- and nineteen-year-olds' driving records are the worst. They are involved in more fatal car accidents than any other group.

   _____

   _____

3. It has been demonstrated that when a car goes over 50 miles per hour, it uses half its fuel to overcome the wind resistance to it.

   _____

   _____

4. They claim that 60 percent of the price of food goes to cover the cost of transportation.

   _____

   _____

5. License plates were first issued in Paris by the police in 1893. The first American plates were issued in New York State in 1901. This shows license plates are an old idea.

   _____

   _____

6. The first national auto show was organized in Boston in 1900. You could see cars from thirty-one manufacturers.

_____

_____

7. More than 6,000 cars a year are stolen in Texas alone for illegal export to Mexico. More than 100,000 cars are stolen each year in New York City. That is why our insurance rates in those places are so high.

_____

_____

8. They say there are 1,000 springs of various kinds in each new car.

_____

9. You have about 200 pounds of plastic in the average car.

_____

Revising to Eliminate Misuse of you

EXERCISE **10-3**

(10e)

Revise this paragraph to eliminate the inappropriate use of *you*. Begin by changing "You have to be careful" to "Everyone has to be careful." Then change further uses of *you* to suitable nouns or pronouns. It may be necessary to change some verbs in order to have them agree with new subjects.

You have to be careful when buying on credit. Otherwise, you may wind up so heavily in debt that it will take years to straighten out your life. Credit cards are easy for you to get if you are working, and many finance companies are eager to give you installment loans at high interest rates. Once you are hooked, you may find yourself taking out loans to pay your loans. When this happens, you are doomed to being forever in debt.

There are, of course, times when using credit makes sense. If you have the money (or will have it when the bill comes), a credit card can enable you to shop without carrying cash. You may also want to keep a few gasoline credit cards with you in case your car breaks down on the road. Using credit will allow you to deal with other emergencies (tuition, a broken water heater) when you lack the cash. You can also use credit to take advantage of sales. However, you need to recognize the difference between a sale item you need and one you want. If you cannot do this, you may find yourself dealing with collection agents, car repossessors, or even bankruptcy lawyers.

11 | *Agreement*

11a Understanding subject–verb agreement

Subject–verb agreement occurs at least once per sentence. To function correctly, subjects and verbs must match in number (singular or plural) and in person (first, second, or third).

> The human **brain weighs** about three pounds. [*brain* = singular subject in the third person; *weighs* = singular verb in the third person]

> Human **brains weigh** about three pounds. [*brains* = plural subject in the third person; *weigh* = plural verb in the third person]

A QUICK REVIEW OF PERSON FOR AGREEMENT

The **first person** is the speaker or writer. *I* (singular) and *we* (plural) are the only subjects that occur in the first person.

Singular   *I* see a field of fireflies.

Plural   *We* see a field of fireflies.

The **second person** is the person spoken or written to. *You* (both singular and plural) is the only subject that occurs in the second person.

Singular   *You* see a shower of sparks.

Plural   *You* see a shower of sparks.

The **third person** is the person or thing being spoken or written of. Most rules for subject–verb agreement involve the third person. A subject in the third person can vary widely—for example, *student* and *students* (singular and plural people), *table* and *tables* (singular and plural things), and *it* and *they* (singular and plural pronouns).

Singular   The **scientist sees** a cloud of cosmic dust.

　　　　　　 She (he, it) sees a cloud of cosmic dust.

Plural   The **scientists see** a cloud of cosmic dust.

　　　　　　 They see a cloud of cosmic dust.

11b Using the final -s or -es either for plural subjects or for singular verbs

Subject–verb agreement often involves one letter: *s*. The key is the difference between the -*s* added to subjects and the -*s* added to verbs.

Plural subjects are usually formed by adding -*s* or -*es* to singular nouns. **Singular verbs** in the present tense of the third person are formed by adding -*s* or -*es* to the simple form—with the exceptions of *be (is)* and *have (has)*.

Visualizing how the *s* works in agreement can help you remember when it is needed. The -*s* (or -*es* when the word already ends in -*s*) can take only one path at a time, either the top or the bottom, as in this diagram.

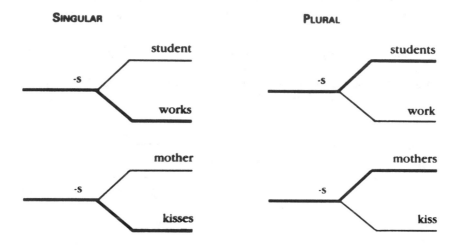

Even though the final -*s* does not appear in some subjects, the principle of the memory device holds. This final -*s* does not appear in the following situations: in subjects that are plural without an -*s* (such as *people, children*); in plural personal pronouns (*we, you, they*); in the plural demonstrative pronouns (*these, those*); and in certain indefinite pronouns when they are used as plurals (*few, some, more, many, most, all*).

> A **person** on a diet often **misses** sweets.
>
> **People enjoy** candy or cake after meals.
>
> **They learn** to substitute fruit for pastry.

♣ USAGE ALERT: Do not add -*s* to the third-person singular main verb after a modal auxiliary verb (a helping verb such as *can, might, must, would*—see 8e). ♣

11c For agreement, ignore words between a subject and verb

Words that separate the subject from the verb can cause confusion about what the verb should agree with. To locate the subject of the sentence, ignore prepositional phrases or phrases that start with *including, together with, along with, accompanied by, in addition to, except,* or *as well as.*

The best **workers** in the bookkeeping department **have** received raises.

The top-selling sales **representative**, along with her husband, **is going** to visit San Diego as a bonus.

11d Using verbs with subjects connected with *and*

When two or more subjects are joined by *and*, they function as a group; therefore, they need a plural verb.

Soda and iced tea are popular summer drinks.

My friend and I prefer cold milk.

However, if the word *each* or *every* precedes subjects joined by *and*, use a singular verb.

Each cat and dog in the animal shelter **deserves** a home.

When *each* or *every* follows subjects joined by *and*, however, it does not affect the basic rule: use a plural verb for subjects joined by *and*:

The ASPCA and the Humane Society each **need** our support.

The one exception to the *and* rule occurs when the parts combine to form a single thing or person.

Beans and rice is a popular vegetarian dish.

My husband and business partner keeps our tax records.

11e Making the verb agree with the subject closest to it

When you join subjects with *or* or *nor* or correlative conjunctions, *either . . . or, neither . . . nor, not only . . . but (also)*, make the verb agree with the subject closest to it. Unlike *and*, these conjunctions do not create plurals. For the purpose of agreement, ignore everything before the final subject.

~~Neither Benny Goodman nor~~ **Louis Armstrong is** heard on the radio often.

~~Either the Andrews Sisters or~~ **Frank Sinatra was** my mother's favorite singer.

11f Using verbs in inverted word order

In questions, the verb comes before the subject. Be sure to look ahead to check that the subject and verb agree.

Is jazz popular?

Expletive constructions postpone the subject by using *there* or *here* plus a form of the verb *be*. Check ahead in such sentences to identify the subject, and make the form of *be* agree with the subject.

There were many **bands** that played swing in the forties.
There is still a dedicated **audience** for this music.

Introductory *it* plus a form of the verb *be* can be an expletive construction as well, but one that always takes a singular verb.

It is young musicians who strive to capture the sound of the Big Bands.

11g Using verbs with indefinite pronouns

Indefinite pronouns do not refer to any particular person, thing, or idea. They take their meanings from context. Indefinite pronouns are usually singular, and therefore they take singular verbs. Here is a list of singular indefinite pronouns:

each	everyone	no one
every	everybody	nobody
one	everything	nothing
either	anyone	someone
neither	anybody	somebody
another	anything	something

Everybody talks about the weather but **no one does** a thing about it.
No matter what **someone forecasts, something** different **seems** to happen.

Two indefinite pronouns, *both* and *many*, are always plural and require a plural verb.

Both of them **accept** the decision.

A few indefinite pronouns—*none, some, more, most, any,* and *all*—may be either singular or plural, depending on the meaning of the sentence.

All of the weather forecasts we hear **are** based on probabilities.
We hate bad weather, but **some is** inevitable.

11h Using verbs in context for collective nouns

A **collective noun** names a group of people or things: *family, group, audience, class, number, committee, team*. When the group acts as one unit, use a singular verb. When the members of the group act individually, use a plural verb.

The **jury is** hearing evidence. [*Jury* refers to a single unit, so the verb is singular.]
The **jury disagree** on a verdict. [The jury members take separate action, so the verb is plural.]

11i Making a linking verb agree with the subject—not the subject complement

Even when the **subject complement** (7m–1) that follows a linking verb (7c) differs in number (singular and plural) from the subject, the verb must agree with the subject.

The best **part** of the week **is** Saturday and Sunday.

but

Saturday and Sunday are the best part of the week.

11j Using verbs that agree with the antecedents of *who, which*, and *that*

Who, which, and *that* have the same form in singular and plural, so you must find their antecedents (10a) before you can decide whether the verb is singular or plural.

The **tenants who move** into this apartment will need to paint it. [*Who* refers to *tenants*, so the verb *move* is plural.]
The **tenant who moves** into this apartment will need to paint it. [*Who* refers to *tenant*, so the verb *moves* is singular.]

Be especially careful to identify the antecedent of *who, which*, or *that* when you see *one of the* or *the only one of the* in a sentence.

George Boyd is one of the **tenants who want** to hire a new janitor. [*Who* refers to *tenants*, so *want* is plural.]
George Boyd is the only **one** of the tenants **who wants** to hire a new janitor. [*Who* refers to *one*, so *wants* is singular.]

11k Using singular verbs with subjects that specify amounts and with singular subjects that are in plural form

Subjects that refer to times, sums of money, distance, or measurement are considered singular and take singular verbs.

Seventy-five cents is the toll over the bridge.
One and six-tenths kilometers makes a mile.

Many words that end in *-s* or *-ics* are singular in meaning despite their plural appearance. These include *news, ethics, economics, mathematics, physics, politics, sports, statistics* (as a course of study).

Mathematics is necessary for many daily tasks.
Athletics demands total commitment.

In contrast, other words are plural even though they refer to one thing. These include *jeans, pants, scissors, clippers, tweezers, eyeglasses, thanks, riches*.

The **scissors are** on the desk.

11l Using singular verbs for titles of written works, companies, and words as terms

Arm and Hammer is a popular brand of baking soda.
Cats, the musical, **is** based on a book of poems by T. S. Eliot.

11m Understanding pronoun–antecedent agreement

The form of most pronouns depends on what their **antecedents** are (10a), so the connection between a pronoun and its antecedent must be clear. These connections are reflected by agreement in number (singular or plural), person (first, second, or third), and gender (male or female).

Singular pronouns must refer to singular antecedents, and plural pronouns must refer to plural antecedents.

The **ocean** has **its** own plant and animal life.
The **oceans** have **their** own plant and animal life.

First-person pronouns must refer to first-person antecedents, second-person pronouns to second-person antecedents, and third-person pronouns to third-person antecedents.

Beginning **divers** have to watch **their** [third person: not *your*] instructors for directions.

11n Using pronouns with antecedents connected with *and*

Two or more antecedents joined by *and* require a plural pronoun, even if each antecedent by itself is singular.

Miami and San Francisco are centers of ocean exploration because of **their** coastal locations.

When *each* or *every* precedes singular nouns joined by *and*, use a singular pronoun.

Each scuba diver and sailor hopes to locate a sunken treasure for **herself** or **himself.**

Also when the singular nouns joined by *and* refer to the same person or thing, use a singular pronoun.

Our **captain and diving instructor** warned us to stay near **her**.

11o Making the pronoun agree with the nearest antecedent

Antecedents joined by the conjunctions *or* or *nor*, or correlative conjunctions (such as *either . . . or, neither . . . nor*), often mix masculine and feminine or singular and plural nouns. To find the needed pronoun, ignore everything before the final antecedent.

~~Either the seals or~~ the **porpoise** will do **its** act.
~~Either the porpoise or~~ the **seals** will do **their** act.
~~Neither Bob nor~~ **Jane** likes to share **her** training methods.
~~Neither Jane nor~~ **Bob** likes to share **his** training methods.

11p Using pronouns with indefinite-pronoun antecedents

Indefinite pronouns (see 11g for a list) are usually singular. When they are, the pronouns that refer to them should also be singular.

Everyone should know **his or her** Social Security number.
No one can be expected to know **his or her** driver's license number.

11q Avoiding sexist pronoun use

Until about twenty-five years ago the masculine pronoun was used to refer to indefinite pronouns as well as to nouns and pronouns that name general categories to which any person might belong: *Everyone should admit his mistakes.* Today people are more conscious that *he, his, him,* and *himself* exclude women. Many writers try to avoid using masculine pronouns to refer to the entire population.

HOW TO AVOID USING ONLY THE MASCULINE PRONOUN TO REFER TO MALES AND FEMALES TOGETHER

Solution 1 Use a pair—but try to avoid a pair more than once in a sentence or in many sentences in a row.

Everyone hopes that **he or she** will win the scholarship.

A successful doctor knows that **he or she** has to work long hours.

Solution 2 Revise into the plural.

Many people hope that **they** will win the scholarship.

Successful doctors know that **they** have to work long hours.

Solution 3 Recast the sentence.

Everyone hopes to win the scholarship.

Successful doctors should expect to work long hours.

Some indefinite pronouns can be either singular or plural, depending on the meaning of the sentence. When the indefinite pronoun is plural, then the pronouns that refer back to it should be plural.

Many students do not realize they have a talent for mathematics. **Some** have learned this attitude from **their** parents.

11r Using pronouns with collective-noun antecedents

A **collective noun** names a group of people or things: *family, group, audience, class, number, committee, team,* and the like. When the group acts as one unit, use a singular pronoun to refer to it. When the members of the group act individually, use a plural pronoun.

The **committee** has elected **its** new chairperson. [The *committee* is acting as one unit, so the pronoun is singular.]

The **committee** expressed **their** opinions about the election campaign. [The *committee* is acting as individuals, so the pronoun is plural.]

Making Subjects and Verbs Agree

A: Fill in the blanks on the right with the present-tense forms of the verbs in parentheses. Be sure each verb agrees in person and number with the subject of the sentence. (11b)

EXAMPLE   The Cuna Indians (to produce) an unusual kind of art.   *produce*

1. Cuna Indians (to occupy) the San Blas Islands off the coast of Panama.   _____

2. The outside world (to associate) them with distinctive women's clothing.   _____

3. Cuna women (to wear) blouses containing two panels of appliqued cloth.   _____

4. The Cuna word *mola* (to refer) to either a blouse or one of its panels.   _____

5. The Cuna (to work) their molas in reverse applique.   _____

6. Traditional applique (to consist) of turning under edges of a piece of fabric and sewing it onto a larger piece.   _____

7. Molas (to use) a different technique.   _____

8. A Cuna woman (to baste) together several layers of cloth of different colors.   _____

9. She then (to cut) through all but the bottom layer.   _____

10. When turned under, the upper layers (to reveal) contrasting colors.   _____

B: Fill in the blanks on the right with the appropriate present-tense forms of the verbs in parentheses. (11c–e)

EXAMPLE   Most resources of the earth (to be) not renewable.   *are*

1. Neither coffee grounds nor an apple core (to need) to be thrown out.   _____

2. Food waste, along with grass clippings, (to make) good compost.   _____

3. Many items from your garbage (to be) recyclable.   _____

4. Aluminum cans, plastic jugs, and glass bottles (to deserve) a second life.   _____

5. One of the most tedious jobs (to seem) to be sorting garbage.   _____

6. Yet rewards from such work (to be) immeasurable.   _____

7. Every recycled bottle and can (to mean) a saving of resources.   _____

8. Not only an adult but also a child (to be) capable of helping the environment.   _____

9. Learning what to recycle, as well as being willing to do it, (to become) necessary.   _____

10. You and I each (to be) expected to do our part.   _____

C: Circle the subjects and underline the verbs. If the verb does not agree with the subject, cross it out and write the correct form on the line to the right. If the verb does agree, write *correct* on the line. (11f,i)

EXAMPLE (Kyoto) the historic capital of Japan, ~~are~~ really many cities in one.   ___*is*___

1. Has Ken and Sara ever visited Japan?   _____
2. There is several places they should see.   _____
3. It is cities like Kyoto that transmit Japanese culture.   _____
4. Japanese history seems alive here.   _____
5. There is more than two thousand temples in Kyoto.   _____
6. In the city are also castles and luxurious residences.   _____
7. There is peaceful Zen gardens.   _____
8. Japanese art and architecture reveals the history of the empire.   _____
9. Yet there is also a very modern city.   _____
10. From all over the world comes visitors to Kyoto.   _____

D: Fill in the blanks on the right with the present-tense forms of the verbs in parentheses. (11g,h)

EXAMPLE   Most of Chicago's visitors (to be) impressed by its architecture.   ___*are*___

1. The Chicago School (to be) a group of architects at the turn of the century.   _____
2. Some (to be) known throughout the world.   _____
3. Not everyone in the group (to be) considered a genius.   _____
4. Yet all (to have) contributed to the appearance of the city.   _____
5. A number of buildings (to be) considered architectural landmarks.   _____
6. Many (to share) certain features like Chicago windows.   _____
7. One of the most famous styles (to be) Frank Lloyd Wright's Prairie House.   _____

8. A tour group visiting Chicago today (to be) sure to enjoy   _____
   a drive down the Magnificent Mile.
9. A family often (to prefer) a walking tour.   _____
10. Few (to be) exempt from the charms of a constantly   _____
    building city.

E: Circle the antecedent of each italicized *who, which,* or *that.* Then fill in the blanks on the right with the appropriate present-tense forms of the verbs in parentheses. (11j)

EXAMPLE   The *Book of Kells* is one of many (manuscripts) *that*   *belong*
              (to belong) to Trinity College, Dublin.

1. Its source is a mystery *that* (to continue) to baffle   _____
   scholars.
2. Anyone *who* (to see) it marvels at its brilliant   _____
   illumination.
3. The book, *which* (to be) considered a masterpiece,   _____
   contains full-page illustrations of the Gospels.
4. No one *who* (to study) the book can fail to be impressed   _____
   by it.
5. The paintings, *which* (to be) done in minute detail, retain   _____
   their vivid colors.
6. There is also decoration *that* (to appear) to have no   _____
   relationship to the text.
7. Some of the pictures, *which* (to stem) from unknown   _____
   origins, seem strange for a religious book.
8. One does not expect birds *that* (to wear) ecclesiastical   _____
   garb.
9. Nor does one expect the humor *that* (to pervade) some   _____
   of the illustrations.
10. The text, *which* (to be) written in beautiful script,   _____
    combines two translations.

F: Fill in the blanks on the right with the appropriate present-tense forms of the verbs in parentheses. (11k,l)

EXAMPLE   Two and a half centimeters (to equal)   *equals*
              approximately one inch.

1. Six dollars (to seem) like a lot of money to see just one   _____
   movie.
2. The news (to be) available 24 hours a day on some radio   _____
   and television stations.

3. *Bonnie and Clyde* (to show) moviegoers the violent rise and fall of a Depression-era gang. _____

4. Twenty-five-thousand miles (to be) the circumference of the earth at the equator. _____

5. When there are children in a home, scissors (to belong) in a safe place. _____

6. Four hundred and fifty-four grams (to make) one pound. _____

7. Simon & Schuster (to publish) books through its many divisions, including Prentice Hall. _____

8. Physics (to deal) with the basic principles governing our universe. _____

9. Eyeglasses (to get) lost easily because once we take them off we cannot see well enough to look for them. _____

10. Dun and Bradstreet (to rate) businesses so people can see if a company is a safe investment. _____

G: Fill in the blanks on the right with the appropriate present-tense forms of the verbs in parentheses. (11a-l)

EXAMPLE   Everyone (to dream) during sleep. _____*dreams*_____

1. No one (to know) why we (to dream). _____
   _____

2. Dreams (to occur) during a special kind of sleep, known as REM. _____

3. REM (to stand) for Rapid Eye Movement. _____

4. A total of about two hours a night (to get) spent in this dream state. _____

5. There (to be) many theories about why people dream and what the rapid movement of our eyeballs (to mean). _____
   _____

6. Some (to suggest) that REM sleep occurs when the brain rids itself of unnecessary images. _____

7. According to this theory, dreams (to represent) random signals. _____

8. Others (to believe) that dreaming helps the brain establish patterns for thinking. _____

9. Human newborns, they say, (to spend) about half their sleep time dreaming. _____

10. The babies, who (to receive) huge amounts of new information every day, may be developing plans for processing what they see and hear. _____

11. In contrast, the elderly (to devote) only fifteen percent of their sleep time to dreaming. _____

12. Why we dream and what dreams mean (to form) a big mystery. _____

172

13. Psychologists (to think) dreams help people deal with   _____
    emotional issues.
14. The population often (to lack) the time necessary to   _____
    cope with complicated emotional situations.
15. For example, people in the middle of divorce often (to   _____
    have) long, detailed dreams.
16. In contrast, people with peaceful lives generally (to   _____
    claim) their dreams are dull.
17. Sigmund Freud said that dreams (to protect) us from   _____
    painful truths.
18. There (to exist) a radical new theory which (to propose)   _____
    that dreams do something entirely different.   _____
19. While awake, people (to learn) about the environment,   _____
    but in dreams the flow of new information about the
    world is cut off.
20. Each dream (to combine) new information with   _____
    information already in the brain, and new ways of
    dealing with the world (to be) rehearsed.   _____

Making Pronouns and Antecedents Agree

Select a personal pronoun that agrees with the subject of each of these sentences. Write your answers on the lines to the right. Some items have more than one correct answer.

EXAMPLE   The group has _____ meeting here.   _____*its*_____

1. Anyone can get _____ name in the news.   _____

2. None of the checks were cashed; _____ finally expired.   _____

3. The chef cut _____ on the thumb while peeling carrots.   _____

4. A person should insure _____ valuables.   _____

5. The family has _____ eye on a new house.   _____

6. The codebreakers shared _____ secrets.   _____

7. Everybody has _____ own dreams and goals.   _____

8. One can be happy only if _____ has respect for _____ .   _____
_____

9. Children never realize how loud _____ can be.   _____

10. The senior class wore _____ rings proudly.   _____

11. My mother and her sister took _____ vacation together.   _____

12. Either Mike or John wears a patch over _____ eye.   _____

13. All are welcome; _____ just need to call for directions to the party.   _____

14. Neither documentaries nor the news is given enough money by _____ network.   _____

15. San Jose and San Diego get _____ names from Spanish.   _____

16. Either Eleanor Roosevelt or Ellen Wilson is believed to have covered for _____ husband during presidential emergencies.   _____

17. Cars cost more than _____ owners expect them to.   _____

18. Venus and Mars have _____ orbits nearer to Earth than to any other planets.   _____

19. The band starts _____ tour tomorrow night.   _____

20. Any of the candidates could win; _____ are very much alike.   _____

174

Revising Sentences
for Agreement

Revise each of these passages so that all pronouns agree with their antecedents in person, number, and gender. You may also have to change verbs or other words. Some sentences can be revised in more than one way. Take the time to try several, and select the version you like best.

EXAMPLE   The human population creates most environmental problems because they have minimum requirements for food and space.
The human population creates most environmental problems because it has minimum requirements for food and space.

1. The number of people that needs to be absorbed into the United States each month is 150,000. They are made up of 120,000 births and 30,000 immigrants.

   _____

2. All need to have basic services. He needs food, clothing, and shelter.

   _____

3. A higher birth rate and a greater survival rate are modern trends. Together, it makes the world population double in 35 years.

   _____

4. Either disease or war may be the result, some people say. They will be ways of reducing the population.

   _____

5. There are theories about how many people the earth can support, but it varies from 500,000 (10 percent of the current population) to 15 billion (about three times the current population).

   _____

6. Anyone in a world of 15 billion people would not have many luxuries in their lives.

   _____

7. Life in the poorest tropical countries is horrible. They are often very short and miserable.

   _____

8. The food supply in these countries is already too small, but rapidly growing populations means they will become even less adequate.

   _____

9. Nobody can be sure of the outcome if we do not make some changes. They can be sure, however, that more people will go hungry.

   _____

10. Neither the dependence on only a few grain crops nor the beef-eating habit is likely to last much into the future. They are too wasteful of food resources.

    _____

11. China and India have a combined population of over two billion. Those are more than one-third of the world's people.

    _____

12. To make room for more towns, some tropical countries are cutting down its rain forests.

    _____

13. Third World governments must take steps to use the forest wisely, or they will disappear.

    _____

12 | *Using Adjectives and Adverbs*

12a Distinguishing between adjectives and adverbs

Both **adjectives** and **adverbs** are **modifiers**—words or groups of words that describe other words. Because adjectives and adverbs function similarly in sentences, distinguishing between them is sometimes difficult.

ADJECTIVE	The **quick** messenger delivered the payroll.
ADVERB	The messenger **quickly** delivered the payroll.

The key to distinguishing between adjectives and adverbs is that they modify different types of words or groups of words.

SUMMARY OF DIFFERENCES BETWEEN ADJECTIVES AND ADVERBS

WHAT ADJECTIVES MODIFY	EXAMPLE
nouns	The **busy** *lawyer* rested.
pronouns	*She* felt **triumphant**.

WHAT ADVERBS MODIFY	EXAMPLE
verbs	The lawyer *spoke* **quickly**.
adverbs	The lawyer spoke **very** *quickly*.
adjectives	The lawyer was **extremely** *busy*.
independent clauses	**Therefore**, *the lawyer rested.*

Adjectives and adverbs are sometimes confused because of the *-ly* ending. In many cases, an adverb is formed by adding *-ly* to an adjective: *soft, softly; grand, grandly; beautiful, beautifully.* However, even though many adverbs end in *-ly*, some do not: *well, very, worse.* Also some words that end in *-ly* are adjectives: *lively, friendly.* The *-ly* ending, therefore, is not a foolproof way to identify adverbs.

To determine whether an adjective or an adverb is called for, see how the word functions in its sentence. If a noun or pronoun is being modified, use an adjective. If a verb, adjective, or other adverb is being modified, use an adverb.

12b Using adverbs—not adjectives—to modify verbs, adjectives, and other adverbs

Only adverbs modify verbs. You should avoid the nonstandard use of adjectives in the place of adverbs.

No It snowed **heavy** last night. [Adjective *heavy* cannot modify verb *snowed.*]

Yes It snowed **heavily** last night. [Adverb *heavily* modifies the verb *snowed.*]

Good–well: The words *good* and *well* can be confusing. As an adjective, *good* can modify nouns or noun substitutes.

The **good** news spread. [Adjective *good* modifies noun *news.*]

The reopened factory would be **good** for the town. [Adjective *good* modifies noun phrase *the reopened factory.*]

Good cannot modify verbs. Only *well*, an adverb, can modify verbs.

No The project started off **good**. [Adjective *good* cannot modify verb *started off.*]

Yes The project started off **well**. [Adverb *well* modifies verb *started off.*]

Yes The **good** project started off **well**.

One exception exists: *well* is used as an adjective to describe conditions of health.

I don't feel **well**.
The patient is **well**.

Only adverbs modify adjectives and other adverbs.

No This is a **true fattening** dessert. [Adjective *true* cannot modify adjective *fattening.*]

Yes This is a **truly fattening** dessert. [Adverb *truly* modifies adjective *fattening.*]

12c Not using double negatives

A **double negative** is a statement that contains two negative modifiers. Negative modifiers include *no, never, not, none, nothing, hardly, scarcely,* and *barely.* They should not occur in the same sentence.

No Some people do **not** have **no** pity for the needy.

Yes Some people do **not** have any pity for the needy.

No They **never** donate **no** food.

Yes They **never** donate food.

No She could **not hardly** pay the rent.

Yes She could **hardly** pay the rent.

12d Using adjectives—not adverbs—as complements after linking verbs

Linking verbs indicate a state of being or a condition. They serve to connect the subject to a word that renames or describes it. If the subject is being described after a linking verb, an adjective is needed. If, however, the verb is being described, an adverb is needed.

The bee was **angry**. [Adjective *angry* describes the subject *bee* after linking verb *was*.]

The bee attacked **angrily**. [Adverb *angrily* describes the action verb *attacked*.]

Bad–badly: The words *bad* (adjective) and *badly* (adverb) are often misused with linking verbs, especially verbs related to the senses, such as *feel*. Only the adjectives *bad* or *good* are correct when a verb is operating as a linking verb.

FOR DESCRIBING A FEELING	The coach felt **bad**. [not *badly*]
FOR DESCRIBING A SMELL	The locker room smelled **bad**. [not *badly*]
FOR DESCRIBING A SOUND	The half-time band sounded **good**. [not *well*]

12e Using correct comparative and superlative forms of adjectives and adverbs

By using special forms of adjectives and adverbs, you can make comparisons. Most adjectives and adverbs show degrees of comparison by means of *-er* and *-est* endings or by being combined with the words *more* and *most*. (All adjectives and adverbs show diminishing or negative comparison by combining with the words *less* and *least: less jumpy, least jumpy; less surely, least surely*.)

FORMS OF COMPARISON FOR REGULAR ADJECTIVES AND ADVERBS	
FORM	**FUNCTION**
Positive	Used for a statement when nothing is being compared
Comparative	Used when only two things are being compared—with *-er* endings or *more* (or *less*)
Superlative	Used when three or more things are being compared—with *-est* ending or *most* (or *least*)

On the following page is a list that contrasts the three forms. Consider the messages of comparison in the sentences after the list.

POSITIVE	COMPARATIVE	SUPERLATIVE
green	greener	greenest
happy	happier	happiest
selfish	less selfish	least selfish
beautiful	more beautiful	most beautiful

Her tree is **green**.

Her tree is **greener** than his tree.

Her tree is the **greenest** one on the block.

The choice of whether to use *-er/-est* or *more/most* depends largely on the number of syllables in the adjective or adverb. With **one-syllable words**, the *-er/-est* endings are most common: *large, larger, largest* (adjective); *far, farther, farthest* (adverb). With **words of three or more syllables**, *more/most* are used: *energetic, more energetic, most energetic*. With **adverbs of two or more syllables**, *more/most* are used: *easily, more easily, most easily*. With **adjectives of two syllables**, practice varies. Often you will form comparatives and superlatives intuitively, based on what you have heard or read for a particular adjective. If neither form sounds natural for a given adjective, consult your dictionary for the recommended form.

Be careful not to use a **double comparative** or **double superlative**. The words *more* or *most* cannot be used if the *-er* or *-est* ending has been used.

Some comparative and superlative forms are irregular. Learn this short list.

IRREGULAR COMPARATIVES AND SUPERLATIVES

POSITIVE (1)	COMPARATIVE (2)	SUPERLATIVE (3+)
good (adjective)	better	best
well (adjective and adverb)	better	best
bad (adjective)	worse	worst
badly (adverb)	worse	worst
many	more	most
much	more	most
some	more	most
little	less	least

12f Avoiding too many nouns as modifiers

Sometimes nouns can modify other nouns: *bird watching, fishing pole, fire drill*. These terms create no problems, but when nouns pile up in a list of modifiers, it can be difficult to know which nouns are being modified and which nouns are doing the modifying.

No   I misplaced my **electric garage door opener rebate coupon**.

YES   I misplaced **the coupon needed to get a rebate on the electric opener for my garage door**.

Identifying Adjectives and Adverbs

EXERCISE **12-1**

(12a,b,d)

On the lines to the right, identify each of the italicized words as an adjective or adverb. (Following common usage, the titles of books also appear in italics; however, these are nouns, never adjectives or adverbs.)

EXAMPLE   Sinclair Lewis was the *first* American to win the
Nobel Prize for Literature.   *adjective*

1. Agatha Christie is famous for her *mystery* novels. _____
2. She *also* wrote romantic novels, under a pen name. _____
3. Joseph Conrad was a *highly* respected English writer. _____
4. His *native* language was Polish. _____
5. He *always* had trouble speaking but not writing English. _____
6. *Gone with the Wind* was Margaret Mitchell's *only* book. _____
7. Upton Sinclair wrote *The Jungle* hoping to improve conditions in the *Chicago* stockyards. _____
8. In *his* book he called for large social and economic reforms. _____
9. Sinclair's work led *directly* to regulations governing food purity. _____
10. Each year, U.S. publishers introduce about 30,000 *different* books. _____
11. The *typical* American book author earns less than $5,000 a year from writing. _____
12. The U.S. Government Printing Office is a *major* publisher. _____
13. It has *6,300* employees. _____
14. Only *recently* have women authors been widely accepted. _____
15. Many nineteenth-century English female authors became *widely* popular writing under men's names. _____
16. George Eliot was *really* Mary Anne Evans, while Charlotte Brontë wrote as Currer Bell and her sister Emily Brontë wrote as Ellis Bell. _____
17. *Other* famous writers have also used pen names. _____
18. George Orwell was *actually* the pen name of Englishman Eric Arthur Blair. _____

19. Popular *romance* novelist Barbara Cortland also publishes under the name Barbara Hamilton McCorquodale. _____

20. Even Agatha Christie *sometimes* chose a pseudonym: Mary Westmacott. _____

Distinguishing Adjectives from Adverbs

From the choices in parentheses, select the correct modifier for each sentence. Write your answers on the lines to the right.

EXAMPLE   Aspirin can cause a (severe, severely) upset stomach in some people.   _____*severely*_____

1. Pain sufferers (annual, annually) spend a quarter of a billion dollars on aspirin. _____

2. Over 200 kinds of headache medicines containing aspirin are (available, availably). _____

3. Many of us feel taking aspirin can make us (good, well). _____

4. However, aspirin has many (serious, seriously) side effects. _____

5. Aspirin (common, commonly) causes bleeding in the stomach. _____

6. This can make us feel (bad, badly). _____

7. Bleeding occurs when an undissolved aspirin tablet lies on the (delicate, delicately) stomach wall. _____

8. For most of us, the amount of blood lost is not (dangerous, dangerously). _____

9. However, some (slow, slowly) dissolving tablets can cause prolonged bleeding, leading to great discomfort. _____

10. (High, Highly) quality aspirin dissolves more quickly and is less likely to cause a problem. _____

11. Aspirin has a (lengthy, lengthily) history. _____

12. Our (ancient, anciently) ancestors chewed the leaves and bark of the willow tree. _____

13. They contain a substance (chemical, chemically) related to aspirin. _____

14. Aspirin itself was introduced as a painkiller and fever reducer more (recent, recently). _____

15. Coming on the market in 1899, it (quick, quickly) _____

became the best-selling nonprescription drug in the world.

16. The tablet form so (popular, popularly) today was introduced by Bayer in 1915. _____

17. Taking an aspirin a day has (late, lately) been claimed to be good for the heart. _____

18. Some research shows that men who take aspirin (regular, regularly) after a heart attack are less likely to have another attack. _____

19. No one knows why this is so, but some healthy people have been (quick, quickly) to start taking aspirin daily. _____

20. Doctors advise us to think (careful, carefully) before we do this because there is no evidence that aspirin prevents first heart attacks. _____

Using Comparatives and Superlatives

EXERCISE **12-3**

(12e)

A: Fill in the comparative and superlative forms of the adjectives and adverbs listed on the left.

	Comparative	Superlative
EXAMPLE tall	taller	tallest
1. bad	_____	_____
2. badly	_____	_____
3. forgiving	_____	_____
4. free	_____	_____
5. good	_____	_____
6. gracefully	_____	_____
7. handsome	_____	_____
8. hot	_____	_____
9. little	_____	_____
10. loudly	_____	_____
11. many	_____	_____
12. much	_____	_____
13. powerfully	_____	_____
14. pretty	_____	_____

15. *quickly*   _____ _____
16. *some*   _____ _____
17. *sweetly*   _____ _____
18. *sympathetically* _____ _____
19. *talented*   _____ _____
20. *well*   _____ _____

B: Use the adjectives and adverbs above in sets of sentences that show how the three forms are related to changes in meaning. Use your own paper.

EXAMPLE   I am tall. (positive)

I am taller than my sister. (comparative)

I am the tallest person in my family. (superlative)

Writing with Adjectives and Adverbs

Write a paragraph describing someone, something, or someplace wonderful. Some suggestions: your favorite restaurant, your favorite movie star, an exciting amusement park, your most treasured possession.

Be sure to have a topic sentence (4b). Develop your idea with four to six sentences, each containing strong and appropriate adjectives and adverbs. Try not to use so many modifiers in any one sentence that the main idea gets lost. Use your own paper.

13 | *Sentence Fragments*

A **sentence fragment** is part of a sentence punctuated as though it were a complete sentence. You can avoid writing sentence fragments if you recognize the difference between a fragment and a complete sentence.

13a Testing for sentence completeness

If you write sentence fragments frequently, you need a system to check that your sentences are complete. Here is a test to use if you suspect that you have written a sentence fragment.

TEST FOR SENTENCE COMPLETENESS

1. **Is there a verb?** If not, there is a sentence fragment.
2. **Is there a subject?** If not, there is a sentence fragment.
3. **Do the subject and verb start with a subordinating word—and lack an independent clause to complete the thought?** If they do, there is a sentence fragment.

QUESTION 1: Is there a verb?

If there is no verb, you are looking at a sentence fragment.

FRAGMENT	Yesterday the math lab hiring tutors.
REVISED	Yesterday the math lab **was** hiring tutors.
FRAGMENT	Today the math lab hiring tutors.
REVISED	Today the math lab **is** hiring tutors.
FRAGMENT	Chosen for their math ability.
REVISED	The tutors **are** chosen for their math ability.
REVISED	Chosen for their math ability, the tutors also **work** well with other students.
FRAGMENT	Each tutor to work with eight students.
REVISED	Each tutor **works** with eight students.
REVISED	Each tutor **is assigned** to work with eight students.

QUESTION 2: Is there a subject?

If there is no subject, you are looking at a sentence fragment. To find a subject, ask a "who?" or "what?" question about the verb.

FRAGMENT	Worked in the library. [Who worked? Unknown]
REVISED	**The students** worked in the library.

Every sentence must have its own subject. A sentence fragment without a subject often results when the missing subject is the same as the subject in the previous sentence.

No	In September, the new dormitories were opened. **Were occupied immediately.**
YES	In September, the new dormitories were opened. **They were occupied immediately.**

Imperative statements—commands and some requests—are an exception. Imperative statements imply the word *you* as the subject.

Sit down! = (You) sit down!

QUESTION 3: Do the subject and verb start with a subordinating word— and lack an independent clause to complete the thought?

If the answer is yes, you are looking at a sentence fragment. Clauses that begin with subordinating words are called **dependent clauses**, as explained in 7o–2. To be part of a complete sentence, a dependent clause must be joined to an independent clause.

One type of subordinating word is a **subordinating conjunction**. Some of the most frequently used are *after, although, because, if, when, where*, and *until*.

FRAGMENT	**If** I see him.
REVISED	**If** I see him, I'll give him your message.
FRAGMENT	**Where** the park is.
REVISED	The city will build a hospital **where** the park is.

♣ PUNCTUATION ALERT: When a dependent clause starting with a subordinating conjunction comes before an independent clause, a comma always separates the clauses. ♣

Another type of subordinating word is a **relative pronoun**. The most common relative pronouns are *who, which*, and *that*.

FRAGMENT	The class **that** we wanted.
REVISED	The class **that** we wanted was full.
FRAGMENT	The students **who** registered early.
REVISED	The students **who** registered early got the classes they wanted.

Questions are an exception—they can begin with words such as *when, where, who*, and *which* without being sentence fragments.

When is the meeting?
Who is your favorite author?

13b Revising dependent clauses punctuated as sentences

To correct a dependent clause punctuated as a sentence (see the discussion of Question 3 in 13a), you can do one of two things: (1) You can join the dependent clause to an independent clause that comes directly before or after—sometimes you will need to add words so that the combined sentence makes sense. (2) You can drop the subordinating conjunction or relative pronoun and, if necessary, add words to create an independent clause.

FRAGMENT	Students often change their majors. **When they start taking courses.**
REVISED	Students often change their majors when they start taking courses. [joined into one sentence]
REVISED	Students often change their majors. They start taking courses and realize they are unhappy. [subordinating conjunction dropped to create an independent clause]
FRAGMENT	The chemistry major is looking for a lab partner. **Who is dependable.**
REVISED	The chemistry major is looking for a lab partner who is dependable. [joined into one sentence]

13c Revising phrases punctuated as sentences

To correct a phrase punctuated as a sentence (see the discussions of Questions 1 and 2 in 13a), either you can rewrite it to become an independent clause by adding the missing subject or verb, or you can join it to an independent clause that comes directly before or after.

A phrase containing a **verbal** (a *gerund*, an *infinitive*, a *past participle*, or a *present participle*) but no verb is not a sentence.

FRAGMENT	The college administration voted last week. **To offer a new program in nursing.**
REVISED	The college administration voted last week to offer a new program in nursing. [joined into one sentence]
REVISED	The college administration voted last week. The members decided to offer a new program in nursing. [rewritten]
FRAGMENT	**Speaking to the students.** The dean explained the new program.
REVISED	Speaking to the students, the dean explained the new program. [joined into one sentence]

REVISED	The dean spoke to the students. She explained the new program. [rewritten]
FRAGMENT	**Seated in the auditorium.** The students listened carefully.
REVISED	Seated in the auditorium, the students listened carefully. [joined into one sentence]
REVISED	The students were seated in the auditorium. They listened carefully. [rewritten]

A **prepositional phrase** contains a preposition (for a complete list see 7g), its object, and any modifiers.

FRAGMENT	She planned to take Biology 102. **During summer session.**
REVISED	She planned to take Biology 102 during summer session. [joined into one sentence]
REVISED	She planned to take Biology 102. It was offered in summer session. [rewritten]

An **appositive** is a word or word group that renames a noun or group of words functioning as a noun.

FRAGMENT	Many students liked the biology professor. **A teacher of great skill and patience.**
REVISED	Many students liked the biology professor, a teacher of great skill and patience. [joined into one sentence]
REVISED	Many students liked the biology professor. She was a teacher of great skill and patience. [rewritten]

Compound predicates contain two or more verbs, plus their objects and modifiers, if any. To be part of a complete sentence, a predicate must have a subject. If the second half of a compound predicate is punctuated as a sentence, it is a sentence fragment.

FRAGMENT	The professor was always available for conferences. **And answered students' questions clearly.**
REVISED	The professor was always available for conferences and answered students' questions clearly. [joined into one sentence]
REVISED	The professor was always available for conferences. And she always answered students' questions clearly. [rewritten]

Revising Fragments

A: Explain what is wrong with each fragment and then rewrite it as a complete sentence.

EXAMPLE   graduating in June
There is no subject and "graduating" is not a conjugated verb.
I am graduating in June.

1. beside the rice cooker

   _____

   _____

2. attends a soccer game

   _____

   _____

3. whoever breaks the piñata

   _____

   _____

4. considered the best in her class

   _____

   _____

5. and plans to study Swahili

   _____

   _____

6. my favorite of all desserts

   _____

   _____

7. studying constantly

   _____

   _____

8. when Ahmed entered the university

_____

_____

9. where our carpool picks us up

_____

_____

10. Kofi hoping for understanding

_____

_____

B: Write two corrected versions of each fragment. Be sure to use the fragment differently in each and identify how you have used it (as illustrated in the parentheses below).

EXAMPLE   eating an orange
          Eating an orange can be messy. (subject)
          Eating an orange, he swallowed a pit. (adjective)

1. when Natasha arrived on campus

_____

_____

2. looks for affordable child care

_____

_____

3. who borrowed my vacuum cleaner

_____

_____

4. to use a fax machine

_____

_____

5. buried under last week's laundry

_____

_____

6. trying to get a visa

   _____

   _____

7. historians and anthropologists

   _____

   _____

8. the instructor who helped me the most

   _____

   _____

9. in the computer lab

   _____

   _____

10. a man shaking hands with his enemy

    _____

    _____

Revising Fragments within Passages

There is one fragment in each passage below. Find it and correct it in whatever way you feel is most appropriate.

EXAMPLE Clothing often indicates a person's social standing. This has been the case for centuries. Although some clothing certainly was inspired by the need for protection from the elements. Even today, style, material, and color all act as social labels.

Clothing often indicates a person's social standing. This has been the case for centuries, although some clothing certainly was inspired by the need for protection from the elements. Even today, style, material, and color all act as social labels.

1. The oldest shoe ever found was a sandal. Which dated from 2000 B.C. It was found in an Egyptian tomb. Sandals were the usual footwear in tropical areas.

   _____

   _____

2. Archaeologists are interested in the clothing of our ancestors. They have discovered hundreds of sandal designs. Each usually representative of a particular culture at a particular time. However, other types of shoes were also worn.

   _____

   _____

3. The oldest nonsandal shoe found has been a leather wrap-around. Shaped like a moccasin. Rawhide lacing could be pulled tight to keep the shoe snugly on the foot. This shoe came from Babylonia.

   _____

   _____

4. Upper-class Greek women favored a similar shoe. The preferred colors were red and white. Roman women also wore red and white closed shoes. And green or yellow ones for special occasions.

   _____

   _____

5. Lower-ranking Roman women wore undyed open sandals. Senators wore brown shoes. With tied black leather straps wound around the lower leg. Consuls, who were high-ranking judges, wore white shoes.

_____

_____

6. Boots were first used by soldiers. The Assyrians created a calf-high laced leather boot. The sole was reinforced with metal. Enabling the Assyrians to walk and fight in relative comfort.

_____

_____

7. Greek and Roman soldiers resisted wearing Assyrian-style boots. They preferred sandals with hobnail soles. To provide better grip and extended wear. They did wear boots for long journeys.

_____

_____

8. Horse-riding cultures adopted boots quickly. They appreciated the boot's sturdiness. And the ability of the boot heel to help their foot stay in the stirrup. Boots became standard combat gear.

_____

_____

9. The heeled boot was the ancestor of modern high-heeled shoes. The original high heels were worn by men in sixteenth-century France. Women's shoe fashions at the time were less dramatic. Because women's feet were covered by floor-length dresses.

_____

_____

10. During this time, the overcrowded cities were filthy. The streets were filled with human and animal waste. The elevation provided by high heels and thick soles kept men out of the muck. And enabled them to stay a bit cleaner.

_____

_____

11. The clogs of Northern Europe served a similar purpose. Worn over good leather shoes in the winter. These wooden shoes protected the wearer from snow and mud. They could also be worn alone in warm weather.

_____

_____

12. King Louis XIV of France was short. During his seventy-two-year reign, the longest in the history of Europe. France was a center of culture and refinement. France was also at its peak of military power.

_____

_____

13. Louis hated being short. To compensate, he wore high-heeled boots. He was imitated by his courtiers. The males as well as the females.

_____

_____

14. Louis' response was to wear even higher heels. His people tried to keep up with him. Once the competition was over. The men returned to their regular height.

_____

_____

15. The female members of Louis' court kept their high heels. Thus beginning the pattern we have today. With rare exceptions, such as in the mid-1970s, men have been expected to keep their feet on the ground. Women still have the choice to wear or not wear high heels.

_____

_____

16. Athletic shoes earned the name "sneakers" because of their rubber bottoms. Which enabled wearers to walk silently, to "sneak" around. The invention of the sneaker depended upon another invention. Charles Goodyear mixed rubber with sulfur to make it more useful.

_____

_____

17. Before this important discovery in the 1860s. Using rubber was impractical because it became sticky when warm and brittle when cold. People immediately realized the value of Goodyear's discovery. Rubber-soled shoes became popular.

_____

_____

18. The first athletic shoes appeared shortly after this. Rubber soles on canvas tops, called Keds. The name came from a blend of *ped*, the Latin word for "foot," and "kid." The brand is still around.

    _____

    _____

19. The first Keds were not very stylish by modern standards. The soles were black. The canvas was brown. In imitation of men's leather shoes.

    _____

    _____

20. Flat soles were standard on sneakers until 1972. In that year, new shoes with a number of startling changes were introduced. Featuring lightweight nylon tops, waffle soles for traction, a wedged heel, and a cushioned mid-sole to reduce impact shock. These shoes began to drive the old ones off the market.

    _____

    _____

Revising Fragments
within Paragraphs

Circle the number of any fragments. Then correct each fragment by connecting it to a main clause or by adding words to complete it. Use your own paper.

A. ¹The Blue Ridge Parkway runs 469 miles. ²Along the crest of mountains in the Appalachian chain. ³It connects two parks. ⁴Shenandoah National Park and Great Smoky Mountains National Park. ⁵The parkway starts in Virginia. ⁶And ends in North Carolina. ⁷Begun by the Works Progress Administration in 1935. ⁸The parkway was completed. ⁹Except for a section around privately owned Grandfather Mountain. ¹⁰Concerned about environmental impact. ¹¹The owner refused to allow any blasting on the mountain. ¹²It was 1987 before the final section, the Linn Cove Viaduct. ¹³Using the latest engineering technology. ¹⁴The viaduct goes around, not over, Grandfather Mountain. ¹⁵Those who drive the parkway. ¹⁶Are not bothered by the speed limit of 45 miles per hour. ¹⁷Driving slowly allows them to appreciate the scenery. ¹⁸To see the many cascades and other natural wonders. ¹⁹One beautiful vista after another. ²⁰In places the distant mountains seem stacked in layers. ²¹Along some stretches of the parkway can be seen catawba rhododendron and mountain laurel. ²²Along others, various wildflowers. ²³In the autumn traffic almost stops on the parkway. ²⁴As people come to enjoy the fall foliage. ²⁵Although most people drive the parkway for the view. ²⁶There are many who come for camping. ²⁷Or for hiking, biking, or studying the wildlife. ²⁸One attraction is Mount Mitchell. ²⁹At 6,684 feet, the highest point east of the Mississippi River. ³⁰It is not surprising. ³¹That visitors return to the parkway year after year.

B. ¹The striped barber pole is a symbol left over from the times. ²When barbers doubled as surgeons. ³As early as the fifth century. ⁴Roman barbers pulled teeth, treated wounds. ⁵And bled patients. ⁶Records show that in 1461 the barbers of London were the only people practicing surgery. ⁷In the city. ⁸However, under Henry VIII, less than a hundred years later. ⁹Parliament passed a law limiting barbers to minor operations. ¹⁰Such as blood letting and pulling teeth. ¹¹While surgeons were prohibited from "barbery and shaving." ¹²The London barbers and surgeons were considered one group until 1745. ¹³In France and Germany, barbers acted as surgeons. ¹⁴Until even more recent times.

¹⁵Barbers usually bled their patients. ¹⁶To "cure" a variety of ailments. ¹⁷Because few people could read in those days. ¹⁸Pictures were commonly used as shop signs. ¹⁹The sign of the barber was a pole painted with red and white spirals. ²⁰From which was suspended a brass basin. ²¹The red represented the blood of the patient. ²²The white the bandage. ²³And the basin the bowl used to catch the blood. ²⁴In the United States, the bowl is often omitted. ²⁵But it is still common on British barber poles. ²⁶Some American barbers added a blue stripe. ²⁷Probably to make the colors match the flag.

14 | *Comma Splices and Fused Sentences*

A **comma splice**, also known as a **comma fault**, occurs when a single comma joins independent clauses. A comma is correct between two independent clauses only when it is followed by a coordinating conjunction (see 7h).

> **COMMA SPLICE**   The car skidded, it hit a mailbox.

A **fused sentence**, also known as a **run-on sentence** or a **run-together sentence**, occurs when two independent clauses are not separated by punctuation nor joined by a comma with a coordinating conjunction.

> **FUSED SENTENCE**   The car skidded it hit a mailbox.

Comma splices and fused sentences are two versions of the same problem: incorrect joining of two independent clauses. If you tend to write comma splices and fused sentences, it may be because you don't recognize them.

HOW TO FIND AND CORRECT COMMA SPLICES AND FUSED SENTENCES

FINDING COMMA SPLICES AND FUSED SENTENCES

1. Look for a pronoun starting the second independent clause.

   No   Thomas Edison was a productive inventor, **he** held over 1,300 U.S. and foreign patents.

2. Look for a conjunctive adverb or other transitional expression starting the second independent clause.

   No   Thomas Edison was a brilliant scientist, **however**, his schooling was limited to only three months of his life.

3. Look for a second independent clause that explains or gives an example of information in the first clause.

   No   Thomas Edison was genius behind many inventions, the phonograph and the light bulb are among the best known.

FIXING COMMA SPLICES AND FUSED SENTENCES

1. Use a period or a semicolon between clauses.
2. Use a comma and a coordinating conjunction between clauses.
3. Use a semicolon and a conjunctive adverb between clauses.

14a Recognizing comma splices and fused sentences

To recognize comma splices and fused sentences, you need to be able to recognize an **independent clause**. As explained in 7o–1, an independent clause contains a subject and a predicate. An independent clause can stand alone as a sentence because it is a complete grammatical unit. A sentence may contain two or more independent clauses only if they are joined properly (with a comma and coordinating conjunction *or* with a semicolon).

14b Using a period or semicolon to correct comma splices and fused sentences

A **period** can separate the independent clauses in a comma splice or fused sentence. A **semicolon** can separate independent clauses that are closely related in meaning (see 25a).

Comma Splice	In the 1880s, Sir Francis Galton showed that fingerprints are unique for each person, he was an English anthropologist.
Corrected	In the 1880s, Sir Francis Galton showed that fingerprints are unique for each person. He was an English anthropologist.
Fused Sentence	Mark Twain used fingerprints to solve murders in *Life on the Mississippi* and *Pudd'nhead Wilson* these were popular books.
Corrected	Mark Twain used fingerprints to solve murders in *Life on the Mississippi* and *Pudd'nhead Wilson*; these were popular books.

14c Using coordinating conjunctions to correct comma splices and fused sentences

When ideas in independent clauses are closely related, you might decide to connect them with a coordinating conjunction that fits the meaning of the material (see 7h). Two independent clauses joined by a coordinating conjunction and a comma form a compound sentence, also known as a coordinate sentence.
♣ PUNCTUATION ALERT: Use a comma before a coordinating conjunction that links independent clauses. ♣

Comma Splice	In 1901, England began fingerprinting criminals, their prints were kept on file with the police.
Corrected	In 1901, England began fingerprinting criminals, **and** their prints were kept on file with the police.
Fused Sentence	Edward Richard Henry, of London's Metropolitan Police, invented a system of classifying fingerprints the FBI uses a version of this original system.

CORRECTED	Edward Richard Henry, of London's Metropolitan Police, invented a system of classifying fingerprints, **and** the FBI uses a version of this original system.

14d Revising one of two independent clauses into a dependent clause to correct a comma splice or fused sentence

You can revise a comma splice or fused sentence by changing one of two independent clauses into a dependent clause. This method is suitable when one idea can be logically subordinated to the other. Sentences composed of one independent clause and one or more dependent clauses are called complex sentences. Inserting an appropriate subordinating conjunction (see 7h) in front of the subject and verb is one way to create a dependent clause.

♣ PUNCTUATION ALERT: Do not put a period after a dependent clause that is not attached to an independent clause, or you will create a sentence fragment (see Chapter 13). ♣

COMMA SPLICE	Immigrants are fingerprinted, most have done nothing wrong.
CORRECTED	Immigrants are fingerprinted **although most have done nothing wrong**.
FUSED SENTENCE	The government wants to identify dangerous criminals they enter the country.
CORRECTED	The government wants to identify dangerous criminals **before they enter the country**.

A relative pronoun can also be used to correct a comma splice or fused sentence by creating a dependent clause.

COMMA SPLICE	Government employees are also fingerprinted, they work on sensitive projects.
CORRECTED	Government employees **who work on sensitive projects** are also fingerprinted. [restrictive dependent clause]

14e Using a semicolon or a period before a conjunctive adverb or other transitional expression between independent clauses

Conjunctive adverbs and other transitional expressions link ideas between sentences. Remember, however, that these words are *not* coordinating conjunctions, so they cannot work with commas to join independent clauses. Conjunctive adverbs and other transitional expressions require that the previous sentence end in a period or semicolon.

Conjunctive adverbs include such words as *however, therefore, also, next, then, thus, furthermore*, and *nevertheless* (see 7f for a fuller list).

COMMA SPLICE	Many people object to being fingerprinted, **nevertheless**, fingerprinting remains a requirement for certain jobs.
CORRECTED	Many people object to being fingerprinted. **Nevertheless**, fingerprinting remains a requirement for certain jobs.

Transitional words include *for example, for instance, in addition, in fact, of course*, and *on the other hand* (see 4d for a fuller list).

FUSED SENTENCE	Not everyone disapproves of fingerprinting **in fact**, some parents have their children fingerprinted as a safety measure.
CORRECTED	Not everyone disapproves of fingerprinting. **In fact**, some parents have their children fingerprinted as a safety measure.

A conjunctive adverb or other transitional expression can appear in various locations within an independent clause. In contrast, a coordinating conjunction can appear only between the independent clauses it joins.

Many people object to being fingerprinted. Fingerprinting, **nevertheless**, remains a requirement for certain jobs.

Many people object to being fingerprinted. Fingerprinting remains, **nevertheless**, a requirement for certain jobs.

Many people object to being fingerprinted. Fingerprinting remains a requirement for certain jobs, **nevertheless**.

Many people object to being fingerprinted, **but** fingerprinting remains a requirement for certain jobs.

Revising Comma Splices EXERCISE **14-1**
and Fused Sentences (14a-e)

A: Correct each comma splice or fused sentence in any of the ways shown in this chapter.

EXAMPLE Many people think of the Middle Ages they think of knights in shining armor.
When many people think of the Middle Ages, they think of knights in shining armor.

1. The term *chivalry* comes from *chevalier* meaning "knight" and is related to *cheval* meaning "horse," thus a knight is an armed horseman.

   _____

   _____

2. Chivalry was more than a code by which a knight lived it became a distinct culture.

   _____

   _____

3. In the Middle Ages birth specified class only knighthood and the church offered social mobility.

   _____

   _____

4. Knighthood was a privilege, not a right, it had to be earned.

   _____

   _____

5. Every knight could confer the rank on another he considered worthy he took responsibility for the one so honored.

   _____

   _____

6. A knight was expected to have his own horse and armor unless he owned land, he had to earn his horse's keep by serving another.

   _____

   _____

7. Many knights pledged fealty to one noble some became mercenaries, hiring themselves as free lances to whoever needed them.

_____

_____

B: Correct each comma splice or fused sentence in the way indicated.

EXAMPLE   Most knights belonged to the landed gentry, they desired knighthood because of its status.
(Make into two separate sentences.)

Most knights belonged to the landed gentry. They desired knighthood
because of its status.

1. Even princes considered knighthood an honor it made them part of a universal fraternity.
(Add a semicolon.)

_____

_____

2. The honor was conferred by tapping the knight on the shoulders with the flat of a sword, after three taps the knight was given a belt and spurs to signify his new rank.
(Make into two separate sentences.)

_____

_____

3. For his part, the knight vowed to uphold the code of chivalry, the code established certain rules of behavior.
(Turn one part into a dependent clause.)

_____

_____

4. The knight promised loyalty to his faith and to his feudal lord he pledged to die willingly for either should death be necessary.
(Add a semicolon and a conjunctive adverb.)

_____

_____

5. He was expected to fight to uphold his ideals he was also expected to show mercy.
(Turn one part into a dependent clause.)

_____

_____

Name _____ Date _____

6. Knighthood is still granted in England it is given for outstanding achievement.
(Add a semicolon.)

_____

_____

7. Today recipients include both men and women their achievements are often related to statesmanship or the arts.
(Add a comma and a coordinating conjunction.)

_____

_____

C: Correct each comma splice or fused sentence in four ways: (1) make each into two separate sentences by inserting a period; (2) add a semicolon; (3) add a coordinating conjunction to create a compound sentence—you will also need to add a comma unless the clauses are very short; (4) add a subordinating conjunction or relative pronoun—you may need to drop a word—to create a complex sentence.

EXAMPLE The didgeridoo is an unusual musical instrument, it was developed by Australian Aborigines.
1. instrument. It was developed . . .
2. instrument; it was developed . . .
3. instrument, for it was developed . . .
4. The didgeridoo, which was developed by Australian Aborigines, is an unusual instrument.

1. To make a didgeridoo, Aborigines choose a long eucalyptus branch, they bury it in the ground.

_____

_____

_____

2. Termites eat out the middle of the branch, the Aborigines then dig it up.

_____

_____

_____

3. They carve the instrument they decorate it with pigments.

_____

_____

_____

_____

4. They play it by blowing into one end it makes a mournful sound.

_____

_____

_____

_____

5. The pitch is low, the sound carries well.

_____

_____

_____

_____

Revising Comma Splices and Fused Sentences within Passages

Find the comma splice or fused sentence in each passage. Correct each in any way shown in this chapter. You may need to change punctuation or wording, but try to keep the meaning of the original passage.

EXAMPLE   Some of the most beautiful temples in the world are those of Angkor. Angkor is a Cambodian region it served as the capital of the ancient Khmer empire between the 9th and 15th centuries. The empire once extended into what are today Vietnam, Laos, and Thailand.
Some of the most beautiful temples in the world are those of Angkor. Angkor is a Cambodian region that served as the capital of the ancient Khmer empire between the 9th and 15th centuries. The empire once extended into what are today Vietnam, Laos, and Thailand.

1. The king Jayavarman II introduced into the empire an Indian royal cult. The cult held that the king was related spiritually to one of the Hindu gods, consequently, the king was thought to fill on earth the role the gods had in the universe.

_____

_____

2. Each king was expected to build a stone temple. The temple, or *wat*, was dedicated to a god, usually Shiva or Vishnu, when the king died, the temple became a monument to him as well.

   _____

   _____

3. Over the centuries the kings erected more than seventy temples within seventy-five square miles. They added towers and gates they created canals and reservoirs for an irrigation system.

   _____

   _____

4. The irrigation system made it possible for farmers to produce several rice crops a year. Such abundant harvests supported a highly evolved culture, the irrigation system and the rice production were what we would call labor-intensive.

   _____

   _____

5. The greatest of the temples in Angkor Wat, it was built by Suryavarman II in the 12th century. Like the other temples, it represents Mount Meru, the home of the Hindu gods. The towers represent Mount Meru's peaks while the walls represent the mountains beyond.

   _____

   _____

6. The gallery walls are covered with bas-reliefs they depict historical events. They show the king at his court, and they show him engaging in activities that brought glory to his empire.

   _____

   _____

7. The walls also portray divine images. There are sculptures of *apsarases*, they are attractive women thought to inhabit heaven. There are mythical scenes on the walls as well.

   _____

   _____

8. One scene shows the Hindu myth of the churning of the Sea of Milk. On one side of the god Vishnu are demons who tug on the end of the long

serpent, on the other are heavenly beings who tug on the other end. All the tugging churns the water.

_____

_____

9. Vishnu is the god to whom Angkor Wat is dedicated. In Hindu myth he oversees the churning of the waters, that churning is ultimately a source of immortality.

_____

_____

10. Another temple is the Bayon, it was built by Jayavarman VII around 1200 A.D. Jayavarman VII was the last of the great kings of Angkor. He built the Bayon in the exact center of the city.

_____

_____

11. The Bayon resembles a step pyramid. It has steep stairs which lead to terraces near the top around its base are many galleries. Its towers are carved with faces which look out in all directions.

_____

_____

12. Jayavarman VII was a Buddhist, the representations on Bayon are different from those on earlier temples. Some scholars think they depict a Buddhist deity with whom the king felt closely aligned.

_____

_____

13. To build each temple required thousands of laborers they worked for years. After cutting the stone in far-off quarries, they had to transport it by canal or cart. Some stone may have been brought in on elephants.

_____

_____

14. Once cut, the stones had to be carved and fitted together into lasting edifices, thus, in addition to requiring laborers, each project needs artisans, architects, and engineers. Each temple was a massive project.

_____

_____

15. Angkor was conquered by the Thais in the 1400s, it was almost completely abandoned. The local inhabitants did continue to use the temples for worship, however, and a few late Khmer kings tried to restore the city.

_____

_____

16. The Western world did not learn about Angkor until the nineteenth century, a French explorer published an account of the site. French archaeologists and conservators later worked in the area and restored some of the temples. More recent archaeologists have come from India.

_____

_____

17. Today the Angkor Conservancy has removed many of the temple statues. Some of the statues need repair, all of them need protection from thieves. Unfortunately, traffic in Angkor art has become big business among people with no scruples. There is even a booming business in Angkor fakes.

_____

_____

18. Theft is just one of the problems Angkor faces today, political upheaval has taken its toll. Although Angkor mostly escaped Cambodia's civil war, some war damage has occurred.

_____

_____

19. More damage has been done by nature, however, trees choke some of the archways, vines strangle the statues, and monsoons undermine the basic structures.

_____

_____

20. Today many Cambodians do what they can to maintain the temples of Angkor. They clean stones or sweep courtyards or pull weeds. No one pays them, they do it for themselves and their heritage.

_____

_____

15 | *Sentences That Send Unclear Messages*

A sentence can seem correct at first glance but still have flaws that keep it from delivering a sensible message. Sentences may be sending unclear messages because of shifts in person and number, in subject and voice, in tense and mood, and between direct and indirect discourse; misplaced modifiers; dangling modifiers; mixed structures; or incomplete structures.

15a Avoiding unnecessary shifts

Unless the meaning or grammatical structure of a sentence requires it, do not shift person and number, subject and voice, and tense and mood. Also, do not shift from indirect to direct discourse within a sentence without using punctuation and grammar to make the changes clear.

1 Staying consistent in person and number

Person in English includes the **first person** (*I, we*), who is the speaker; the **second person** (*you*), who is the person spoken to; and the **third person** (*he, she, it, they*), who is the person or thing being spoken about. Do not shift person within a sentence or a longer passage unless the meaning calls for a shift.

No   **We** need to select a college with care. **Your** future success may depend upon **your** choice. [*We* shifts to *your.*]

Yes   **We** need to select a college with care. **Our** future success may depend upon **our** choice.

Number refers to one (singular) and more than one (plural). Do not start to write in one number and then shift suddenly to the other.

No   A college **freshman** has to make many adjustments. **They** have to work harder and become more responsible. [The singular *freshman* shifts to the plural *they.*]

Yes   College **freshmen** have to make many adjustments. **They** have to work harder and become more responsible.

A common source of confusion in person and number is a shift to the second-person *you* from the first-person *I* or a third-person noun such as *person,* or *people.* You can avoid this error if you remember to reserve *you* for sentences that directly address the reader (10e) and to use third-person pronouns for general statements.

No	The French **president** serves for seven years. **You** can accomplish much in such a long term. [*President*, third person, shifts to *you*, second person.]
Yes	The French **president** serves for seven years. **He** can accomplish much in such a long term.
No	I would be afraid to give someone such power for so long a time. **You** might decide **you** disliked his policies. [*I*, first person, shifts to *you*, second person.]
Yes	I would be afraid to give someone such power for so long a time. I might decide **I** disliked his policies.

2 Staying consistent in subject and voice

The **subject** of a sentence is the word or group of words that acts, is acted upon, or is described: *The bell rings.* The **voice** of a sentence is either active (*The bell rings*) or passive (*The bell is rung*). Whenever possible, use the active voice.

No	The chemistry **student lit** a match too near the supplies, and some pure **oxygen was ignited**. [The subject shifts from *student* to *oxygen,* and the voice shifts from active to passive.]
Yes	The chemistry **student lit** a match too near the supplies, and **he ignited** some pure oxygen.
No	When **people heard** the explosion, **the hall was filled**.
Yes	When **people heard** the explosion, **they filled** the halls.
Yes	**People**, hearing the explosion, **filled** the halls.

3 Staying consistent in tense and mood

Tense refers to the ability of verbs to show time. Tense changes are required when time movement is described: *I expect the concert will start late.* If tense changes are illogical, the message becomes unclear.

No	Traffic accidents **kill** between forty and fifty thousand people as they **drove** on U.S. highways each year. [The tense shifts from the present *kill* to the past *drove*.]
Yes	Traffic accidents **kill** between forty and fifty thousand people as they **drive** on U.S. highways each year.
No	India **loses** few people in traffic accidents. Unfortunately, ten thousand people a year **died** of cobra bites. [The shift occurs between sentences. The present tense *loses* shifts to the past tense *died*.]
Yes	India **loses** few people in traffic accidents. Unfortunately, ten thousand people a year **die** of cobra bites.

Mood refers to whether a sentence is a statement or question (**indicative mood**), a command or request (**imperative mood**), or a conditional or other-than-real statement (**subjunctive mood**). Shifts among moods blur your message. The most common shift is between the imperative and indicative moods.

No   Better home security is available to all of us. First, **install** deadbolt locks on all doors. Next, **you can install** inexpensive window locks. [The verb shifts from the imperative *install* to the indicative *you can install*.]

Yes   Better home security is available to all of us. First, **install** deadbolt locks on all doors. Next, **install** inexpensive window locks.

Yes   Better home security is available to all of us. First **you can install** deadbolt locks on all doors. Next, **you can install** inexpensive window locks.

4 | Avoiding unmarked shifts between indirect and direct discourse

Indirect discourse *reports* speech or conversation; it is not enclosed in quotation marks. **Direct discourse** *repeats* speech or conversation exactly and encloses the spoken words in quotation marks. Sentences that mix indirect and direct discourse without quotation marks and other markers confuse readers.

No   The recruiter said I could advance in the Air Force, but do you really want to enlist? [The first clause is indirect discourse; the second shifts to unmarked direct discourse.]

Yes   The recruiter said I could advance in the Air Force, but asked whether I really wanted to enlist. [indirect discourse]

Yes   The recruiter said I could advance in the Air Force, but asked, "Do you really want to enlist?" [This revision uses direct and indirect discourse correctly.]

15b Avoiding misplaced modifiers

A **misplaced modifier** is a description incorrectly positioned within a sentence, resulting in distorted meaning. Always check to see that your modifiers are placed as close as possible to what they describe. The various kinds of misplaced modifiers are discussed below.

An **ambiguous placement** means that a modifier can refer to two or more words in a sentence. Little limiting words (such as *only, just, almost, even, hardly, nearly, exactly, merely, scarcely, simply*) can change meaning according to where they are placed. Consider how the placement of *only* changes the meaning of this sentence: *Scientists say that the space program is important.*

Only scientists say that the space program is important.

Scientists **only** say that the space program is important.

Scientists say **only** that the space program is important.

Scientists say that **only** the space program is important.

Squinting modifiers also cause ambiguity. A squinting modifier appears to describe both what precedes and what follows it.

No   The dock that was constructed **partially** was destroyed by the storm. [What was partial—the construction or the destruction?]

Yes   The dock that was **partially** constructed was destroyed by the storm.

Yes   The **partially** constructed dock was destroyed by the storm.

Yes   The dock that was constructed was **partially** destroyed by the storm.

Wrong placement means that the modifiers are far from the words they logically modify.

No   The British Parliament passed a law forbidding Scots to wear kilts **in 1746**. [This sentence says kilts could not be worn only in 1746.]

Yes   **In 1746**, the British Parliament passed a law forbidding Scots to wear kilts.

No   This was an attempt, **of which the kilt was a symbol**, to destroy Scottish nationalism. [This sentence says the kilt represented the destruction of Scottish nationalism.]

Yes   This was an attempt to destroy Scottish nationalism, **of which the kilt was a symbol**.

An **awkward placement** is an interruption that seriously breaks the flow of the message. A **split infinitive** is a particularly confusing kind of awkward placement. An infinitive is a verb form that starts with *to: to buy, to sell*.

No   The herb sweet basil was thought **to**, in medieval Europe, **have** strange effects on people who ate it.

Yes   In medieval Europe, the herb sweet basil was thought **to have** strange effects on people who ate it.

Generally, avoid interruptions between subject and verb, between parts of a verb phrase, and between verb and object.

15c Avoiding dangling modifiers

A **dangling modifier** modifies what is implied but not actually stated in a sentence. Dangling modifiers can be hard for a writer to spot because the writer's brain tends to supply the missing information, but the reader cannot supply it, and confusion results.

No   **Learning about bamboo, the plant's versatility** amazed me. [This sentence says the plant's versatility is learning.]

You can correct a dangling modifier by revising the sentence so that the intended subject is expressed.

Yes   **Learning about bamboo,** I was amazed by the plant's versatility.

Yes   **I learned about bamboo** and was amazed by its versatility.

No	When measured, a Japanese scientist recorded four feet of growth in one bamboo plant in twenty-four hours. [The scientist was not measured.]
Yes	When he measured the growth of one bamboo plant, a Japanese scientist recorded four feet of growth in twenty-four hours.

15d Avoiding mixed sentences

A **mixed sentence** has two or more parts that do not make sense together. In a **mixed construction**, a sentence starts out taking one grammatical form and then changes, confusing the meaning.

No	When the Pony Express's riders included Wild Bill Hickok and Buffalo Bill Cody became folk heroes. [The opening dependent clause is fused with the independent clause that follows.]
Yes	The Pony Express's riders included Wild Bill Hickok and Buffalo Bill Cody, who became folk heroes. [*When* has been dropped, making the first clause independent; and *who* has been added, making the second clause dependent and logically related to the first.]
No	To novelists, such as Ned Buntline, romanticized their adventures. [A prepositional phrase, such as *to novelists,* cannot be the subject of a sentence.]
Yes	Novelists, such as Ned Buntline, romanticized their adventures. [Dropping the preposition *to* clears up the problem.]
Yes	To novelists, such as Ned Buntline, their adventures were romantic. [Inserting a logical subject, *their adventures,* clears up the problem; an independent clause is now preceded by a modifying prepositional phrase.]

In **illogical predication**, sometimes called **faulty predication**, the subject and predicate do not make sense together.

No	The **job** of the Pony Express riders **delivered** the mail from Saint Joseph, Missouri, to Sacramento, California.
Yes	The Pony Express **riders delivered** the mail from Saint Joseph, Missouri, to Sacramento, California.
Yes	The **job** of the Pony Express riders **was to deliver** the mail from Saint Joseph, Missouri, to Sacramento, California.

Illogical predication is the problem in several common, informal constructions: *is when, is where,* and *reason is because.* Avoid these constructions in academic writing.

No	Across dangerous territory **is where** the riders traveled.
Yes	The riders traveled across dangerous territory.
No	**One reason** the Pony Express was so popular **was because** usual mail delivery took six weeks.
Yes	**One reason** the Pony Express was so popular **was that** usual mail delivery took six weeks.
Yes	The Pony Express was so popular **because** usual mail delivery took six weeks.

15e Avoiding incomplete sentences

An **incomplete sentence** is missing words, phrases, or clauses necessary for grammatical correctness or sensible meaning. Do not confuse an incomplete sentence with an elliptical construction. An **elliptical construction** deliberately leaves out words that have already appeared in the sentence: *I have my book and Joan's [book]*. The chief rule for an elliptical comparison is that the words left out must be exactly the same as the words that do appear in the sentence.

No   When migrating, most **birds travel** 25 to 30 miles per hour, but **the goose** 60 miles per hour. [The word *travel* cannot take the place of *travels*, needed in the second clause.]

Yes   When migrating, most **birds travel** 25 to 30 miles per hour, but the **goose travels** 60 miles per hour.

No   Flying **in fog** and **water**, many migrating birds perish.

Yes   Flying **in fog** and **over water**, many migrating birds perish.

In writing a comparison, be sure to include all words needed to make clear the relationship between the items or ideas being compared.

No   Young people learn languages faster. [*Faster* indicates a comparison, but none is stated.]

Yes   Young people learn languages faster than adults do.

No   Some employers value bilingual employees more than people who speak only English. [not clear: Who values whom?]

Yes   Some employers value bilingual employees more than they value people who speak only English.

No   A French speaker's enjoyment of Paris is greater than a nonspeaker. [*Enjoyment* is compared with a *nonspeaker*; a thing cannot be compared logically with a person.]

Yes   A French speaker's enjoyment of Paris is greater than a nonspeaker's.

No   Unfortunately, foreign languages have such a reputation for difficulty. [In academic writing, comparisons begun with *such*, *so*, and *too* must be completed.]

Yes   Unfortunately, foreign languages have such a reputation for difficulty that many students are afraid to try to learn one.

Small words—articles, pronouns, conjunctions, and prepositions—that are needed to make sentences complete sometimes slip into the cracks. If you tend accidentally to omit words, proofread your work an extra time solely to find them.

No   Naturalists say squirrel can hide as much twenty bushels food dozens of spots, but it rarely remembers where most of food is hidden.

Yes   Naturalists say **a** squirrel can hide as much **as** twenty bushels **of** food **in** dozens of spots, but it rarely remembers where most of **its** food is hidden.

Revising to Eliminate Shifts

A: Revise this paragraph to eliminate shifts in person and number. The first sentence should become "The next time you watch a western movie, notice whether it contains any sign language." Use your own paper.

    The next time I watch a western movie, notice whether it contains any sign language. Some people consider sign language the first universal language. Although few people use them today, it is a Native American language with a lengthy history. You can find some tribal differences, but basic root signs are clear to everyone who studies it.

    Sign language differs from the signage used by hearing-impaired people. For instance, he indicates the forehead to mean *think* while a Sioux pointed to the heart. You also use extensive facial expression in speaking to someone with a hearing loss while Native Americans maintained a stoic countenance. She believed the signs could speak for itself. Ideally you made the signs in round, sweeping motions. They tried to make conversation beautiful.

B: Revise this paragraph to eliminate shifts in verb tense. The first sentence should read "No one knows why sailors *wear* bell-bottom pants." Use your own paper.

    No one knows why sailors wore bell-bottom pants. However, three theories were popular. First, bell-bottoms will fit over boots and keep sea spray and rain from getting in. Second, bell-bottoms could be rolled up over the knees, so they stayed dry when a sailor must wade ashore and stayed clean when he scrubbed the ship's deck. Third, because bell-bottoms are loose, they will be easy to take off in the water if a sailor fell overboard. In boot camp, sailors were taught another advantage to bell-bottoms. By taking them off and tying the legs at the ends, a sailor who has fallen into the ocean can change his bell-bottom pants into a life preserver.

C: Identify the shift in each passage by writing its code on the line to the right: *1* for a shift in person or number, *2* in subject or voice, *3* in tense, *4* in mood, or *5* in discourse (confusing direct and indirect quotation). Then revise each sentence to eliminate the shift.

EXAMPLE   When people speak of a fisherman knit sweater, you mean one from the Aran Isles.   ___1___

When people speak of a fisherman knit
sweater, they mean one from the Aran Isles.

1. The Aran Isles are situated off the coast of Ireland. Galway is not far from the Isles.   _____

_____

2. An islander has a difficult life. They must make their living by fishing in a treacherous sea.   _____

_____

3. They use a simple boat called a *curragh* for fishing. It is also used to ferry their market animals to barges.   _____

_____

4. Island houses stood out against the empty landscape. Their walls provide scant protection from a hostile environment.   _____

_____

5. In 1898 John Millington Synge first visited the Aran Isles. They are used as the setting for *Riders to the Sea* and other of his works. _____

_____

6. Whether people see the Synge play or Ralph Vaughan Williams' operatic version of *Riders to the Sea*, you will feel the harshness of Aran life.   _____

_____

7. The mother Maurya has lost her husband and several sons. They are all drowned at sea.   _____

_____

8. When the body of another son is washed onto the shore, his sister identifies it from the pattern knitted into his sweater.   _____

_____

9. Each Aran knitter develops her own combination of patterns. The patterns not only produce a beautiful sweater, but they will have a very practical purpose. _____

_____

10. The oiled wool protected the fishermen from the sea spray while the intricate patterns offer symbolic protection as well as identification when necessary. _____

_____

11. When you knit your first Aran Isle sweater, you should learn what the stitches mean. Don't choose a pattern just because it is easy. _____

_____

12. A cable stitch represents a fisherman's rope; winding cliff paths are depicted by the zigzag stitch. _____

_____

13. Bobbles symbolize men in a *curragh* while the basket stitch represented a fisherman's creel and the hope that it will come home full. _____

_____

14. The tree of life signifies strong sons and family unity. It was also a fertility symbol. _____

_____

15. When someone asks you did you knit your Aran Isle sweater yourself, you can proudly say that you did and you also chose the patterns. _____

_____

Eliminating Misplaced and Dangling Modifiers

A: Underline each misplaced modifier. Then revise the sentence, placing the modifier where it belongs.

EXAMPLE   Inexperienced people are afraid to paint their own homes <u>often.</u>
*Inexperienced people are **often** afraid to paint their own homes.*

1. To paint one's house frequently one must do it oneself.

2. All homeowners almost try to paint at one time or another.

3. They try to usually begin on a bedroom.

4. They think no one will see it if they botch the job by doing so.

5. Most people can learn to paint in no time.

6. The uncoordinated should only not try it.

7. People have a distinct advantage that have strong arm muscles.

8. Prospective painters can always exercise lacking strength.

9. Novices need to carefully purchase all supplies, such as brushes, rollers, and drop cloths.

10. They must bring home paint chips exactly to match the shade desired.

11. It takes as much time nearly to prepare to paint as it does to do the actual job.

12. Painters are in for a surprise who think they are done with the last paint stroke.

13. Painters need to immediately clean their own brushes and put away all equipment.

_____

14. They can be proud of their accomplishment in the long run.

_____

15. Then can they enjoy only the results of their labor.

_____

16. Painting one's own home can, when all is said and done, be extremely satisfying.

_____

B: Revise each sentence to eliminate dangling modifiers. You may have to add or change a few words. If a sentence is acceptable as written, write *correct* on the line.

EXAMPLE   Advising a group of young women in his neighborhood, many discussions focusing on love problems were led by Samuel Richardson.
Advising a group of young women in his neighborhood, Samuel Richardson led many discussions focusing on love problems.

1. Playing the role of a caring and wise father, the girls were told by Richardson how to handle various situations.

_____

_____

2. To help the girls, letters to their suitors were sometimes written for them by Richardson.

_____

_____

3. After writing a number of successful letters, the idea of writing a book of model letters occurred to Richardson.

_____

_____

4. To prepare the book, it included letters written as if from adults to sons, daughters, nieces, and nephews.

_____

_____

5. When ready to send advice, a letter was copied out by a parent, and just the names changed.

   _____

   _____

6. Bought by many, Richardson was a successful author.

   _____

   _____

7. While working on one letter, enough ideas for a whole book occurred to Richardson.

   _____

   _____

8. By writing a series of letters between a girl and her faraway parents, young readers would be entertained and instructed.

   _____

   _____

9. Upon finishing *Pamela, or Virtue Rewarded* in 1740, a new form of literature had been invented by Richardson.

   _____

   _____

10. After years of development, we call this form the novel.

    _____

11. Being a nasty person, Horace Walpole's only novel wasn't very attractive either.

    _____

12. Imitated by others for over 200 years, his *The Castle of Otranto* was the first gothic novel.

    _____

13. Although badly written, Walpole invented the themes, atmosphere, mood, and plots that have filled gothic novels ever since.

    _____

    _____

14. Featuring gloomy castles filled with dark secrets, people are entertained by gothic movies too.

    _____

    _____

C: Underline all misplaced and dangling modifiers in this paragraph. Then revise the paragraph to eliminate them. You can change or add words and otherwise revise to make the material sensible.

[1]The art of carving or engraving marine articles, sailors developed scrimshaw while sailing on long voyages. [2]Practiced primarily by whalermen, sperm whale teeth were the most popular articles. [3]Baleen was another popular choice which was also called whalebone. [4]A sailor needed something to occupy his time with whaling voyages taking several years. [5]Imagination or available material only limited scrimshaw. [6]All kinds of objects were produced by the scrimshander, canes, corset busks, cribbage boards. [7]From whaling scenes to mermaids the sailor used everything to decorate his work. [8]A sailor doing scrimshaw often drew his own ship. [9]The most frequently depicted ship, the *Charles W. Morgan,* is, at present, a museum ship at Mystic Seaport. [10]It is possible to easily see it on a visit to Connecticut.

Eliminating Mixed Constructions, Faulty Predication, and Incomplete Sentences

A: Revise these mixed sentences to eliminate faulty predication and mixed constructions. It may be necessary to change, add, or omit words.

EXAMPLE Easter is when Russians traditionally exchanged eggs.
On Easter Russians traditionally exchanged eggs.

1. When one thinks of Carl Fabergé created Easter eggs for the tsars.

   _____

2. Because Fabergé was a talented goldsmith was the reason he was able to make exquisite objects.

   _____

3. Working for the court of Imperial Russia was able to combine craftsmanship and ingenuity.

   _____

4. The object of Fabergé pleased his clients by creating unique works of art.

   _____

5. When he included gems in his creations but they did not overshadow his workmanship.

   _____

6. In adapting enameling techniques achieved a level seldom matched by other artisans.

   _____

7. With buyers in Europe expanded his clietele beyond the Russian royal family.

   _____

8. Because he had no money worries meant few restrictions on imagination.

   _____

9. Although Fabergé created other examples of the jeweler's art, but it is the Imperial Easter eggs for which he is most remembered.

   _____

10. In the most famous eggs contained surprises inside—a hen, a ship, a coach.

_____

11. When one egg opened to reveal a model of a palace.

_____

12. Because the most ambitious creation represented an egg surrounded by parts of a cathedral.

_____

13. An artist is when one practices an imaginative art.

_____

14. One reason Fabergé is so admired is because he was a true artist.

_____

B: Revise these incomplete sentences to supply any carelessly omitted words or to complete compound constructions and comparisons clearly. Write *correct* if the sentence has no errors.

EXAMPLE   Cuneiform was system of writing with wedgelike marks.
*Cuneiform was **a** system of writing with wedgelike marks.*

1. The use of cuneiform began and spread throughout ancient Sumer.

_____

2. This picture language of the Sumerians is thought to be older than the Egyptians.

_____

3. Like hieroglyphics, early cuneiform used easily recognizable pictures represent objects.

_____

4. When scribes began using a wedge-shaped stylus, greater changes occurred.

_____

5. The new marks were different.

_____

6. They had become so stylized.

_____

7. Early Sumerian tablets recorded practical things such lists of grain in storage.

_____

8. Some tablets were put clay envelopes that were themselves inscribed.

_____

9. Gradually ordinary people used cuneiform as much as official scribes.

_____

10. *The Epic of Gilgamesh,* written in Akkadian cuneiform, is older than any epic.

_____

11. The Code of Hammurabi recorded in cuneiform a more comprehensive set of laws.

_____

12. No one could decipher cuneiform script until someone discovered the Record of Darius.

_____

13. Because it was written in three languages, it served the same purpose.

_____

14. Today we understand cuneiform as much, if not more than, we understand hieroglyphics.

_____

C: Revise this paragraph, changing, adding, or deleting words as you see best, in order to eliminate mixed and incomplete sentences. Circle the number of the one sentence that contains no errors. Use your own paper.

[1]Although wild rice may be the caviar of grains is not really rice. [2]It is, however, truly wild. [3]One reason is because it needs marshy places in order to thrive. [4]By planting it in man-made paddies can produce abundant crops. [5]Nevertheless, most wild rice grows naturally along rivers and lake shores northern states and Canada. [6]In certain areas only Native Americans are allowed harvest the rice. [7]Connoisseurs think wild rice tastes better than any grain. [8]It is surely the most expensive. [9]Some hostesses serve it with Cornish hens exclusively, but the creative cook, with many dishes. [10]Try it in quiche or pancakes; your guests will be so pleased.

16 | *Conciseness*

Conciseness refers to writing that is direct and to the point. In concise writing, every word contributes to the clear presentation of the author's message.

16a Eliminating wordy sentence structures

1 Revising unnecessary expletive constructions

An **expletive** postpones the subject by putting *it* or *there* plus a form of the verb *be* before the subject. If you remove the expletive and revise slightly, you place the subject in a position of greater impact—the beginning of the sentence.

No	It is fun to taste foods from other cultures.
Yes	Tasting foods from other cultures is fun.
No	There is a new Greek restaurant opening in town.
Yes	A new Greek restaurant is opening in town.

2 Revising unnecessary passive constructions

For most writing, the active voice (see 8n,o) adds liveliness as well as conciseness. When a passive construction (see 8n,o) names the doer of an action, it does so in a phrase starting with *by*. To change a passive sentence into an active sentence, make the noun or pronoun in the *by* phrase the subject of the sentence.

No	The cafeteria was boycotted by students to protest high prices.
Yes	Students boycotted the cafeteria to protest high prices.

You can also revise a sentence from passive to active by finding a new verb. In this technique you keep the same subject but change the verb voice.

Passive	Clint Eastwood **was elected** mayor of Carmel, California.
Active	Clint Eastwood **won** the mayoral election in Carmel, California.

3 | Combining sentences, and reducing clauses and phrases

Often when you revise you can combine sentences or reduce a clause to a phrase or a phrase to a single word, making your writing more concise and your original idea clearer.

Combining sentences: Look carefully at sets of sentences in your draft. You may be able to reduce the information in an entire sentence to a group of words that you can include in another sentence.

TWO SENTENCES	In 1985, Mel Fisher found *Nuestra Señora de Atocha* 40 miles west of Key West, Florida. The *Atocha* was a Spanish treasure ship.
COMBINED SENTENCE	In 1985, Mel Fisher found the Spanish treasure ship *Nuestra Señora de Atocha* 40 miles west of Key West, Florida.
TWO SENTENCES	The *Atocha* was heading for Spain in 1622 when it sank in a hurricane. It was loaded with gold and silver.
COMBINED SENTENCE	The *Atocha* was heading for Spain in 1622 when it sank in a hurricane, along with its load of gold and silver.

Reducing clauses: You can often reduce adjective clauses (see 7o–2) to phrases, sometimes just by dropping the relative pronoun and its verb.

Earlier, Fisher had found the *Santa Margarita*, **which was the *Atocha*'s sister ship**.

Earlier, Fisher had found the *Santa Margarita*, **the *Atocha*'s sister ship**.

Sometimes you can reduce the clause to a single word.

Fisher's find will make **people who invested in his company** rich.

Fisher's find will make **investors** rich.

Creating elliptical constructions (7o–2) is another way to reduce clauses, but be sure to omit only strongly implied words.

While they were searching for the *Atocha*, Fisher's son and daughter-in-law drowned.

While searching for the *Atocha*, Fisher's son and daughter-in-law drowned.

Reducing phrases: You may be able to shorten phrases or reduce them to single words.

In 1966, Fisher had begun to search for **the fleet that the *Atocha* was leading**.

In 1966, Fisher had begun to search for **the *Atocha* fleet**.

In twenty years, Fisher found more than a hundred **ships that had been wrecked**.

In twenty years, Fisher found more than a hundred **shipwrecks**.

4 **Using strong verbs and avoiding nouns formed from verbs**

Your writing will have more impact when you choose strong verbs—verbs that directly convey action—instead of forms of *be* or *have*. Using strong verbs also reduces the number of words in your sentences.

No   The city council **has a plan** to build a new stadium.

Yes   The city council **plans** to build a new stadium.

No   Being home to a professional baseball team **is a way to promote** civic pride.

Yes   Being home to a professional baseball team **promotes** civic pride.

When you look for weak verbs to revise, look too for **nominals**—nouns created from verbs, often by adding suffixes such as *-ance, -ment*, or *-tion*. For clear, concise writing, turn nominals back into verbs.

No   The company **was involved in the importation** of catchers' mitts.

Yes   The company **imported** catchers' mitts.

16b Eliminating unneeded words

Imprecise and showy language creates wordiness. See 21e for advice on recognizing and avoiding showy (pretentious) language. When a writer tries to write very formally or tries to reach an assigned word limit, **padding** usually results. Sentences are loaded down with **deadwood**—empty words and phrases that add nothing but confusion.

Padded   The lifeguards, who watch out for the safety of beachgoers, closed the beach near the water when a shark was sighted and seen.

Concise   The lifeguards closed the beach when a shark was sighted.

Padded   After two hours, a fishing boat full of fishermen reported seeing the shark leave the local area of the shore, so the beach was declared reopened to the public.

Concise   Two hours later, a fishing boat reported seeing the shark leave the area, so the beach was reopened.

On the next page is a chart showing a few of the most common empty phrases. Before you use one of these, be sure it adds to the meaning of your passage. For a more complete list, refer to the *Simon & Schuster Handbook for Writers*, Chapter 16.

GUIDE FOR ELIMINATING EMPTY WORDS AND PHRASES

Empty Word or Phrase	Wordy Example	Revision
as a matter of fact	**As a matter of fact**, statistics show that many marriages end in divorce.	Statistics show that many marriages end in divorce.
because of the fact that	**Because of the fact that** a special exhibit is scheduled, the museum will be open until ten o'clock.	Because of a special exhibit, the museum will be open until ten o'clock.
in fact	**In fact**, the physicist published her results yesterday.	The physicist published her results yesterday.
in view of the fact that	**In view of the fact that** the rainfall was so heavy, we may have flooding.	Because the rainfall was so heavy, we may have flooding.
seems	It **seems** that the union called a strike over health benefits.	The union called a strike over health benefits.
tendency	The team had a **tendency** to lose home games.	The team often lost home games.

16c Revising redundancies

Intentional repetition can create a powerful effect, but unplanned repetition of words or ideas (known as **redundancy**) can make an essay boring.

No   The college is building a new **parking lot** to provide more **parking space.**

Yes   The college is building a new **lot** to provide more **parking space**.

No   The model was **slender in shape** and **tall in height**.

Yes   The model was **slender** and **tall**.

Eliminating Wordy Sentence Structures

Revise these sentences to eliminate wordy sentence structures. You may need to delete expletives, change passive sentences to the active voice, reduce clauses to phrases or phrases to words, and/or replace weak, heavily modified verbs with strong direct verbs.

EXAMPLE It is Art Deco which became an international style in the 1920s and 1930s.

Art Deco became an international style in _____
the 1920s and 1930s. _____

1. Art Deco took its name from an exposition which was held in Paris in 1925.

    _____

2. Art Deco may be defined as a style that used shapes that were bold and streamlined and that experimented with new materials.

    _____

3. In the 1920s Art Deco was influenced by public fascination with technology and the future.

    _____

4. In addition to architecture, which it dominated, the style could be found in designs for glassware, appliances, furniture, and even advertising art.

    _____

5. The Empire State Building and the Chrysler Building are exemplifications of the dynamic style of Art Deco.

    _____

6. After the crash of the stock market in 1929, Art Deco became less extravagant in its expression of modern ideas and themes.

    _____

7. There was a restraint and austerity in the Art Deco of the Great Depression.

    _____

8. Builders of architecture made use of rounded corners, glass blocks, and porthole windows.

    _____

9. They had a liking for roofs that were flat.

_____

10. Buildings that had plain exteriors often were decorated with lavish care inside and had furniture to match.

_____

Eliminating Unneeded Words

Revise these sentences to eliminate unneeded words and phrases.

EXAMPLE   It seems that many cultures considered the first of May the official beginning of summer.
Many cultures considered the first of May
the official beginning of summer.

1. As a matter of fact, the Romans gave sacrifices to the goddess Maia on the first day of the month named for her.

_____

2. It seems that the Celts also celebrated May Day as the midpoint of their year.

_____

3. One of the most important of the May Day celebrations that exist is the Maypole.

_____

4. In a very real sense, the Maypole represented rebirth.

_____

5. In Germany a Maypole tree was often stripped of all but the top branches for the purpose of representing new life.

_____

6. In the case of Sweden, floral wreaths were suspended from a crossbar on the pole.

_____

7. The English had a different type of tradition.

_____

8. Holding streamers attached to the top of the Maypole, villagers danced around it in an enthusiastic manner.

_____

9. In view of the fact that May Day had pagan beginnings, the Puritans disapproved of it.

_____

10. Thus it never had a tendency to become popular in the United States.

_____

Eliminating Redundancies

Revise these passages to eliminate unnecessary repetition of words and redundant ideas. Retain helpful repetition.

EXAMPLE   Stamps are small in size, and it takes many in number to make a good collection.
Stamps are small, and it takes many to make _____
a good collection. _____

1. Many new collectors express astonished amazement at the number of stamps to be collected.

_____

2. They get excited about each and every new stamp they acquire.

_____

3. They hope to make their collections totally complete.

_____

4. Soon it becomes perfectly clear that a complete collection is impossible.

_____

5. Then they may take the pragmatic approach and be practical.

_____

6. They limit their collections by confining them to one country, continent, or decade.

_____

7. At that point in time, their collections will again provide great satisfaction.

_____

8. It is a consensus of opinion that collecting stamps can be educational.

_____

9. It can teach about past history or the geography of the earth.

_____

10. Nevertheless, a new collector should not become discouraged by overstepping possibility and trying to collect too much.

_____

Revising for Conciseness

EXERCISE 16-4

(16a-c)

Revise these paragraphs to eliminate wordiness, pointless repetitions, and redundancies. Combine sentences as necessary. Use your own paper.

A: The deadly bubonic plague was a disease that killed one-third of Europe's population of people. It was in the fourteenth century. This Asian disease came from Asia. It began this way. To begin with, there was a group of merchants from Genoa. They were attacked by infected bandits while they were at a Crimean trading outpost. They became infected. Diseased corpses were thrown over the outpost walls by the bandits, and this was a factor in the merchants catching the plague. Many of the merchants got the disease. They had a tendency to die from the disease. Those who were survivors of the disease went home. The plague was brought back with them. The first European city to have an outbreak was Constantinople in Europe. This happened in 1334. The disease had symptoms of a horrible nature. The disease then spread to the rest of Europe.

B: Auguste Escoffier was the most famous chef at the turn of the century between 1880 and World War I. In a very real sense, he was the leader of the culinary world of his day. Until that point in time, the best chefs were found in private homes. With Escoffier came an era of fine dining at restaurants to which the nobility and wealthy flocked in order to eat well. After Escoffier joined César Ritz, the luxury hotel owner, they worked as a team together to attract such patrons as the Prince of Wales. Ritz had a tendency to make each and every guest feel personally welcome. It was Escoffier who added the crowning touch by preparing dishes made especially for guests. He created dishes for the prince and for celebrities such as those well known in the entertainment world. He concocted a soup which was called *consommé favori de Sarah Bernhardt* for the actress of the same name. There was an opera singer for whom he created *poularde Adelina Patti*. As a matter of fact, another singer was fortunate to have more than one dish named for her. When Nellie Melba, an Australian singer, sang in *Lohengrin*, Escoffier served *pêches melba*, a combination of poached peaches and vanilla ice cream. To commemorate the swans of *Lohengrin*, he served the dessert in a swan that was made of ice. Melba toast was created by Escoffier during one of the periods when Melba was trying to diet. Today despite the fact that many people have not heard of Nellie Melba, they are familiar with melba toast. As a young army chef, Escoffier had to prepare horse meat and even rat meat for the purpose of feeding the troops. It is obvious that he left those days far behind him when he became the most renowned chef of his day.

17 | *Coordination and Subordination*

Coordination and subordination make it possible for your writing style to work together with your meaning. **Coordination** of sentences gives equal weight to your ideas, and **subordination** emphasizes one idea over others.

17a Understanding coordination

A **coordinate** (or **compound**) **sentence** consists of independent clauses (7o–1) joined by a semicolon or a coordinating conjunction (*and, but, for, nor, or, so,* or *yet*). ❖ PUNCTUATION ALERT: Always put a comma before a coordinating conjunction that joins two independent clauses. ❖

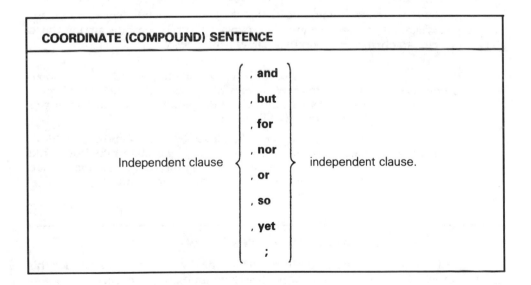

COORDINATE (COMPOUND) SENTENCE

Independent clause { , and / , but / , for / , nor / , or / , so / , yet / ; } independent clause.

Each coordinating conjunction has a specific meaning that establishes the relationship between the ideas in a coordinate sentence.

MEANING OF THE COORDINATING CONJUNCTIONS

CONJUNCTION	MEANING	FUNCTION
and	also, in addition to	to join
but	however	to contrast
for	because	to show cause
nor	an additional negative	to make the second element negative
or	an alternative	to show more than one possibility
so	therefore	to show result
yet	nevertheless	to contrast

Tuition was increasing, **and** the price of the meal plan was going up even more. Her schedule was tight, **but** she knew she needed to get a job.

17b Using coordinate sentences to show relationships

Coordinate sentences communicate that the ideas in each independent clause carry equal weight. At the same time, they explain the relationships among those ideas more effectively than a group of separate sentences would.

UNCLEAR RELATIONSHIPS	We planned a picnic. It rained. We had brought a lot of food. We had to make other arrangements. The food would spoil. We went to the ballfield in the park to use the dugout. It was full of water. We all went home.
CLEAR RELATIONSHIPS	We planned a picnic, **but** it rained. We had brought a lot of food, **so** we had to make other arrangements, **or** the food would spoil. We went to the ballfield in the park to use the dugout, **but** it was full of water, **so** we all went home.

17c Using coordinate sentences for effect

Coordination can be used to pile up details for dramatic effect. Consider this passage, in which coordinate sentences present an unfolding of events.

Scott woke up before the alarm went off. He was hungry, **but** he skipped breakfast. He raced to the showroom, **and** then he had to stand in the cold for fifteen minutes waiting for the place to open. Finally, the manager arrived, **but** before he could put the key in the lock, Scott blurted out, "I got this card; it says my car has arrived."

17d Avoiding the misuse of coordination

Coordination is illogical when ideas in the joined independent clauses are not related and when ideas do not unfold in a purposeful sequence. Avoid illogically coordinated sentences.

No   Bicycles are becoming a popular means of transportation, **and** they are dangerous on city streets. [Each independent clause is true, but the ideas are not related.]

Yes   Bicycles are becoming a popular means of transportation, **yet** the crowded conditions on city streets can make riding them dangerous.

Like all good techniques, coordination can be used too often. Overused coordination can result from writing down whatever comes into your head and not revising later. Avoid overusing coordination.

No   Hawaii is famous for its coral, **and** some of it is very shiny and hard, **so** it can last indefinitely. Some Hawaiian coral is black, **and** some is gold or pink, **and** Hawaii has $10 million a year in coral sales, **but** worldwide sales are $500 million a year.

Yes   Hawaii is famous for its coral. Some of it is very shiny and hard enough to last indefinitely. Hawaiian coral comes in black, gold, and pink. Although Hawaii has $10 million a year in coral sales, worldwide sales are $500 million a year.

No   Laughter seems to help healing, **so** many doctors are prescribing humor for their patients, **and** some hospitals are doing the same. Comedians have donated their time to several California hospitals, **and** the nurses in one large hospital in Texas have been trained to tell each patient a joke a day.

Yes   Laughter seems to help healing. Many doctors and hospitals are prescribing humor for their patients. Comedians have donated their time to several California hospitals, and the nurses in one large hospital in Texas have been trained to tell each patient a joke a day.

17e Understanding subordination

A sentence that uses subordination contains at least two clauses: (1) an **independent clause** (7o–1), which can stand on its own as a sentence, and (2) a **dependent clause** (7o–2), which cannot stand alone. Subordination joins related but separate items so that one is featured—the one in the independent clause.

Some dependent clauses start with **subordinating conjunctions**, words such as *after, before, until, when, so that* and *although*. ❖ PUNCTUATION ALERTS: (1) When a dependent clause that starts with a subordinating conjunction occurs before the independent clause, separate the clauses with a comma. (2) When such a clause follows the independent clause, separate the clauses with a comma *unless* the dependent clause is essential to the meaning of the independent clause (24e). ❖

While tuition had increased, the price of the meal plan had gone up even more.
Although her schedule was tight, she knew she needed to get a job.

Some dependent clauses start with **relative pronouns**, such as *who, which*, and *that*. Dependent clauses that begin with relative pronouns are called **relative clauses** (or **adjective clauses**). They either follow or interrupt the independent clauses they modify. ❖ PUNCTUATION ALERT: When an adjective clause is nonrestrictive—that is, when the clause is not essential to the meaning of the sentence—separate it from the independent clause with commas. ❖

Tuition, **which was high**, increased again.
The student, **who was already on a tight schedule**, needed to get a job.

17f Choosing the subordinating conjunction appropriate to your meaning

Each subordinating conjunction expresses a different relationship between the major and minor ideas in the subordinate sentences.

SUBORDINATING CONJUNCTIONS AND THE RELATIONSHIPS THEY IMPLY	
Time	*after, before, once, since, until, when, whenever, while*
Reason or Cause	*as, because*
Result or Effect	*in order that, so that*
Condition	*if, even if, provided that, unless*
Concession	*although, even though, though*
Location	*where, wherever*
Choice	*rather than, than, whether*

Notice how a change in the subordinating conjunction can change your meaning.

After you have been checked in, you cannot leave the security area without a pass. [time limit]

Because you have been checked in, you cannot leave the security area without a pass. [reason]

Unless you have been checked in, you cannot leave the security area without a pass. [condition]

Although you have been checked in, you cannot leave the security area without a pass. [concession]

17g Using subordination to show relationships

Subordination directs your reader's attention to the idea in the independent clause, while using the ideas in the dependent clause to provide context and support. Subordination communicates relationships among ideas more effectively than a group of separate sentences does.

UNCLEAR RELATIONSHIPS	I waited at the bus station. I thought I saw Marcia. She was my baby-sitter fifteen years ago. I was gathering the courage to approach her. She boarded a bus and was gone.
CLEAR RELATIONSHIPS	As I waited at the bus station, I thought I saw Marcia, who was my baby-sitter fifteen years ago. While I was gathering the courage to approach her, she boarded a bus and was gone.

17h Avoiding the misuse of subordination

Subordination is illogical when the subordinating conjunction does not make clear the relationship between the independent and dependent clauses. Avoid illogical subordination.

No	Before some states made wearing seat belts mandatory, the number of fatal automobile accidents fell. [illogical: The fatality rate fell as a result of, not prior to, the seat belt laws.]
YES	After some states made wearing seat belts mandatory, the number of fatal automobile accidents fell.
No	Because he was deaf when he wrote them, Beethoven's final symphonies were masterpieces. [illogical: It was not Beethoven's deafness that led to his writing symphonic masterpieces.]
YES	Although Beethoven was deaf when he wrote his final symphonies, they are musical masterpieces.

Like all good writing techniques, subordination can be overused. Overusing subordination means crowding together too many images or ideas, so that readers become confused and lose track of the message. Avoid overusing subordination.

No	As a result of water pollution, many shellfish beds, which once supported many families that had lived in the areas for generations, are being closed, which is causing hardships for these families.
Yes	As a result of water pollution, many shellfish beds are being closed. This is causing hardships for the many families that have supported themselves for generations by harvesting these waters.
No	A new technique for eye surgery, which is supposed to correct nearsightedness, which previously could be corrected only by glasses, has been developed, although many doctors do not approve of it because it can create unstable eyesight.
Yes	A new technique for eye surgery, which is supposed to correct nearsightedness, has been developed. Previously, nearsightedness could be corrected only by glasses. Because it can create unstable eyesight, many doctors do not approve of it, however.

17i Balancing subordination and coordination

Coordination and subordination are not always used in separate sentences. **Compound-complex sentences**, combine coordination with subordination to make sentences that flow.

> Since only a few people are supposed to have this mathematical mind, part of what makes us so passive in the face of our difficulties in learning mathematics is that we suspect all the while we may not be one of "them," and we spend our time waiting to find out when our nonmathematical minds will be exposed.
>
> —Sheila Tobias, *Overcoming Math Anxiety*

Combining Sentences with Coordination

EXERCISE 17-1

(17a-d)

Combine these sentences using coordination. For the first five sentences, use the coordinating conjunction given; for the rest, use whatever coordinating conjunction you feel is most appropriate. It may be necessary to add or change a few words, but major rewriting is not needed.

EXAMPLE   *TV Guide* was not the first television magazine with local listings.
It has become the most popular. (but)
TV Guide *was not the first television magazine with local listings,*
but it has become the most popular.

1. In 1952 publisher Walter H. Annenberg heard that someone was considering starting a national television magazine.
He became interested in the idea himself. (and)

_____

2. He wanted to learn about his competition.
He had one of his assistants find out if such magazines already existed. (so)

_____

3. The assistant found local television magazines being published in New York, Philadelphia, Chicago, and Los Angeles.
Annenberg bought them all. (;)

_____

4. Articles to appear in the first issue were written quickly.
There was no supply of already completed work to rely on. (for)

_____

5. One of the first people hired was sportswriter Red Smith.
This was before he won a Pulitzer Prize for sports reporting. (but)

_____

6. Starting the magazine was hard work.
One decision was not hard at all.

_____

7. *I Love Lucy* was the most popular show on the air in 1953.
The star, Lucille Ball, had just given birth to a baby boy.

_____

8. The whole country had followed Lucy's pregnancy.
   The editors decided to take advantage of this interest and to feature the
   baby, Desi Arnaz, Jr.

   _____

9. They could not ignore the baby's popularity.
   They could not ignore Lucy's popularity.

   _____

10. The cover had a big picture of Desi, Jr.
    It had a smaller picture of Lucy in the upper right-hand corner.

   _____

11. From the beginning *TV Guide* has been a national magazine.
    It has different editions, giving local listings.

   _____

12. Sales fell soon after the first, successful issue.
    Summer had come.
    People preferred to sit outside in the cool night air rather than watch
    television in their hot living rooms.

   _____

13. The editors had to have a sudden great idea.
    The magazine would fail.

   _____

14. They needed to increase interest in their subject.
    They decided to devote one issue to the new shows scheduled for the
    1953–54 season.

   _____

15. That first Fall Preview issue sold out.
    It started a tradition that is repeated at the start of every new television
    season.

   _____

Combining Sentences
with Subordination

Combine these sentences using subordination. For the first five sentences, use the subordinating conjunction or relative pronoun given; for the rest, use whatever subordinating conjunction or relative pronoun you feel is most appropriate. Some items have more than one correct answer, but most make sense only one way, so decide carefully which sentence comes first and where to place the subordinating conjunction or relative pronoun. It may sometimes be necessary to add or change a few words, but major rewriting is not needed.

EXAMPLE   Readers in the 1920s wanted to be well-informed. No one had the
time or money to read all the popular magazines. (although)

*Although readers in the 1920s wanted to be well-informed, no one
had the time or money to read all the popular magazines.*

1. DeWitt Wallace was a minister's son.
   He had an idea for a new magazine. (who)

   _____

2. Wallace planned to select the most important articles in all the magazines,
   condense them, and gather them in one place.
   People could keep up-to-date. (so that)

   _____

3. He prepared a sample issue without knowing something.
   He could get a publisher. (whether)

   _____

4. He sent two hundred copies of his magazine to possible financial backers.
   None of them offered to help him. (after)

   _____

5. Wallace and his fiancée got married.
   They continued to work on the magazine. (before)

   _____

6. They prepared for their wedding.
   They continued to condense magazine articles.

   _____

7. They printed a notice offering subscriptions.
   They mailed it to thousands of people.

   _____

8. They returned from their honeymoon two weeks later.
   They found 1,500 people had sent in money for subscriptions.

   _____

9. They now had plenty of customers.
   They got to work immediately on the first issue of *Reader's Digest*.

   _____

10. They found success.
    They had a new problem.

    _____

11. In the beginning other magazines were glad to have their articles reprinted.
    The Wallaces did not pay them for the articles.

    _____

12. The other magazines considered a reprinted article good publicity.
    Reader's Digest became successful enough to be competition.

    _____

13. The *Reader's Digest* began to take away readers and advertising fees.
    Many magazines refused to give permission for any more reprints.

    _____

14. For a while, Wallace paid for articles to be written for other small
    magazines with the understanding that he would be able to reprint them.
    He needed articles, and some of his best sources had been cut off.

    _____

15. The practice was stopped in the 1950s.
    Many people complained, saying the policy was dishonest.

    _____

Expanding Sentences with Coordination and Subordination

Add to each sentence below in two ways. First add an independent clause, using a coordinating conjunction. Then add a dependent clause beginning with either a subordinating conjunction or a relative pronoun.

EXAMPLE Traveling by balloon is exciting.

Traveling by balloon is exciting, and I hope to do it again soon.

Traveling by balloon is exciting because the wind is unpredictable.

1. Public transportation in the city is inadequate.

_____

_____

2. Teaching a nervous partner to dance can be frustrating.

_____

_____

3. The park looked especially beautiful at sunset.

_____

_____

4. Never buy a stereo without listening to it first.

_____

_____

5. Exercise can be fun.

_____

_____

6. Mexican food is tasty.

_____

_____

7. Watching a tape at home with friends is better than going to the movies.

_____

_____

8. The cost of food keeps going up.

   _____

   _____

9. A small car may be difficult to handle in rough weather.

   _____

   _____

10. Keeping a pet in an apartment requires compromises.

    _____

    _____

Using Coordination and Subordination in a Paragraph

These paragraphs are full of choppy sentences. Revise them using coordinating and subordinating conjunctions so that the sentences are smoother and more fully explain the relationships between ideas. Many correct versions are possible. Take the time to try several, and select the version you like best.

Senet is a game. It was played by ancient Egyptians. It was very popular. Egyptians began putting senet boards into tombs as early as 3100 B. C. Tomb objects were intended for use in the afterlife. They give us a good idea of daily life.

Many senet boards and playing pieces have been found in tombs. The hot, dry air of the tombs preserved them well. Tomb paintings frequently show people playing the game. Hieroglyphic texts describe it. Numerous descriptions of the game survive. Egyptologists think it was a national pastime.

Senet was a game for two people. They played it on a board marked with thirty squares. Each player had several playing pieces. They probably each had seven. The number did not matter as long as it was the same for both. Opponents moved by throwing flat sticks. The sticks were an early form of dice. Sometimes they threw pairs of lamb knuckles instead. Players sat across from each other. They moved their pieces in a backward S line. The squares represented houses. They moved through the houses.

By the New Kingdom the game began to take on religious overtones. The thirty squares were given individual names. They were seen as stages on the journey of the soul through the netherworld. New Kingdom tomb paintings showed the deceased playing senet with an unseen opponent. The object was to win eternal life. The living still played the game. They played it in anticipation of the supernatural match to come.

18 | *Parallelism*

18a Understanding parallelism

Parallelism is related to the concept of parallel lines in geometry. In writing, parallelism calls for the use of equivalent grammatical forms to express equivalent ideas. Parallel forms match words with words in the same form, phrases with similar phrases, or clauses with other clauses composed of the same verb forms and word orders.

Parallelism helps you communicate that two or more items in a group are equally important and makes your writing more graceful. For this reason, it is a good idea to avoid the error of faulty **parallelism**—using nonequivalent grammatical patterns.

PARALLEL WORDS	A triathlon includes **running, swimming, and cycling**. [The *-ing*s are parallel in form and equal in importance.]
PARALLEL PHRASES	Training requires **an intense exercise program** and **a carefully regulated diet**. [The phrases are parallel in structure and equal in importance.]
PARALLEL CLAUSES	Most people prefer to watch the triathalon rather than participate **because the triathalon is so difficult** and **because their couches are so comfortable**. [The clauses starting with *because* are parallel in structure and equal in importance.]

18b Using words in parallel form

Words in lists or other parallel structures must occur in the same grammatical form. Be sure to use such matching forms for parallel items.

No	The warm-up includes **stretches, sit-ups**, and **sprinting**.
YES	The warm-up includes **stretches, sit-ups**, and **sprints**.
YES	The warm-up includes **stretching, doing sit-ups**, and **sprinting**.
No	The strikers had tried **pleading, threats**, and **shouting**.
YES	The strikers had tried **pleading, threatening**, and **shouting**.
YES	The strikers had tried **pleas, threats**, and **shouts**.

247

18c Using phrases and clauses in parallel forms

Phrases and clauses in parallel structures must occur in the same grammatical form. Be sure to use such matching forms for parallel items.

No   The kitchen crew **scraped the grill, the salt shakers were refilled,** and **were taking out the trash**.

Yes The kitchen crew **scraped the grill, refilled the salt shakers**, and **took out the trash**.

18d Using parallel structures with coordinating and correlative conjunctions and with *than* and *as*

Whenever you join words, phrases, or clauses with coordinating conjunctions or correlative conjunctions (7h), be sure that they occur in parallel form.

Happiness is good health **and** a bad memory

—Ingrid Bergman

We are the carriers of health and disease—**either** *the divine health of courage and nobility* **or** *the demonic disease of hate and anxiety*.

—Joshua Loth Liebman

Absence *diminishes little passions* **and** *increases great ones*, **as** wind *extinguishes candles* **and** *fans a fire*.

—François de La Rochefoucauld

18e Repeating function words in parallel elements

To strengthen the effect of parallelism, repeat words that begin parallel phrases or clauses. Such words include prepositions (7g), articles (*a, an, the*), and the *to* of an infinitive (7d).

To *find* a fault is easy; **to** *do* better may be difficult.

—Plutarch

Use parallel clauses beginning with *and who, and whom*, or *and which* when they follow clauses beginning with *who, whom* or *which*.

I have in my own life a precious friend, a woman of 65 **who has** lived very hard, **who is** wise, **who listens** well, **who has** been where I am and can help me understand it; **and who represents** not only an ultimate ideal mother to me but also the person I'd like to be when I grow up.

—Judith Viorst, "Friends, Good Friends—and Such Good Friends"

18f Using parallel, balanced structures for impact

Parallel structures characterized by balance serve to emphasize the meaning that sentences deliver. Balanced, parallel structures can be words, phrases, clauses, or sentences.

Deliberate, rhythmic repetition of parallel, balanced word forms and word groups reinforces the impact of a message. (For information about misused repetition, see 16c.) Consider the impact of this famous passage:

> **Go back to** Mississippi, **go back to** Alabama, **go back to** South Carolina, **go back to** Georgia, **go back to** Louisiana, **go back to** the slums and ghettos of our northern cities, knowing that somehow this situation can and will be changed.
>
> —Martin Luther King, Jr., "I Have a Dream"

King's structures reinforce the power of his message. An ordinary sentence would have been less effective: "Return to your homes in Mississippi, Alabama, South Carolina, Georgia, Louisiana, or the cities, and know that the situation will be changed."

A **balanced sentence** has two parallel structures, usually sentences, with contrasting content. A balanced sentence is a coordinate sentence (see 17a), characterized by opposition in the meaning of the two structures, sometimes with one cast in the negative: *Mosquitos do not bite, they stab.*

18g Using parallel sentences in longer passages for impact

Parallel sentences in longer passages provide coherence (4d). The carefully controlled repetition of words and word forms creates a pattern that enables readers to follow ideas more easily.

18h Using parallelism in outlines and lists

Items in formal outlines and lists should be in parallel structure. Without parallelism, the information may not be clear to the reader and may not communicate that the items are equally important. (For information about developing outlines, see 2o).

Outline not in parallel form

TYPES OF FIRE EXTINGUISHERS

I. The Class A Type

    A. Contains water or water-chemical solution

    B. For fighting wood, paper, or cloth fires

II. Class B

    A. Foam, dry chemicals, or carbon dioxide "snow"

    B. Use against grease or flammable-liquid fires

18h

III. Class C

    A. Containing dry chemicals

    B. Electrical fires

Outline in parallel form

TYPES OF FIRE EXTINGUISHERS

  I. **Class** A

    A. **Contains** water or water-chemical solution,

    B. **Fights** wood, paper, or cloth fires

 II. **Class** B

    A. **Contains** foam, dry chemicals, or carbon dioxide "snow"

    B. **Fights** grease or flammable-liquid fires

III. **Class** C

    A. **Contains** dry chemicals,

    B. **Fights** electrical fires

List not in parallel form

HOW TO ESCAPE A FIRE

1. Feel the door for heat, and don't open it if it is hot.
2. You should open the door slowly.
3. Smoke?
4. If there is smoke, close the door and leave by another door or window.
5. If there is no other exit—try crawling under the smoke.
6. Be sure to use the stairs; the elevator should be avoided.
7. The fire department.
8. Reenter the building? No!

List in parallel form

HOW TO ESCAPE A FIRE

1. **Feel** the door for heat; **do** not **open** it if it is hot.
2. **Open** the door slowly.
3. **Check** the hall for smoke.
4. **If there is** smoke, **close** the door and **leave** by another door or window.
5. **If there is** no other exit, **crawl** under the smoke.
6. **Use** stairs, never an elevator.
7. **Call** the fire department.
8. **Do** not **reenter** the building.

EXERCISE **18-1**
_____

Identifying Parallel Elements

(18a-f)

Underline parallel words, phrases, and clauses.

EXAMPLE   Many ancient writers <u>in Greece</u> and <u>in Rome</u> wrote about underwater ships.

1. They hoped these ships would be used for exploration and travel.
2. Leonardo Da Vinci felt that humanity would be destroyed by a great flood because of its proud and evil ways.
3. Therefore, just as earlier he had made plans for a helicopter, he made plans for an underwater ship.
4. However, the first working submarine was designed by a British mathematician and built by a Dutch inventor.
5. It was designed in 1578, built in 1620, and successfully tested from 1620 to 1624.
6. This submarine was equipped with oars, so it could be used either on the surface or below the surface.
7. King James I of England actually boarded the submarine and took a short ride.
8. James's praise soon made submarines the talk of the town and the focus of scientific investigation.
9. A much later model featured goatskin bags attached to holes in the bottom of the ship. When the vessel was to submerge, the bags would fill with water and pull the ship downward; when the vessel was to rise, a twisting rod would force water from the bags, and the lightened ship would surface.
10. David Bushnell, a student at Yale during the American Revolution, designed and built a war-submarine, the *Turtle*.
11. It was intended to sneak up on British warships and attach explosives to their hulls.
12. Despite successful launching and steering, the *Turtle* failed on its only mission when the pilot was unable to attach the explosives to the British target ship.
13. The first successful wartime submarines were developed by the South in the Civil War: small, four-person ships called "Davids" and a full-sized submarine called the "Hunley."
14. New submarines were designed throughout the nineteenth century, but providing dependable power and seeing to navigate remained problems for years.
15. The development of the gasoline engine and the invention of the periscope solved these problems before the beginning of World War I.

Writing Parallel Elements

Fill in the blanks with words, phrases, or clauses, as appropriate.

EXAMPLE Her hobbies include *hiking, playing tennis,* and *listening to jazz.*

1. He keeps gaining weight because he loves _____ but hates
   _____.

2. Many Americans would like to travel to both _____ and
   _____.

3. _____ a television is easier than _____ one.

4. After graduation, I plan to get a good job, _____ , and
   _____.

5. A new factory, which will _____ and _____ , is
   opening across town.

6. A successful picnic has no _____ and no _____ .

7. The best food in town is found at _____ and _____ .

8. The student who _____ and _____ will speak at
   graduation.

9. It is better to _____ than never _____ .

10. I'll take math at either _____ or _____ .

11. She is on the run all day: _____ , _____ , and
    _____.

12. After the _____ and _____ received a pay raise, the
    ambulance drivers demanded one too.

13. When her child wandered off in the department store, the woman looked
    for him _____ , _____ , and _____ .

14. Professional dancers have to be _____ and _____ .

15. I want to marry someone who _____ and _____ .

19 | *Variety and Emphasis*

19a Understanding variety and emphasis

Your writing style has **variety** when your sentence lengths and patterns vary. Your writing style has **emphasis** when your sentences are constructed to reflect the relative importance of your ideas. Variety and emphasis are closely related. They represent the joining of form and meaning.

19b Varying sentence length

If you vary your sentence length, you signal distinctions among your ideas so that your readers can understand the focus of your material. Also you avoid the monotony created by an unvarying rhythm.

Strings of too many short sentences rarely establish relationships and levels of importance among ideas. Such strings suggest that the writer has not thought through the material and decided what to emphasize.

> **No** Ants are much like human beings. It is embarrassing. They farm fungi. They raise aphids as livestock. They launch armies into wars. They use chemical sprays to alarm and confuse enemies. They capture slaves.

> **Yes** Ants are so much like human beings as to be an embarrassment. They farm fungi, raise aphids as livestock, launch armies into wars, use chemical sprays to alarm and confuse enemies, capture slaves.
>
> —Lewis Thomas, "On Societies as Organisms"

Too often, compound sentences are only short sentences strung together with *and* or *but*, without consideration of the relationships among the ideas. Consider this passage, which babbles along.

> **No** Sodium is an element and some people think it is the same as salt, but sodium is just one element in salt, and it also contains chlorine.

> **Yes** Sodium is an element. Some people think it is the same as salt; however, sodium is just one element in salt. In fact, salt also contains chlorine.

As can be seen in the passage below, you can emphasize one idea among many others by expressing it in a sentence noticeably different in length or structure from the sentences surrounding it.

> Mistakes are not believed to be part of the normal behavior of a good machine. **If things go wrong, it must be a personal, human error, the result of fingering, tampering, a button getting stuck, someone hitting the wrong key.** The computer, at its normal best, is infallible. I wonder whether this can be true.
>
> —LEWIS THOMAS, "To Err Is Human"

19c Using an occasional question, mild command, or exclamation

To vary your sentence structure and to emphasize material, you can call on four basic sentence types. The most typical English sentence is **declarative:** it makes a statement—it declares something. A sentence that asks a question is called **interrogative.** Occasional questions help you involve your reader. A sentence that issues a mild or strong command is called **imperative.** Occasional mild commands are particularly helpful for gently urging your reader to think along with you. A sentence that makes an exclamation is called **exclamatory.**

Consider the following examples from *Change!* by Isaac Asimov.

QUESTION	The colonization of space may introduce some unexpected changes into human society. **For instance, what effect will it have on the way we keep time?** Our present system of time keeping is a complicated mess that depends on accidents of astronomy and on 5,000 years of primitive habit.
MILD COMMAND	**Consider the bacteria.** These are tiny living things made up of single cells far smaller than the cells in plants and animals.
EXCLAMATION	**The amazing thing about the netting of the coelacanth was that till then zoologists had been convinced the fish had been extinct for 60 million years!** Finding a living dinosaur would not have been more surprising.

19d Choosing the subject of a sentence according to your intended emphasis

Because the subject of a sentence establishes the focus for that sentence, choose a subject that corresponds to the emphasis you want to communicate.

The following sentences, each of which is correct grammatically, contain the same information. Consider, however, how changes of the subject (and its verb) influence meaning and impact.

> Our **poll shows** that most voters prefer Jones. [emphasis on the poll]
>
> Most **voters prefer** Jones, according to our poll. [emphasis on the voters]
>
> **Jones is preferred** by most voters, according to our poll. [emphasis on Jones]

19e Adding modifiers to basic sentences for variety and emphasis

Sometimes you may want a very short sentence for its dramatic effect, but you usually need to modify simple subjects and verbs. (The parentheses below tell where in the workbook you can find the definitions of each term.)

BASIC SENTENCE	Traffic stopped.
ADJECTIVE (7E, 12)	**Rush-hour** traffic stopped.
ADVERB (7F, 12)	Traffic stopped **suddenly**.
PREPOSITIONAL PHRASE (7N)	**In the middle of rush hour**, traffic stopped **on the bridge**.
PARTICIPIAL PHRASE (7N)	**Blocked by an overturned tractor-trailer**, traffic stopped, **delaying hundreds of travelers**.
ABSOLUTE PHRASE (7N)	**The accident blocking all lanes**, traffic stopped.
ADVERB CLAUSE (7o–2)	**Because all lanes were blocked**, traffic stopped **until the trailer could be removed**.
ADJECTIVE CLAUSE (7o–2)	Traffic, **which was already slow**, stopped.

19f Inverting standard word order

Standard word order in the English sentence places the subject before the verb: *The **mayor walked** into the room*. Because this pattern is so common, it is set in people's minds. Any variation from the pattern creates emphasis. Inverted word order places the verb before the subject. *Into the room **walked the mayor**.* Used too often, inverted word order can be distracting, but used sparingly, it can be very effective.

19g Repeating important words or ideas to achieve emphasis

Repeating carefully chosen words can help you to emphasize your meaning, but choose for repetition only those words that contain a main idea or that use rhythm to focus attention on a main idea.

> **Happiness** is never more than partial. There are no pure states of mankind. Whatever else **happiness** may be, it is neither in having nor in being, but in becoming. What the Founding Fathers declared for us as an inherent right, we should do well to remember, was not **happiness** but the *pursuit* of **happiness**.
>
> —JOHN CIARDI, "Is Everybody Happy?"

Varying Sentence Beginnings by Varying Subjects

Revise each sentence so that it begins with the word or words given.

EXAMPLE   A look at our history shows that Americans have enjoyed following the latest fads.
Americans: *Americans have enjoyed following the latest fads throughout our history.*

1. Parents usually think the dances their teenagers like are strange.
   The dances: _____

2. In the early 1900s, fifteen women were fired by the management of the magazine where they worked.
   In the early 1900s, the management: _____

3. They had offended management by dancing the Turkey Trot during their lunch hour.
   Their offense: _____

4. Other popular dances of the period included the Grizzly Bear, the Kangaroo Dip, and the Bunny Hug.
   The Grizzly Bear: _____

5. Alvin "Shipwreck" Kelly invented flagpole sitting.
   Flagpole sitting: _____

6. No one knows the source of his nickname.
   The source: _____

7. Pie plates from the Frisbee Baking Company were the first Frisbees.
   The first Frisbees: _____

8. A Harvard student began a goldfish swallowing fad in 1939.
   The goldfish swallowing fad: _____

9. Reporters saw him swallow a live three-inch fish.
   He: _____

10. Australians invented the Hula Hoop for use in gym classes.
    The Hula Hoop: _____

Expanding Sentences with Modifiers

A: Expand these simple sentences in the ways stated in parentheses.

EXAMPLE   The moon was shining.
          (prepositional phrase) *The moon was shining through the trees.*

1. The sofa is wearing out.

   (adjective) _____

   (adverb clause) _____

   (participial phrase) _____

2. My father swam daily.

   (adverb) _____

   (adjective clause) _____

   (absolute phrase) _____

3. The performance was splendid.

   (prepositional phrase) _____

   (adjective) _____

   (adverb clause) _____

4. The snow fell silently.

   (participial phrase) _____

   (adverb) _____

   (adjective clause) _____

5. Lewis finished writing the concerto.

   (absolute phrase) _____

   (prepositional phrase) _____

   (adjective) _____

B: Add the several elements given to each of the following sentences.

EXAMPLE The astronaut was welcomed home.
    (adjective modifying *astronaut*; adverb modifying *was welcomed*;
    prepositional phrase modifying *home*)
    The *brave* astronaut was *warmly* welcomed home *from space*.

1. The celebration included a parade.
   (adjectives modifying *celebration* and *parade*; prepositional phrase modifying *parade*)

   _____

2. The crowd was dressed in shorts and shirts.
   (absolute phrase; adjective modifying *shirts*)

   _____

3. The mayor stopped traffic.
   (adjective clause modifying *mayor*; adverb clause)

   _____

4. The astronaut rode in a car.
   (adjectives modifying *astronaut* and *car*; adverb modifying *rode*)

   _____

5. Youngsters tried to get autographs.
   (adverb clause; adjective clause modifying *youngsters*)

   _____

6. The mayor gave a speech.
   (absolute phrase; two adjectives modifying *speech*)

   _____

7. Everyone cheered.
   (two adverb clauses)

   _____

8. The celebration ended.
   (prepositional phrase modifying *ended*)

   _____

9. Everyone headed home.
   (participial phrase modifying *everyone*)

   _____

10. The street cleaners came out.
    (prepositional phrase modifying *came out*; adverb clause)

    _____

Revising to Emphasize the Main Idea

Using sentence combining, revise each passage into one or two sentences that emphasize its main idea. To do this, select the most effective subject for the sentence, stay in the active voice whenever possible, use a variety of sentence types (simple, compound, complex, compound-complex) and modifiers, and change clauses into phrases where practical.

EXAMPLE   Elizabeth Blackwell was a teacher. She was bored with teaching. She wanted to become a doctor. She had trouble qualifying for medical school.
Elizabeth Blackwell was bored with teaching and wanted to become a doctor, but she had trouble qualifying for medical school.

1. There was only one way to gain the knowledge she needed. She became a governess for doctors' families. She used her spare time. She studied their medical books.

   _____

   _____

2. She was turned down by eleven medical schools. She was finally accepted by Geneva Medical College in New York in 1848. The faculty let the students vote whether or not to accept her. They voted her in as a joke.

   _____

   _____

3. Blackwell was a good student. She received her degree in 1849. She could not find work in U.S. hospitals. She went to Europe to work.

   _____

   _____

4. She returned to New York in 1851. She wanted to open her own practice. No one would rent her office space. She bought her own house. It became the New York Infirmary for Women and Children.

   _____

   _____

5. The infirmary had an all-female staff. It was the first all-female hospital in the world. It offered internships to women medical students. It was the first to do this too.

   _____

   _____

20 | *Understanding the Meanings of Words*

20a Using dictionaries

Good dictionaries show how language has been used and is currently being used. Such dictionaries give not only a word's meaning, but also much additional important information.

An individual dictionary entry usually includes the following information: spelling; word division into syllables (syllabication); pronunciation; parts of speech; grammatical forms (plurals, parts of verbs including irregular forms, etc.); word origin; meanings; related words (nouns, adjectives); synonyms; words used in sample sentences; usage labels; and idioms that include the word.

The spelling is given first, with the word usually divided into syllables by centered dots. The pronunciation follows. Here you will sometimes see unusual symbols, such as /ə/, the **schwa** or "uh" sound. These symbols are explained in a pronunciation key, usually located in the dictionary's introduction or at the bottom of each page. The part of speech comes next. It is usually abbreviated, such as *n* for *noun* or *vt* for *transitive verb*. The dictionary also gives the principal parts of each word (for regular verbs, the *-ed* form for past tense and past participle, the *-ing* form for the present participle). The word's history (known as the etymology) usually follows. The word's meanings come next. If a word can be used as more than one part of speech, the meanings are grouped according to the parts of speech. Usage labels give additional important information, indicating which words are *slang, poetic*, or *dialect*.

Dictionaries come in several varieties. **Unabridged** ("unshortened") dictionaries have the most in-depth, accurate, complete, and scholarly entries of the various kinds of dictionaries. They give many examples of a word's current uses and changes in meanings over time. They also include infrequently used words that other dictionaries may omit.

Abridged ("shortened") dictionaries contain only the most commonly used words. They are convenient in size and economical to buy. These are the most practical reference books for writers and readers.

A number of specialized dictionaries focus on single areas, such as slang, word origins, synonyms, usage, or almost any other aspect of language. Whatever your interest, a specialized dictionary is probably available. Ask your reference librarian to point out what you need.

20b Choosing exact words

Careful writers pay close attention to **diction**—word choice. To choose the most appropriate and accurate word, a writer must understand the word's denotation and connotation.

When you look up a new word in the dictionary to find out exactly what it means, you are looking for its **denotation**. Words with the same general definition may have subtle differences of meaning. These differences enable you to choose precisely the right word, but they also obligate you to make sure you know what meanings your words convey. For example, describing someone as *lean* or *slender* is far different from calling that person *skinny*.

Connotation refers to the ideas implied but not directly indicated by a word. Connotations convey emotional overtones beyond a word's direct definition. What first comes to mind when you see the word *blood*? To some people *blood* represents war or injury while to others it is a symbol of family or ethnic identity; to people in the healing professions, *blood* may be interpreted as a symbol of life. Good writers understand the additional layer of meaning connotations deliver to specific audiences.

Specific words identify individual items in a group (*grape, orange, apple, plum*), whereas **general** words relate to an overall group (*fruit*). **Concrete** words identify persons and things that can be detected by the senses—seen, heard, tasted, felt, smelled (the *crisp, sweet red apple*). **Abstract** words denote qualities, concepts, relationships, acts, conditions, or ideas (*delicious*). Writers must use all these types of words. Effective writers, however, make sure to supply enough specific, concrete details to breathe life into generalizations and abstractions.

20c Increasing your vocabulary

Here are a few techniques you can use to make new words you encounter part of your vocabulary.

TECHNIQUES FOR BUILDING YOUR VOCABULARY

1. Using a highlighter pen, mark all unfamiliar words in your textbooks and other reading material. Then define the words in the margin so you can study the meaning in context. Copy new words onto index cards or into a special notebook.

2. Listen carefully to learn how speakers use the language. Jot down new words and later look them up. Write each new word and its definitions on an index card or in a special notebook.

3. Set aside time each day to study the new words. You can carry your cards or notebook in your pocket to study in spare moments during the day.

4. Use mnemonics to memorize words (see 22a). Set a goal of learning *and using* eight to ten new words a week.

5. Every few weeks go back to the words from previous weeks. Make a list of any words you do not still remember and study them again.

---

1 Knowing prefixes and suffixes

Prefixes are syllables in front of a **root** (base) word that modify its meaning. *Per (thoroughly)* placed before the root *form (to make* or *do)* gives *perform* ("to do thoroughly"). **Suffixes** are syllables added to the end of a root word that modify its meaning. For example, *ice* has the various forms of adjective, adverb, and noun when suffixes are added: *icy, icily, icicle, icing*.

Roots are the central parts of words to which prefixes and suffixes are added. Once you know, for example, the Latin root *bene* (*well, good*), you can decode various forms: *benefactor, benediction*.

Knowing common prefixes and suffixes is an excellent way to learn to figure out unfamiliar words. The following charts list some of the most common prefixes and suffixes.

PREFIXES

Prefix	Meaning	Example
anti-	against	antiballistic
contra-	against	contradict
extra-	more	extraordinary
hyper-	more	hyperactive
super-	more	supernatural
ultra-	more	ultraconservative
dis-	not	disagree
il-	not	illegal
im-	not	immoral
in-	not	inadequate
ir-	not	irresponsible
mis-	not	misunderstood
non-	not	noninvolvement
un-	not	unhappy
semi-	half	semicircle
mono-	one	monopoly
uni-	one	uniform
multi-	many	multitude
poly-	many	polygamy
ante-	before	antebellum
pre-	before	prehistoric
post-	after	postscript
re-	back	return
retro-	back	retroactive
sub-	under	submissive
trans-	across	transportation
inter-	between	interpersonal
intra-	inside	intravenous
auto-	self	autobiography
mal-	poor	malnutrition
magni-	great	magnificent
omni-	all	omnipotent
ab-	from	abstain

NOUN SUFFIXES

SUFFIX	MEANING	EXAMPLE
-tion	act of	*integration*
-hood	state of	*childhood*
-ness	state of	*kindness*
-ship	state of	*friendship*
-tude	state of	*solitude*
-dom	state of	*freedom*
-eer	a doer of	*auctioneer*

VERB SUFFIXES

SUFFIX	MEANING	EXAMPLE
-ate	to make	*integrate*
-ify	to make	*unify*
-ize	to make	*computerize*
-en	to cause to be	*broaden*

ADJECTIVAL SUFFIXES

SUFFIX	MEANING	EXAMPLE
-able	able to be	*comfortable*
-ible	able to be	*compatible*
-ate	full of	*fortunate*
-ful	full of	*tactful*
-ous	full of	*pompous*
-y	full of	*gloomy*
-less	without	*penniless*
-like	characteristic of	*doglike*
-ly	characteristic of	*saintly*

2 Using context clues to figure out word meanings

The familiar words that surround an unknown word can give you hints about the new word's meaning. These **context** clues include four main types.

1. **Restatement** context clue: You can figure out an unknown word when a word you know repeats the meaning: *The dieter was* **enervated**. *He was even too weakened to do his exercises. Enervated* means "weakened."

2. **Contrast** context clue: You can figure out an unknown word when an opposite or contrast is presented: *We expected Uncle Roy to be* **omnivorous**, *but he turned out to be a picky eater. Omnivorous* means "eating any sort of food." The explanatory contrast is *but he turned out to be a picky eater*.

3. **Example** context clue: You can figure out an unfamiliar word when an example or illustration relating to the word is given: *The Board of Directors made the vice-president the* **scapegoat**, *saying that the pollution was a result of her policies. Scapegoat* means "one who bears the blame for mistakes of others."

4. **General sense** context clue: An entire passage can convey a general sense of a new word. For example, *After a series of victories, the tennis star came to think of herself as* **invincible**. You can figure out that *invincible* has something to do with winning consistently.

Keep in mind that a specific context will reveal only one of many possible meanings of a word. Once you have deciphered a meaning from context clues, check the exact definition of the word in a dictionary.

Name _____ Date _____

Using the Dictionary

A: Using a college-level dictionary, rewrite each word to indicate capitalization, syllabication, hyphens, and spaces between words; use a dot to represent a break between syllables.

	Spelling	Pronunciation
EXAMPLE bolognese	Bo · lo · gnese	bō' lə nēz'
1. brogue		
2. broadminded		
3. cornmeal		
4. dahlia		
5. gypsy		
6. headache		
7. headstart		
8. incunabula		
9. inveigh		
10. peripatetic		

B: Give the meaning of these abbreviations and symbols. Consult your college-level dictionary if you are unsure.

EXAMPLE adj. _adjective_

1. *Afr.* _____
2. *alt.* _____
3. *AmInd.* _____
4. *art.* _____
5. *Celt.* _____
6. *ger.* _____
7. *Gr.* _____
8. *<* _____
9. *IE.* _____
10. *i.e.* _____

11. *cf.* _____
12. *Colloq.* _____
13. *exc.* _____
14. *ff.* _____
15. *G.* _____
16. *L.* _____
17. *ME.* _____
18. *** _____
19. *pp.* _____
20. *var.* _____

C: Give the past and past participle forms of these irregular verbs.

	Past	Past Participle
EXAMPLE send	sent	sent
1. have	_____	_____
2. do	_____	_____
3. eat	_____	_____
4. choose	_____	_____
5. drink	_____	_____
6. go	_____	_____
7. fly	_____	_____
8. know	_____	_____
9. pay	_____	_____
10. let	_____	_____

D: Give the comparative and superlative forms of these adjectives and adverbs.

	Comparative	Superlative
EXAMPLE kind	kinder	kindest
1. kindly	_____	_____
2. good	_____	_____
3. well	_____	_____
4. bad	_____	_____
5. badly	_____	_____
6. intelligent	_____	_____
7. intelligently	_____	_____
8. happily	_____	_____
9. grateful	_____	_____
10. loudly	_____	_____

E: Give the plural forms of these nouns. If your dictionary gives more than one form, list them all in the order given.

EXAMPLE alligator _____ *alligators, alligator* _____

1. scarf _____
2. llama _____
3. salmon _____
4. nucleus _____
5. formula _____

6. phenomenon _____
7. index _____
8. kibbutz _____
9. bandit _____
10. château _____

F: Carefully read the etymologies of these words in your dictionary. Then list (a) each word's original language and (b) its original meaning. Do not use abbreviations.

EXAMPLE house   a. *Old English hus*
                 b. *house*

1. wife   a. _____
                 b. _____

2. husband   a. _____
                 b. _____

3. son   a. _____
                 b. _____

4. daughter   a. _____
                 b. _____

5. marry   a. _____
                 b. _____

6. mango   a. _____
                 b. _____

7. cherry   a. _____
                 b. _____

8. tomato   a. _____
                 b. _____

9. pepper   a. _____
                 b. _____

10. onion   a. _____
                 b. _____

G: Find out what you can about the origin of each of these words.

EXAMPLE   sandwich
           after John Montagu, fourth Earl of Sandwich (1718–1792), who was
           said to have eaten these in order not to leave the gambling table
           for meals

1. cardigan _____
2. quixotic _____
3. pants _____
4. bedlam _____
5. saxophone _____
6. pasteurize _____
7. dunce _____
8. guillotine _____
9. hamburger _____
10. mentor _____

H: List all the parts of speech that each word below can serve as. How many meanings does
   each part of speech have? Do not count the meanings of idiomatic expressions using these
   words.

EXAMPLE   nest   _noun, 6 meanings; intransitive verb, 3 meanings; transitive_
                   verb, 3 meanings

1. orange _____
2. period _____
3. practice _____
4. go _____
5. turn _____

I: What usage label does your dictionary assign to each of these words? If no label is given,
   write _no label._

EXAMPLE   prithee   _archaic_

1. into (meaning _involved in_) _____
2. hot (meaning _stolen_) _____
3. rare (meaning _scattered_) _____
4. lift (meaning _elevator_) _____
5. ere (meaning _before_) _____

270

Understanding Differences in Denotation and Connotation

A: Underline the most appropriate word from the pair given in parentheses. If you are unsure, consult your dictionary's synonymy. (A synonymy is a paragraph comparing and contrasting words.)

EXAMPLE   The sky was (<u>clear</u>, transparent), with not a cloud in sight.

1. The sergeant (instructed, commanded) his men to clean the barracks.
2. The plane remained (complete, intact) after passing through the severe storm.
3. The dictator was (conquered, overthrown) by his own brother.
4. Astronomy calls for great (accuracy, correctness).
5. After he fell into the cesspool, his suit was so (soiled, foul) it could not be cleaned.
6. The inheritance was (divided, doled out) among her sisters.
7. The crowd (dissipated, dispersed) once the ambulance took away the accident victim.
8. The tenants (withheld, kept) their rent in protest over the long-broken boiler.
9. Most fashion models are (lofty, tall).
10. The patient was (restored, renovated) to health by physical therapy.
11. Because of his (immoderate, exorbitant) behavior, the young man was thrown out of the restaurant.
12. The committee voted to (eliminate, suspend) voting on the budget until the missing members could be located.
13. The coach talked to the team in the (capacity, function) of a friend.
14. The family (donated, bestowed) its time to help restore the fire-damaged day-care center.
15. The practical joker (tittered, guffawed) as his victim slipped on a banana peel.
16. The professor (praised, eulogized) the class for its good work on the midterm examination.
17. Sometimes people offer (premiums, rewards) to help capture dangerous criminals.
18. The guest wondered if it would be (impolite, boorish) to ask for a third piece of pie.
19. The man (clandestinely, secretly) took his wife's birthday present into the attic.
20. The lifeguard's (skin, hide) was dry from overexposure to the sun.

B: The following words are synonymous, but not all are equally appropriate in every situation. Check the precise meaning of each word, and then use each in a sentence. Your dictionary may have a synonymy (a paragraph comparing and contrasting all the words) listed under one of the words, so check all the definitions before writing your sentences.

EXAMPLE   laughable   *The travel book was laughable because the author had never left the tour bus.*

        amusing   *We spent an amusing afternoon riding in an old, horse-drawn carriage.*

        droll   *The political commentator had a droll sense of humor.*

        comical   *The clowns in the circus were truly comical.*

1. danger _____

   peril _____

   hazard _____

   risk _____

2. rich _____

   wealthy _____

   affluent _____

   opulent _____

3. speak _____

   talk _____

   converse _____

   discourse _____

4. think _____

   reason _____

   reflect _____

   speculate _____

   deliberate _____

5. irritable _____

   choleric _____

   touchy _____

   cranky _____

   cross _____

Using Concrete, Specific Language

A: Reorder the words in each list so they move from most general to most specific.

EXAMPLE cola   _beverage_

soda   _soda_

Coca-Cola   _cola_

beverage   _Coca-Cola_

1. sandwich   _____
   food   _____
   cheese sandwich _____
   Swiss cheese on rye _____

2. A&P   _____
   store   _____
   business   _____
   supermarket   _____

3. bill   _____
   record club charges _____
   letter   _____
   mail   _____

4. clothing   _____
   jeans   _____
   pants   _____
   stone-washed jeans _____

5. land   _____
   tropical paradise _____
   islands   _____
   Hawaii   _____

6. cookbook   _____
   The Joy of Cooking _____
   how-to book   _____
   book   _____

7. lion   _____
   hunter   _____
   cat   _____
   animal   _____

8. television show _____
   entertainment   _____
   family comedy   _____
   The Cosby Show _____

9. The Blue Boy   _____
   painting   _____
   art   _____
   portrait   _____

10. sports   _____
    100-yard dash _____
    running   _____
    track   _____

B: The italicized word or phrase in each sentence below is too abstract or general. Replace it with a word (or words) that is more specific or concrete. Use the lines to the right.

EXAMPLE   The *beast* escaped from the zoo.

ferocious leopard

1. He's very proud of his new *car*. _____
2. They planted *bushes* along the edge of the walk. _____
3. The milk tasted *funny*. _____
4. Proudly, she *walked* onto the stage. _____
5. My aunt lives in *the South*. _____
6. *Somebody* asked me to deliver these roses to you. _____
7. She wrote a book about *history*. _____
8. A *bird* flew into the classroom. _____
9. To be successful, an accountant must be *good*. _____
10. The Coast Guard chased the *criminals*. _____
11. The dancer *hurt* her ankle. _____
12. He received *jewelry* as a birthday present. _____
13. The engine made a *strange* sound. _____
14. He thought Economics class was *a pain*. _____
15. The nurse was very *nice* to the patients. _____
16. After practice, we went to *a movie*. _____
17. His new dining room set was delivered *damaged*. _____
18. The building is a *mess*. _____
19. I want to get a *good* job after graduation. _____
20. The doctor gave *everyone* a booklet about how to quit smoking. _____

Using Prefixes and Suffixes

A: Add a prefix to each of these roots to form a synonym of the word or phrase in parentheses.

EXAMPLE (away)   _ab_sent

1. (use incorrectly)   _____apply

2. (without pausing)   _____stop

3. (coming before)   _____ceding

4. (make over)   _____model

5. (move something from one place to another)   _____fer

6. (immortal)   _____dying

7. (a person's own signature)   _____graph

8. (make something appear greater than it is)   _____fy

9. (knowing only one language)   _____lingual

10. (having many parts)   _____ple

11. (in all places at the same time)   _____present

12. (having more than one husband or wife)   _____gamy

B: Add a suffix to each of these roots to form a synonym of the word or phrase in parentheses. Indicate any necessary changes in spelling.

EXAMPLE   (state of being a child)   child*hood*

1. (state of being happy)   happy_____

2. (resembling a wolf)   wolf_____

3. (act of expanding)   expan_____

4. (act of being dedicated)   dedica_____

5. (resembling heaven)   heaven_____

6. (one who climbs mountains)   mountain_____

7. (one who flies)   aviat_____

8. (to make hard)   hard_____

9. (state of having the skill of a leader)   leader_____

10. (state of being wise)   wis_____

11. (to make larger)   magn_____

12. (able to be afforded)   afford_____

EXERCISE 20-5

Using Context Clues

(20c)

Using context clues, write the probable meaning of each italicized word. Then check the definitions in the dictionary. Finally, revise any of your definitions that are inaccurate.

EXAMPLE   According to folklore, coffee has been popular since the ninth century.
Supposedly, an Ethiopian goatherd found his flock jumping around
after eating coffee beans, and when he tried some he began
gamboling along with them.
jumping around _____

1. Of all the natural *commodities* in world trade, coffee ranks second in dollar value, coming after petroleum.

   _____

2. Twenty-five million people in fifty exporting countries rely on coffee for their *sustenance*.

   _____

3 This is *singular*, as coffee has almost no nutritional value.

   _____

4. Except for Brazil, which consumes a third of its own crop, coffee-producing nations are *loath* to encourage coffee drinking at home.

   _____

5. There are greater *fiscal* benefits in exporting coffee.

   _____

6. Coffee prices rose *precipitously* in 1975 and 1979, when killing frosts destroyed many of Brazil's coffee trees.

   _____

7. The custom of *imbibing* coffee instead of eating it probably began in Yemen about A.D. 1000.

   _____

8. Coffee had an *invigorating* effect: helping people stay awake all night when they needed to.

   _____

9. For *teetotal* Muslims, coffee provided a lift they were forbidden to get from alcohol.

_____

10. Coffee was considered so *requisite* that old Turkish law allowed a wife to sue for divorce if her husband did not keep the home supplied with coffee.

_____

11. Some doctors say that excessive coffee *consumption* presents health risks.

_____

12. For example, too much coffee may *exacerbate* ulcers or high blood pressure.

_____

13. However, the studies often disagree, so the results are considered *inconclusive*.

_____

14. Meanwhile, specialty coffees *proliferate*, providing just the right accompaniment for any meal.

_____

15. For some, coffee drinking has become an *aesthetic* experience, part of the good life.

_____

21 | *Understanding the Effect of Words*

To use words well, you have to make careful choices. Your awareness of your purpose in writing, your audience, and the situation in which you are writing should influence your choice of words.

21a Using appropriate language

Good writers pay special attention to **diction** (word choice), making certain that the words they use communicate their meaning as clearly and convincingly as possible.

Informal levels and highly formal levels of writing use different vocabulary and sentence structures, and the two differ clearly in **tone**. Tone reflects the attitude of the writer toward the subject and audience. It may be highly formal, informal, or in between. Different tones are appropriate for different audiences, subjects, and purposes. An **informal** tone occurs in casual conversation or letters to friends. A highly **formal** tone, in contrast, occurs in public and ceremonial documents, such as proclamations and treaties. Informal language, which creates an informal tone, may use slang, colloquialisms, and regionalisms. In addition, informal writing may include sentence fragments, contractions, and other casual forms. Medium-level language uses general English—not too casual, not too scholarly. Unlike informal language, medium-level language is acceptable for academic writing. This level uses standard vocabulary (for example, *learn* instead of the informal *wise-up*), conventional sentence structure, and few or no contractions. Highly formal language uses many long words derived from Latin and a flowery style. Academic writing and most writing for general audiences should range from medium to somewhat formal levels of language.

The language standards you are expected to use in academic writing are those of a book like this workbook. Such language is called **standard English**, because it follows established rules of grammar, sentence structure, punctuation, and spelling. This language is also called **edited American English**. Standard English is not a fancy dialect for the elite. It is a practical set of rules about language use that most educated people observe.

Slang consists of newly created words and new meanings attached to established words. Slang words and phrases usually pass out of use quickly: *hip, cool, fresh*. **Colloquial language** is characteristic of casual conversation and informal writing: *The pileup on Route 23 halted traffic*. **Regional (dialectal) language** is specific to some geographic areas: *They had nary a dime to their name*. These usages are not appropriate for academic writing.

To communicate clearly, choose words that demonstrate your fairness as a writer. When you are talking about a subject on which you hold strong opinions, do not slip into biased or emotionally loaded language. Suppose you were arguing against a proposed increase in tuition. If you write that the president of the college is "a blood-sucking dictator out to destroy the lives of thousands of innocent young people," a neutral audience will doubt your ability to think rationally and write fairly about the subject.

21b Avoiding sexist language

Sexist language assigns roles or characteristics to people on the basis of sex. Such practices unfairly discriminate against both sexes. Sexist language inaccurately assumes that all nurses and homemakers are female (and therefore refers to them as "she") and that all physicians and wage earners are male (and therefore refers to them as "he"). One of the most widespread occurrences of sexist language is the use of the pronoun *he* to refer to someone of unidentified sex. Although traditionally *he* has been correct in such a general situation, using only masculine pronouns to represent the human species excludes females. You can avoid this problem by using the techniques suggested in the following chart.

HOW TO AVOID SEXIST LANGUAGE

1. Avoid using only the masculine pronoun to refer to males and females together:
    a. Use a pair of pronouns, but try to avoid strings of pairs in a sentence or in several consecutive sentences.

    No A doctor cannot read much outside **his** specialty.

    Yes A doctor cannot read much outside **his or her** specialty.

    b. Revise into the plural.

    No A successful doctor knows that **he** has to work long hours.

    Yes Successful doctors know that **they** have to work long hours.

    c. Recast the sentence to omit the gender-specific pronoun.

    No Everyone hopes that **he will** win the scholarship.

    Yes Everyone hopes **to win** the scholarship.

2. Avoid using *man* when men and women are clearly intended in the meaning.

    No Man is a social animal.

    Yes People are social animals.

HOW TO AVOID SEXIST LANGUAGE (*Continued*)

---

3. Avoid stereotyping jobs and roles by gender when men and women are included.

    No chairman; policeman; businessman; statesman
    Yes chair, chairperson; police officer; businessperson, business executive; diplomat, prime minister, etc.

    No teacher . . . she; principal . . . he
    Yes teachers . . . they; principals . . . they

4. Avoid expressions that exclude one sex.

    No mankind; the common man; man-sized sandwich; old wives' tale
    Yes humanity; the average person; huge sandwich; superstition

5. Avoid using degrading and insulting labels.

    No lady lawyer; gal Friday; career girl; coed
    Yes lawyer; assistant; professional woman; student

21c Using figurative language

Figurative language uses one idea or image to explain another by creating comparisons and connections. The most common figures of speech are similes and metaphors.

A **simile** states a direct comparison between two otherwise dissimilar things. It sets up the comparison by using the words *like* or *as*. A disagreeable person might be said to be *as sour as unsweetened lemonade.*

A **metaphor** implies a comparison between otherwise dissimilar things without using *like* or *as*: *The new tax bill bled lower-income families of their last hope.*

Be careful not to create an inappropriate and silly image, such as in *The rush hour traffic bled out of all the city's major arteries*. Cars are not at all like blood and their movement is not similar to the flow of blood, so the metaphor ends up confusing rather than explaining. Also be careful not to create **mixed metaphors**, illogical combinations of images: *Milking the migrant workers, the supervisor bled them dry*. Here the initial image is of taking milk from a cow, but the final image is of blood, not milk.

21d Avoiding clichés

A **cliché** is an overused, worn-out expression that has lost its ability to communicate effectively. Some comparisons that were once clever have grown old and worn out: *dead as a doornail, gentle as a lamb*. Do not take the easiest phrase, the words that come immediately to mind. If you have heard them over and over again, so has your reader. Rephrasing clichés will improve your writing.

281

21e Avoiding artificial language

Always try to make what you are saying as clear as possible to your readers. Extremely complex ideas or subjects may require complex terms or phrases to explain them, but in general the simpler the language, the more likely it is to be understood.

Pretentious language is too showy and sometimes silly, calling unsuitable attention to itself with complex sentences and long words: *I had a portion of an Italian comestible for the noontime repast* [Translation: I had a slice of pizza for lunch]. Plain English that communicates clearly is far better than fancy English that makes the reader aware that you are showing off.

Jargon is specialized vocabulary of a particular group—words that an outsider would not understand. Whether or not the word is considered jargon depends on purpose and audience. For example, when a sportswriter uses words such as *gridiron* and *sacked*, a football fan understands them with no difficulty. Specialized language evolves in every field: professions, academic disciplines, business, even hobbies. However, using jargon unnecessarily or failing to explain it is showy and artificial.

Euphemisms attempt to avoid harsh reality by using pleasant-sounding, "tactful" words. Although they are sometimes necessary to spare someone's feelings, euphemisms drain meaning from truthful writing. People use unnecessary euphemisms to describe socially unacceptable behavior: *Barry bends the rules* instead of *Barry cheats*. They use euphemisms to hide unpleasant facts: *She really likes her liquor* instead of *She is a drunk*. Euphemisms like these fool no one. Except in the rare cases where delicate language is needed—to soften the pain of death, for example—keep your language free of euphemisms.

Doublespeak is artificial, misleading language. For example, people who strip and sell stolen cars might call themselves "auto dismantlers and recyclers" selling "predismantled previously owned parts." Such language is distorting and dishonest. To use doublespeak is to use words that hide the truth, a highly unethical practice that tries to control people's thoughts. For example, in 1984 the U.S. State Department announced it would no longer use the word *killing* in its official reports about human rights in other countries. *Killing* was replaced with *unlawful or arbitrary deprivation of life*. This practice forces readers into thinking inaccurately. Such misuses of language have terrible social and political effects.

Like doublespeak, **bureaucratic language** is confusing. Unlike doublespeak, it is not intended to mislead. Rather, it is carelessly written, stuffy, overblown language, as shown by the following memo:

> You can include a page that also contains an Include instruction. The page including the Include instruction is included when you paginate the document but the included text referred to in its Include instruction is not included.

Recognizing Levels of Formality

Different levels of formality are appropriate in different situations. Decide which level (informal, medium, between medium and formal, and formal) best fits each of these situations.

	Level of Formality
EXAMPLE a letter requesting the list of winners in a sweepstakes	*medium*
1. a note to a friend asking him or her to take a package to the post office for you	_____
2. a lab report for chemistry	_____
3. a petition to have a candidate's name added to the election ballot	_____
4. an invitation to a veteran to speak to your daughter's sixth grade class about his experiences in Viet Nam	_____
5. the valedictorian's speech at a college graduation ceremony	_____

Now select three of these documents, each calling for a different level of formality, and write them. Use your own paper.

Avoiding Slang, Colloquial, and Overly Formal Language

Underline the word in each sentence that best suits an academic style. You may need to check your dictionary for usage labels.

EXAMPLE   That academic advisor fails to motivate students because she is (stuck-up, <u>aloof</u>).

1. My anthropology professor is a brilliant (guy, man).
2. The food in the main dining hall is barely (edible, comestible).
3. (Prithee, Please) shut off the lights when leaving classrooms.
4. The Dean of Faculty will (address, parley with) the audience at graduation.
5. (Regardless, Irregardless) of the weather, the honors and awards ceremony will be held on Thursday evening.
6. All students must wear skirts or (britches, slacks) under their graduation robes.

7. The elevator is reserved for faculty and (educands, students) with passes.
8. Remind your guests to park their (cars, wheels) in the visitors' lot.
9. Anyone parking a (motorcycle, chopper) on campus should chain it to the rack in the parking field.
10. Relatives may stay overnight in the (dormitories, dorms) provided they have written in advance and (checked in, touched base) with the house parents before 10 P.M.

Revising Sentences for Appropriate Language

EXERCISE **21-3**

(21a)

Revise these sentences using language appropriate for academic writing.

EXAMPLE   William Burke and William Hare were these murderers who hung around Edinburgh, Scotland, during the prior century.
William Burke and William Hare were murderers who preyed on the people of Edinburgh, Scotland, during the last century.

1. At that time, the docs and med students in Scotland needed bodies to cut up in order to figure out how to handle diseases.

_____

2. However, mighty tough laws made it hard to procure enough bodies.

_____

3. Copping stiffs from boneyards to sell to the medicos was an easy way to make a buck, but risky.

_____

4. Hare ran a boarding house, and when one of his roomers kicked the bucket, he and Burke sold the body.

_____

5. It was a cinch.

_____

6. These guys took to luring travelers to their pads, getting them cock-eyed on booze, and then wringing their necks.

_____

7. In nine months, they packed off fifteen suckers at up to £14 a pop.

_____

8. However, the fadeaway of the sixteenth victim was ascertained.

_____

9. Burke, Hare, and their cronies were nabbed.

_____

10. Hare ratted on his mate and got off; Burke was the guest of honor at a necktie party.

_____

Revising Slanted Language

Here is the opening paragraph of a very slanted letter to the editor. Revise it, using moderate language. Try to convince the reader that you are a reasonable person with a valid argument.

The Morning Telegram
Anytown, U.S.A. 00001

Dear Editor:
    I just read your ridiculous article on the proposed opening of a hazardous waste storage depot just outside town. Are you crazy? Anyone who would propose such a deadly project has no soul. Those city council members who are sponsoring this monstrous facility obviously have the brains of fruit flies. If they had bothered to do a little research, they would have discovered that dreadful things can happen to any poor community that lets such a depot be forced upon it.

Revising for Appropriate Figurative Language

Revise these sentences by replacing clichéd, inappropriate, or mixed metaphors with fresh, appropriate figures of speech. You may want to reduce the number of figures of speech in a sentence, or you may sometimes feel a message is best presented without any figurative language.

EXAMPLE   The police set up a statewide dragnet, certain the killer could not drop through the cracks.
        The police set up a statewide dragnet, certain that the killer could not escape. [A net cannot have cracks.]

1. My uncle has a grip like a vise.

_____

2. He held her in an embrace as inescapable as flypaper.

   _____

3. The fingers of the waves danced on the shore.

   _____

4. As soon as she entered her studio, the flames of creativity swept over her like an advancing iceberg.

   _____

5. They talked us into going to an expensive restaurant, so we went, reluctantly, like lambs going to the slaughter.

   _____

6. Having no backbone is his Achilles' heel.

   _____

7. Like a vise, he caught her eye, turned her head, and swept her off her feet.

   _____

8. I burned the midnight oil studying until 6 A.M.

   _____

9. The train rushed at us like a scared rabbit.

   _____

10. After I painted myself in the corner, I felt like a trapped rat.

    _____

11. The situation came to a head, so an investigation was set afoot.

    _____

12. The mailman licked the prowler and held him for police.

    _____

13. He wore his heart on his sleeve and bared his soul to her.

    _____

14. This painting is pretty as a picture.

    _____

15. The meteorologist's explanation of what causes mist was foggy.

    _____

EXERCISE 21-6

Using Figurative Language

(21c,d)

Using new, appropriate figures of speech, write a sentence describing each of the following.

EXAMPLE   a fast train
Disappearing like the vapor trail of a jet, the train sped into
the distance.

1. a graceful horse

   _____

2. a run-down shack

   _____

3. a terrible dance band

   _____

4. greasy french fries

   _____

5. being awakened by your alarm clock

   _____

6. a professor who requires too much work

   _____

7. a salesperson with a phony smile

   _____

8. a hot day in the city

   _____

9. something that is very late

   _____

10. an unpleasant singing voice

   _____

Eliminating Artificial Language

A: "Translate" these sentences into standard academic English by eliminating inappropriate jargon and euphemisms. You may need to refer to your dictionary.

EXAMPLE   We received two inches of precipitation last night.
We got two inches of rain (or snow) last night.

1. After falling, the child sustained a severe hematoma of the patella.

   _____

2. Operators of automotive vehicles should be sure to utilize their seat belts before engaging engines.

   _____

3. Although she was in a family way, she continued in the fulfillment of her familial and employment responsibilities.

   _____

4. The municipal public-thoroughfare contamination controllers are on unauthorized, open-ended leave.

   _____

5. The dean has asked department heads to interface with him.

   _____

B: Find a piece of published writing that you feel uses pretentious language, unnecessary jargon, unnecessary euphemisms, doublespeak, and/or bureaucratic language. Likely sources are newsletters, business memos and reports, political mailings, solicitations for charity, and sales brochures. Be prepared to say in what ways the language is artificial and what problems that language can create for readers. Then rewrite the piece using appropriate language. Submit the original and your revision to your instructor.

22 | *Spelling and Hyphenation*

One reason English spelling can be difficult is that our words have come from many sources. We have borrowed words from Latin, Greek, French, Spanish, and many other languages. Because of these various origins, plus differences in the ways English-speaking people pronounce words, it is unwise to rely on pronunciation in spelling a word.

What we can rely on, however, is a system of proofreading, studying, and learning spelling rules. With a little time and effort, English spelling can be mastered.

22a Eliminating careless spelling errors

Many spelling errors are not *spelling* errors at all. They are the result of illegible handwriting, slips of the pen, or typographical errors ("typos"). While you may not be able to change your handwriting completely, you can make it legible enough so that readers know what words you are writing. Careful proofreading is required to catch typos. When you reread your papers, you are likely to read what you meant to write rather than what is actually on the page because the brain tends to "read" what it expects to see. When proofreading for typos, then, try reading the page backwards, from the last sentence to the first. Using a ruler to help you focus on one line at a time is also effective.

If you are unsure how to spell a word but you do know how it starts, look it up in the dictionary. If you do not know how to spell the beginning of a word, think of a synonym, and look that word up in a thesaurus.

When you come across unfamiliar words in a textbook, highlight or underline them as you read. Then, after you have finished reading, go back and memorize the correct spelling.

As you discover words you frequently misspell, print each carefully on a card, highlighting the problem area by using larger print, a different-colored ink, or a highlighter.

Mnemonic devices, techniques to improve memory, can also help you to remember the spelling of difficult words:

The princi**pal** is your **pal**. A princi**ple** is a **rule**.

The w**ea**ther is cl**ea**r. **Whe**ther is **wh**at.

22b Spelling homonyms and commonly confused words

Many words sound similar to or exactly like others (*its/it's, morning/mourning*). Words that sound alike are called **homonyms**. To avoid using the wrong word, look up unfamiliar homonyms in the dictionary, and then use mnemonic devices to help you remember their meanings.

Some expressions may be written either as one word or two, depending on meaning:

An **everyday** occurrence is something that happens **every day**.

The guests were there **already** by the time I was **all ready**.

When we were **all together** there were five of us **altogether**.

We were there for **a while** when the host said dinner would be **awhile** longer.

Maybe the main course will be sushi, but it **may be** tofuburgers.

When we went **in to** dinner, he walked **into** the table.

Two expressions, however, are *always* written as two words: *all right* (not *alright*) and *a lot* (not *alot*).

HOMONYMS AND NEAR SOUNDALIKES

accept / except	hole / whole
advice / advise	human / humane
affect / effect	its / it's
aisle / isle	know / no
already / all ready	later / latter
altar / alter	lead / led
altogether / all together	lessen / lesson
angel / angle	lightning / lightening
are / hour / our	loose / lose
ascent / assent	maybe / may be
assistance / assistants	meat / meet
bare / bear	miner / minor
board / bored	of / off
brake / break	passed / past
breath / breathe	patience / patients
buy / by	peace / piece
capital / capitol	personal / personnel
choose / chose	plain / plane
cite / sight / site	principal / principle
clothes / cloths	quiet / quite / quit
coarse / course	rain / reign / rein
complement / compliment	right / rite / write
conscience / conscious	road / rode
council / counsel	scene / seen
dairy / diary	sense / since
dessert / desert	stationary / stationery
device / devise	than / then
dominant / dominate	there / they're / their
die / dye	through / threw / thorough
dying / dyeing	to / too / two
fair / fare	weak / week
formally / formerly	weather / whether
forth / fourth	where / were / wear
gorilla / guerrilla	which / witch
hear / here	whose / who's
heard / herd	your / you're / yore

22c Spelling plurals

Regular plurals: In general, add *-s* to form a plural: *desks, tables*. If a word ends in *-ch, -s, -sh, -x,,* or *-z*, add *-es: patches, dresses, flashes, waxes, buzzes*. Words ending in *-o* preceded by a consonant take the *-es* plural: *heroes, tomatoes*. Words ending in *-o* preceded by a vowel take the *-s* plural: *ratios, videos*. There are exceptions to these two rules, many of which are music terms taken from Italian: *contraltos, solos, pianos, tobaccos*. A few words ending in *-o* may take either the *-s* or *-es* plural: *cargoes/cargos, volcanoes/volcanos, zeroes/zeros*.

Words ending in -f or -fe: In general, change the *-f* to *-ve* before adding *-s: leaf/leaves, wife/wives*. There are three exceptions to this rule: *belief/beliefs, motif/motifs, safe/safes*. These exceptions avoid confusion with the singular verbs *believes* and *saves* and the plural noun *motives*. When the word ends in *-ff* or *-ffe*, simply add *-s: giraffe/giraffes, staff/staffs*.

Compound nouns: In general, place the *-s* or *-es* at the end of a compound noun: *attorney generals, capfuls, nurse-midwives*. If, however, the major word in the compound is the first word, add the *-s* or *-es* to the first word: *professors emeritus, passersby, sisters-in-law*.

Internal changes: Some words change internally to form the plural: *man/men, child/children, mouse/mice, foot/feet, ox/oxen*.

Foreign plurals: Words borrowed from other languages usually form their plurals according to the rules of that language. Latin words ending in *-um* or *-on* usually form their plurals by changing the *-um* or *-on* to *-a: curriculum/curricula, medium/media, datum/data, criterion/criteria*. For Latin words ending in *-us*, the plural is *-i: alumnus/alumni, syllabus/syllabi*.

Plurals retaining singular form: Some words are spelled the same in both singular and plural forms. Usually these are the names of animals or grains: *deer, elk, fish, rice, wheat*.

22d Spelling words with prefixes

Prefixes are syllables placed in front of base words, either changing or adding to the word's meaning. Prefixes do not alter the spelling of the base word: *un + reliable = unreliable*; *re + locate = relocate*. For a list of prefixes and their meanings, see 20c–1.

22e Spelling words with suffixes

A **suffix** is an ending added to the basic form of a word, to change either the tense (*-d*, *-ed*) or the part of speech. Spelling problems arise when different suffixes sound alike or when changes must be made in the base word before the suffix is added.

-able, -ible: These two suffixes cause problems because there are no reliable rules for their use. More words end in *-able: comfortable, probable, treatable.* Still, some common words end in *-ible: irresistible, audible.* The best rule to follow with these two endings is when in doubt, look up the word.

-ally/-ly: Both endings turn words into adverbs: *-ally* is added to words ending in *-ic (logically, tragically); -ly* is added to words not ending in *-ic (quickly, slowly).*

-ance, -ence, -ant, -ent: These endings do not occur according to any rules. Some words end in *-ance: observance, reluctance.* Some words end in *-ence: convenience, correspondence.* Once you know whether a noun ends in *-ance* or *-ence,* you will know whether its adjective form ends in *-ant* or *-ent: observant, reluctant, convenient, correspondent.*

-cede, -ceed, -sede: Only one word ends in *-sede: supersede.* Only three words end in *-ceed: exceed, proceed, succeed.* The rest end in *-cede: precede, recede, secede.*

-d ending: When the *-d* ending is not clearly pronounced at the end of past-tense verbs and adjectives, the wrong form of the word may be written. Watch out for incorrect forms such as *prejudice person* (instead of *prejudiced person*) and *use to* (instead of *used to*).

Final e: Drop the final *e* before a suffix beginning with a vowel (*arrange + -ing = arranging*), but keep it if the suffix begins with a consonant (*arrange + -ment = arrangement*). Often a final *e* "softens" the sound of a preceding *c* or *g* (soft *c* sounds like *s,* soft *g* like *j*). In such cases, the final *e* is retained with suffixes beginning with *a* or *o,* in order to retain the soft sound of the consonant: *service + -able = serviceable; outrage + -ous = outrageous.* Some words retain the final *e* to prevent confusion with other words: *dye + -ing = dyeing,* to avoid confusion with *dying.* For the few exceptions to the basic rule for final *e,* simply memorize their spelling: *argument, awful, truly, wisdom.*

Final y: If the final *y* is preceded by a consonant, change the *y* to *i* before adding a suffix unless the suffix begins with *i; try + -ed = tried; try + -ing = trying.* If the final *-y* is preceded by a vowel, retain the *-y* when adding any suffix: *employ + -ed = employed; employ + -ing = employing; employ + -er = employer.* Common exceptions to this rule are the past tenses of *lay, pay,* and *say: laid, paid,* and *said.*

Doubling final consonants: If a one-syllable word ends in a consonant preceded by a single vowel, double the final consonant before adding a suffix: *flip* + *-ing* = *flipping*. With two-syllable words, an additional rule applies: double the final consonant only if the last syllable of the stem is accented. Thus, adding *-ing* to the word *refer* produces *referring* (final *r* doubled), but adding *-ence* produces *reference* (final *r* not doubled) because in *referring* the accent is on the last syllable of *refer*, while in *reference* the accent is on the first syllable.

22f Using the *ie, ei* rule

Generally, you can rely on the old rhyme: "*i* before *e*, except after *c*, or when sounded like *ay*, as in *neighbor* and *weigh*": *field, believe, grief; receive, ceiling, conceit; neigh, vein, eight.* There are, however, a few common exceptions that are worth memorizing: *counterfeit, foreign, forfeit, either, neither, leisure, seize, weird, height, sleight, ancient.*

22g Using hyphens correctly

1 Hyphenating at the end of a line

Try not to divide words at the end of a line, but when you must do so, follow these guidelines.

GUIDELINES FOR DIVIDING WORDS AT END OF LINE

1. Never divide short words, and never divide single-syllable words at the end of a line, no matter how long the word: *cleanse*, not *cle-anse*.
2. Always divide words between syllables. The dictionary listing of a word shows its syllables clearly: *helicopter*, for example, appears in the dictionary as *he li cop ter*.
3. Never leave or carry over only one or two letters on a line: *alive*, not *a-live*.
4. Follow rules for double consonants. Suffixes usually create added syllables. If a base word ends in a double consonant, divide the word *after* the double consonant: *success-ful*, not *succes-sful*. If a single consonant is doubled when the suffix is added, then divide the word *between* the double consonants: *omit-ting*, not *omitt-ing*.
5. Never violate pronunciation when dividing words. Not all word endings create syllables. The *-ed* ending, for example, often simply adds the sound of the consonant *d* to a word. If you divide such a word before the *-ed* ending, you create a new syllable: *com-pelled*, not *compell-ed*.

---

2 | Dividing words with prefixes

Most prefixes form **closed words**, or words written as one (*semi + sweet = semisweet*). When you divide a word with a prefix, it is preferable to divide after the prefix (unless the prefix has only one or two letters) rather than between other syllables: *mis-understood* not *misunder-stood*.

A few prefixes require hyphens. When you divide a word with a prefix attached by a hyphen, always divide after the prefix.

all-, ex-, quasi-,* and *self-: These prefixes usually come before complete words and require hyphens: *all-inclusive, ex-husband, quasi-judicial, self-assured*.

Proper nouns and numbers: When the main word is a proper noun or number, the prefix is followed by a hyphen: *all-American, pre-1950*.

Compound main words: When the main word is a compound, the prefix is followed by a hyphen: *anti-gun control*.

Avoiding confusion: Sometimes it is necessary to hyphenate a prefix in order to avoid confusion, either in meaning or pronunciation. If a prefix added to a word causes it to look exactly like another word, the prefix must be followed by a hyphen: *re-creation* vs. *recreation*.

3 | Hyphenating compound words

A **compound word** consists of two or more words used together to form one word. When a compound acts as a modifier *before* a noun, it is usually hyphenated: *fast-paced lecture, long-term commitment*. When the same modifier comes after the noun, however, there is no hyphen: *The lecture was fast paced*. Some terms have become clear enough that they do not require hyphens: *genetic engineering laboratory, health insurance policy, junior high school, state sales tax*.

The hyphen is omitted in several other situations: when the first word in the compound ends with *-ly*, when the first word is a comparative or superlative, or when the compound is a foreign phrase: *happily married couple, lowest common denominator, ad hoc committee*.

A hyphen is placed between the two parts of a combined unit of measurement: *kilowatt-hours, light-years*.

Most compound titles are not hyphenated (*state senator, vice principal*), but many are. Hyphenated titles usually are national names, actual double titles, or three-word titles: *Italian-American, father-in-law, director-producer*.

4 Using hyphens with spelled-out numbers

Fractions: Hyphens are used between the numerator and the denominator of fractions, unless a hyphen already appears in either or both: *three-hundredths (3/100)*, but *two three-hundredths (2/300)*.

Double-digit numbers: Hyphens are used between the two parts of all double-digit numbers, whether those numbers are written alone or as part of larger numbers: *sixty-two, five hundred sixty-two*.

Combined numbers and words: When numbers and words are combined to form one idea or modifier, a hyphen is placed between the number and the word: *50-minute class*. If the word in the modifier is possessive, omit the hyphen: *one week's work*.

Recognizing Homonyms and Commonly Confused Words

Underline the word within parentheses that best fits each sentence.

EXAMPLE   When (your, <u>you're</u>) in New York, be sure to visit the Museum of Natural History.

1. The winners of the World Series (road, rode) down Main Street in a parade.
2. After reading murder mysteries all summer, she decided to (right, write) one herself.
3. While I was cleaning, I found some (loose, lose) change under the sofa cushions.
4. Thunder and (lightning, lightening) kept the campers awake all night.
5. The young woman put a lock on her (dairy, diary) when she realized her roommate had been reading it.
6. A square has four right (angels, angles).
7. The runners stood (altogether, all together) near the starting line, waiting for the signal to take (their, there) places.
8. The trip was great, (accept, except) for the day the car broke down in the (dessert, desert).
9. The broken-hearted man wrote to the (advice, advise) columnist.
10. Going to college can (altar, alter) a person's view about many things.
11. The play was an (hour, our) long.
12. The neighborhood (counsel, council) agreed to patrol the park at night.
13. Professional bakers have special (devices, devises) that help them make (peaces, pieces) of pastry easily.
14. The amount of oxygen in the air (lessens, lessons) as climbers reach higher levels.
15. Scott Kamiel (maybe, may be) the best pitcher we have ever had.
16. Prince Charles will (reign, rein) as the next King of England.
17. Do you know (whose, who's) car is blocking the driveway?
18. The last (scene, seen) of the movie was filmed from a helicopter.
19. He hid the last chocolate bar (where, were) his brothers could not find it.
20. Everything costs more now (than, then) it used (to, too).
21. Some days the smog in Los Angeles is so thick that the people can scarcely (breath, breathe), and the paramedics have more (patients, patience) than they can handle.

22. Sundaes are popular (deserts, desserts), even though we all (no, know) they are fattening.
23. Signs in the library request (quiet, quite).
24. By the time the tourists' hot air balloon landed it was (all ready, already) too late for them to return to the hotel in time for dinner.
25. (Gorillas, Guerrillas) blew up roads in an attempt to stop the shipment of weapons to the (capital, capitol).

Writing Sentences with Homonyms and Commonly Confused Words

EXERCISE **22-2**

(22b)

Use each word below in a sentence that clearly demonstrates its meaning.

EXAMPLE its *Every plan has its disadvantages.*

it's *It's too late to go out for pizza.*

1. already _____

all ready _____

2. its _____

it's _____

3. than _____

then _____

4. they're _____

their _____

there _____

5. to _____

two _____

too _____

6. your _____

you're _____

7. passed _____

past _____

8. quiet _____

    quite _____

9. through _____

    threw _____

    thorough _____

10. whose _____

    who's _____

Writing Plural Nouns

Write the plural forms of these nouns.

EXAMPLE lamp   _____*lamp*_____

           attorney at law *attorneys at law*

1. orange	_____		11. mother-in-law	_____
2. kiss	_____		12. datum	_____
3. stray	_____		13. ice skate	_____
4. life	_____		14. herself	_____
5. radio	_____		15. echo	_____
6. pair	_____		16. half	_____
7. speech	_____		17. child	_____
8. fly	_____		18. woman	_____
9. monkey	_____		19. phenomenon	_____
10. piano	_____		20. mouse	_____

Adding Prefixes

Combine these prefixes and roots.

EXAMPLE   re + start   _____*restart*_____

1. un + able   _____
2. mis + spell   _____
3. anti + freeze   _____
4. pre + determine   _____
5. extra + ordinary   _____
6. super + human   _____
7. trans + form   _____
8. sub + marine   _____
9. re + appear   _____
10. uni + cycle   _____

What rules govern the combining of prefixes and roots?

_____

_____

_____

Name _____   Date _____

Adding Suffixes

A: Combine these suffixes and roots. If in doubt about the spelling, look up the word in your dictionary.

EXAMPLE awake + ing   ___*awaking*___

1. motivate + ion   _____
2. guide + ance   _____
3. notice + able   _____
4. grace + ful   _____
5. true + ly   _____
6. accurate + ly   _____
7. mile + age   _____
8. argue + ment   _____
9. drive + ing   _____
10. outrage + ous   _____

What basic rules govern the combining of roots ending in *e* and suffixes?

_____

_____

B: Combine these suffixes and roots. If in doubt about the spelling, look up the word in your dictionary.

EXAMPLE carry + ing   ___*carrying*___

1. duty + ful   _____
2. play + ing   _____
3. dry + er   _____
4. supply + ed   _____
5. noisy + est   _____
6. stray + ed   _____
7. sloppy + er   _____
8. gravy + s   _____
9. happy + ness   _____
10. buy + ing   _____

What basic rules govern the combining of roots ending in *y* and suffixes?

_____

_____

C: Combine these suffixes and roots. If in doubt about the spelling, look up the word in your dictionary.

EXAMPLE   trap + ed   _trapped_

1. grip + ing   _____
2. mend + able   _____
3. steam + ed   _____
4. begin + er   _____
5. plant + ing   _____
6. stop + er   _____
7. pour + ed   _____
8. split + ing   _____
9. occur + ence   _____
10. refer + ence   _____

What basic rules govern the doubling of final consonants when a suffix is added?

_____

_____

Distinguishing Between ei and ie

Fill in the blanks with *ei* or *ie*. Because there are frequent exceptions to the rule, check your dictionary whenever you are in doubt.

EXAMPLE   anc_ie_nt

1. bel____ve   6. f____ld
2. rec____ve   7. counterf____t
3. n____ther   8. w____rd
4. c____ling   9. fr____ght
5. for____gn   10. n____ce

Correcting Common Spelling Errors

Underline the misspelled word in each sentence, and spell it correctly on the line to the right. If a sentence has no misspellings, write *correct* on the line.

EXAMPLE Some exceptions to spelling rules are <u>wierdly</u> irregular.   *weirdly*

1. The letter carrier retired after being biten by the same dog for the seventh time.   _____

2. The counterfeiter pleaded innocent, saying he had been frammed.   _____

3. In the committee's judgment, the fair succeeded because of extremely efficient managment.   _____

4. The scientists received news from a reliable source about an important foriegn discovery.   _____

5. We had hoped to buy a new dinning room set with our winnings from the quiz show we competed on last month.   _____

6. It seems incredable that, after trailing in the polls for weeks, our candidate managed finally to win the election.   _____

7. Running, swimming, and jumping rope are all ways to increase the heart's endurance.   _____

8. Many undocumented aliens have little liesure time because they often hold two or even three jobs, all paying illegally low salaries.   _____

9. Because we did not think the payments were affordable, we reluctantly postponed repairing the leaky ceiling.   _____

10. The disatisfied customers tried to return the chipped benches to the manufacturer, but the factory was permanently closed.   _____

11. The young man received a commendation from the community for his incredibly couragous performance in rescuing disabled children from an overturned bus.   _____

12. When he was layed off from work, he filed a grievance with his union representative and then proceeded to the unemployment office.   _____

13. After carefully painting the attic stairs, my brother-in-law   _____
    realized he had closed off his route of escape, and he
    was traped upstairs until the paint dried.

14. When I was younger, I use to want to take drum   _____
    lessons until I realized how tiring practicing the drums
    could be.

15. The professor stated that she would return illegable   _____
    papers without commenting on them, and she
    encouraged students to type all work carefully.

16. Although the street was usually gloomy, every New   _____
    Year's Eve it magicly transformed itself into a joyful
    scene for a few hours.

17. According to some philosophies, the world is constantly   _____
    changing and it is pointless to expect anything to be
    permanant.

18. The neighborhood children voted to coordinate a   _____
    carwash and use the procedes to buy durable
    playground equipment.

19. The chef advertised in the classified section of the   _____
    newspaper for a relieable dessert-maker.

20. The school aide was payed a bonus for her invaluable   _____
    assistance during the hurricane.

21. In some cultures, it is beleived that the ghosts of   _____
    ancestors take up residence in the family home.

22. One of the most appealing aspects of watching team   _____
    sports is seeing the interraction among the players on
    the field.

23. The most boring part of working in a department store is   _____
    taking part in periodic inventorys of the available
    merchandise.

24. Each autumn, people tragically injure themselves in   _____
    avoidable falls on rain-soaked leafs.

25. *Star Wars* was a very well-received and profitible movie,   _____
    and it set the pattern for many imitations.

Dividing Words
at the Ends of Lines

Using your dictionary, rewrite each word on the line to its right. Use a slash to indicate the best place to divide the word at the end of a line. Some words may be broken in more than one place. Pick the best place, and use dots to indicate all other syllable breaks. If the word cannot be divided, write it out as one unit.

EXAMPLES   signaled   *sig/naled*
           brake   *brake*
           sledgehammer   *sledge/ham·mer*

1. sleepless	_____	21. sleeve	_____
2. slenderize	_____	22. sapsucker	_____
3. referee	_____	23. Polynesia	_____
4. phlegm	_____	24. palace	_____
5. palate	_____	25. nonresident	_____
6. muscle-bound	_____	26. increase	_____
7. indecent	_____	27. however	_____
8. Hollywood	_____	28. gesticulate	_____
9. expiration	_____	29. emerge	_____
10. echo	_____	30. cubic	_____
11. cuckoo	_____	31. colorless	_____
12. cough	_____	32. caretaker	_____
13. butte	_____	33. buttermilk	_____
14. avocado	_____	34. await	_____
15. avoirdupois	_____	35. antacid	_____
16. loose	_____	36. mother-in-law	_____
17. cattail	_____	37. trousseau	_____
18. enroll	_____	38. midget	_____
19. grouch	_____	39. controlling	_____
20. progressing	_____	40. farther	_____

Writing Compound Nouns and Adjectives

Using your dictionary, rewrite each of these compound words as a single word, as a hyphenated word, or as two separate words. If more than one form is correct, be prepared to explain.

EXAMPLE foot ball _____football_____

1. open heart surgery _____
2. free for all _____
3. high school _____
4. pear shaped _____
5. bird house _____
6. accident prone _____
7. pot hole _____
8. bathing suit _____
9. bread winner _____
10. hand made _____

11. head ache _____
12. head cold _____
13. head phone _____
14. head to head _____
15. head stone _____
16. free agent _____
17. free hand _____
18. free form _____
19. free spoken _____
20. free style _____

Using Hyphens in Numbers

Formal usage in the humanities requires that numbers, including common fractions, be written in words. Write out each of these numbers, using hyphens as needed.

EXAMPLE 2102 _____twenty-one hundred and two_____

1. 35 _____
2. ½ _____
3. ⅘ _____
4. 101 _____
5. 1st _____
6. 3457 _____
7. 495 _____

23 | *The Period,*
Question Mark,
and Exclamation Point

23a Using a period at the end of a statement, a mild command, or an indirect question

Most sentences end with a period.

STATEMENT Those who cannot remember the past are condemned to repeat it.

—GEORGE SANTAYANA

MILD COMMAND Be ready at 6:00.

INDIRECT QUESTION I wondered how to select a deserving charity. [Compare with direct question (23c).]

23b Using periods with most abbreviations

Most abbreviations call for periods, but some do not. Typical abbreviations with periods that are acceptable in academic writing include *Dr., Mr., Mrs., Ms., Ph.D., M.D., R.N.,* and *a.m.* and *p.m.* with exact times such as *2:15 p.m.* Abbreviations not requiring periods include postal abbreviations for states, such as *CA* and *NY;* names of some organizations and government agencies, such as *CBS* and *FBI;* and acronyms (initials pronounced as words), such as *NASA* and *CARE.*

♣ PUNCTUATION ALERT: (1) Abbreviations of academic degrees should usually be set off with commas. When they follow city names, abbreviations of states are set off by commas. (2) When the period of an abbreviation falls at the end of a sentence, the period also serves to end the sentence. ♣

23c Using a question mark after a direct question

In contrast to an **indirect question**, which *reports* a question and ends with a period, a **direct question** *asks* a question and ends with a question mark.

> What is the capital of Georgia?
>
> How do I select a deserving charity? [Compare with indirect question (23a).]

♣ PUNCTUATION ALERT: Do not combine a question mark with a comma, a period, or an exclamation point. ♣

No	She asked, "How are you?."
Yes	She asked, "How are you?"

23d Using an exclamation point for a strong command or an emphatic declaration

A strong command gives a very firm order, and an emphatic declaration makes a shocking or surprising statement.

> Wait!   Sit down!   He lost the rent money!

♣ PUNCTUATION ALERT: Do not combine an exclamation point with a comma, a period, or a question mark. ♣

No	"Halt!," shouted the guard.
Yes	"Halt!" shouted the guard.

23e Avoiding the overuse of exclamation points

In academic writing your choice of words, not exclamation points, is expected to communicate the strength of your message. Overusing exclamation points can make your writing appear hysterical.

No	Any head injury is potentially dangerous! Go to the doctor immediately in case of bleeding from the ears, eyes, or mouth! Go if the patient has been unconscious!
Yes	Any head injury is potentially dangerous. Go to the doctor immediately in case of bleeding from the ears, eyes, or mouth, or if the patient has been unconscious.

Supplying Appropriate End Punctuation

5

EXERCISE 23-1

(23a-e)

A: Circle all inappropriate end punctuation: periods, exclamation marks, and question marks. Then on the line to the right, copy the final word of the sentence and add the appropriate end punctuation. If the end punctuation is correct as is, write *correct* on the line.

EXAMPLE   Many people wonder why nurses wear white?   _____ *white.* _____

1. Have you ever wondered why doctors wear blue or green while operating.   _____

2. White is the traditional symbol of purity!   _____

3. It is also easier to keep clean because it shows dirt.   _____

4. Surgeons wore white during operations until 1914?   _____

5. Then one surgeon decided that the sight of red blood against the white cloth was disgusting!   _____

6. He preferred—would you believe?—a spinach green that he felt reduced the brightness of the blood?   _____

7. After World War II, surgeons began using a different shade of green!   _____

8. Called minty green, it looked better under the new lighting used in operating rooms.   _____

9. The latest color is a blue-gray!   _____

10. Why did the doctors change again.   _____

11. Do you believe they did it because this blue shows up better on television than green does.   _____

12. Believe it or not.   _____

13. The surgeons appear on in-hospital television demonstrating new techniques to medical students!   _____

B: Add end punctuation to this paragraph as needed.

Do you know who Theodor Seuss Geisel was Sure you do He was Dr Seuss, the famous author of children's books After ten years as a successful advertising illustrator and cartoonist, Seuss managed to get his first children's book published *And to Think That I Saw It on Mulberry Street* was published in 1937 by Vanguard Press It had been rejected by 27 other publishers I wonder why They certainly were foolish What's your favorite Dr Seuss book Mine is *The Cat in the Hat*, published in 1957 Everyone has a favorite And I do mean *Everyone* His books have been translated into 17 languages, and by 1984 over a hundred million copies had been sold worldwide In fact, in 1984 Seuss received a Pulitzer Prize for his years of educating and entertaining children How fitting Sadly Dr. Seuss died in 1991 We will all miss him

Writing Sentences with
Appropriate End Punctuation

Write a sentence to illustrate each of these uses of end punctuation.

EXAMPLE   an emphatic command
          Wipe that grin off your face!

1. an indirect question

_____

2. a mild command

_____

3. a direct question

_____

4. an abbreviation

_____

5. a declarative sentence containing a direct quotation

_____

6. an exclamation

_____

7. a declarative statement

_____

8. an emphatic command

_____

9. a declarative sentence containing a quoted direct question

_____

10. a declarative sentence containing an indirect quotation

_____

11. a declarative sentence containing a quoted exclamation

_____

24 | *The Comma*

24a Using a comma before a coordinating conjunction that links independent clauses

The coordinating conjunctions—*and, but, for, or, nor, yet*, and *so*—can link two or more independent clauses to create compound sentences. Use a comma before the coordinating conjunction. ♣ COMMA CAUTION: Do not put a comma *after* a coordinating conjunction that links independent clauses. ♣

	and	
	but	
	for	
Independent clause,	**or**	independent clause.
	nor	
	yet	
	so	

Tea contains caffeine, **but** herbal tea does not.

Caffeine makes some people jumpy, **and** it may even keep them from sleeping.

Caffeine is found in colas, **so** heavy cola drinkers may also have trouble sleeping.

♣ COMMA CAUTION: Do not use a comma when a coordinating conjunction links words, phrases, or dependent clauses. ♣

No   More restaurants now carry decaffeinated coffee, and fruit juice.

Yes   More restaurants now carry decaffeinated coffee and fruit juice.

♣ COMMA CAUTION: To avoid creating a comma splice, do not use a comma to separate independent clauses unless they are linked by a coordinating conjunction. ♣

No   Caffeine occurs naturally in many foods, it is even found in chocolate. [These independent clauses have no linking word. The comma cannot substitute for a linking word.]

Yes   Caffeine occurs naturally in many foods, and it is even found in chocolate. [A coordinating conjunction and comma link the two independent clauses.]

When independent clauses containing other commas are linked by a coordinating conjunction, use a semicolon before the coordinating conjunction.

Some herbal teas, such as orange flavored, have become very popular; yet some people, afraid to try anything new, refuse to taste them.

24b Using a comma after an introductory clause, phrase, or word

When a clause, phrase, or word introduces an independent clause, use a comma to signal the end of the introductory element and the beginning of the independent clause.

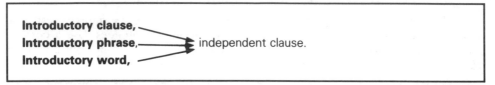

An adverb clause, one type of dependent clause, cannot stand alone as an independent unit. Although it contains a subject and verb, it begins with a subordinating conjunction (7h, 7o–2). Use a comma to set off an adverb clause that introduces an independent clause.

Whenever it rains, the lake floods local streets.

Because federal loans are hard to get, the community will have to get private help.

When an adverb clause comes after the independent clause, do not use a comma.

The lake floods local streets whenever it rains.

The community will have to get private help because federal loans are hard to get.

A **phrase** (7n) is a group of words that cannot stand alone as an independent unit because it lacks a subject, a verb, or both. Use a comma to set off a phrase that introduces an independent clause.

Inside even the cleanest homes, insects thrive. [prepositional phrase]

Carefully using insecticides, we can safely drive the insects out of our homes again. [participial phrase]

Introductory transitional words (see 4d) indicate relationships between ideas in sentences and paragraphs. Use a comma to set off a transitional word or phrase that introduces an independent clause (some writers prefer to omit the comma after single-word transitions).

First, an exterminator must clear the area of open containers of food, pets, and fragile plants.

In addition, he must be careful not to transport insects to new areas when he moves these items.

24c Using commas to separate items in a series

A series is a group of three or more elements—words, phrases, or clauses—that match in grammatical form and have the same importance within a sentence. Use commas between items in a series and before *and* when it is used between the last two items.

---

word, word, and **word**

word, word, word

phrase, phrase, and **phrase**

phrase, phrase, phrase

clause, clause, and **clause**

clause, clause, clause

Citrus fruits include **oranges, tangerines,** and **grapefruits**.

There are many varieties of oranges: **the sweet orange, the Jaffa orange, the navel orange, the mandarin.**

Lemons are good for **flavoring cakes, decorating platters**, and **removing stains**.

When the items in a series contain commas or other punctuation, or when the items are long and complex, separate them with semicolons instead of commas.

Oranges are probably native to tropical Asia, but they spread quickly centuries ago because of the Roman conquest of Asia, Europe, and North Africa; the Arab trade routes; the expansion of Islam throughout the Mediterranean, except for France and Italy; and the Crusades.

24d Using a comma to separate coordinate adjectives

Coordinate adjectives are two or more adjectives that equally modify a noun or noun group. Separate coordinate adjectives with commas or coordinating conjunctions.

---

coordinate adjective, coordinate adjective noun

The sweet orange has **broad, glossy** leaves.

Adjectives are coordinate if *and* can be inserted between them or if their order can be reversed without damaging the meaning of the sentence. Meaning does not change when the example sentence says *broad and glossy leaves* or *glossy, broad leaves*. ♣ COMMA CAUTIONS: (1) Don't put a comma after a final coordinate adjective and the noun it modifies—note that no comma comes between *glossy* and *leaves* in the above example. (2) Don't put a comma between adjectives that are not coordinate: *Six large oranges cost two dollars.* ♣

24e Using commas to set off nonrestrictive (nonessential) elements; not setting off restrictive (essential) elements

Restrictive and nonrestrictive elements are kinds of modifiers. A **nonrestrictive modifier** is also called a **nonessential modifier** because the information it provides about the modified term is "extra." If a nonrestrictive modifier is dropped, a reader can still understand the full meaning of the modified word. Nonrestrictive modifiers are set off with commas.

Nonrestrictive element, independent clause.

Beginning of independent clause, **nonrestrictive element**, end of independent clause.

Independent clause, **nonrestrictive element**.

Believe it or not, the first daily newspaper was a Roman invention.

The *Acta Diurna*, **whose title means "daily events,"** was available every day.

Scribes made multiple copies of each day's political and social news, **which included senate action and the results of gladiatorial games**.

When the nonrestrictive information in these examples is eliminated, the meaning of the modified terms does not change.

The first daily newspaper was a Roman invention.

The *Acta Diurna* was available every day.

Scribes made multiple copies of each day's political and social news.

In contrast, a **restrictive modifier** (also known as an **essential modifier**) cannot be omitted without creating confusion. No commas are used because the information in these passages is part of the basic message of the sentence. ♣ COMMA CAUTION: A restrictive modifier is not extra. Do not use commas to set it off from the rest of the sentence. ♣

Whoever invented paper is unknown.

The Chinese printed **what are considered the first books**.

They invented a white paper **that was made of wood** and a way to transfer a carved image from stone to paper.

Compare the pairs of restrictive and nonrestrictive modifiers that follow.

NONRESTRICTIVE CLAUSE	The world's oldest surviving book printed from wood blocks was published in A.D. 868 by Wang Chieh, **who followed an already long Chinese printing tradition.** [*Who followed an already long Chinese printing tradition* adds information about Wang Chieh, but it is not essential to the sentence.]
RESTRICTIVE CLAUSE	Students **who wish to imitate the woodblock method** do not need many materials. [The clause clarifies which students, so it is essential.]

NONRESTRICTIVE PHRASE	**Before carving**, the student should sketch out a preliminary version of the page. [*Before carving* is a prepositional phrase that explains when to act. However, the sentence is clear without it.]
RESTRICTIVE PHRASE	Marco Polo introduced woodblock printing **to Europe**. [Prepositional phrase is essential to the message.]

An **appositive** (7m–3) is a word or group of words that renames the noun or noun group preceding it. Most appositives are nonrestrictive. Once the name of something is given, words renaming it are not usually necessary to specify or limit it even more.

> Johann Gutenberg, **a German printer living in France**, was the first European to use movable type.

Some appositives, however, are restrictive and are not set off with commas.

> Mr. Jones **the rare book collector** would pay a fortune to own a Gutenberg Bible. [The appositive is essential for distinguishing this Mr. Jones from other Mr. Joneses.]

24f Using commas to set off transitional and parenthetical expressions, contrasts, words of direct address, and tag questions

Words, phrases, or clauses that interrupt a sentence but—like nonrestrictive elements—do not change its basic meaning should be set off, usually with commas. (Parentheses or dashes also set material off.)

Transitional words (such as *however, for example, in addition, therefore*) sometimes express connections within sentences. When they do, they are set off with commas.

> The oldest surviving document of a news event, **in fact**, is a report of a storm and earthquake in Guatemala in 1541. [Transitional expression indicating that the truth is not what one might have expected.]

♣ COMMA CAUTION: When a transitional expression links independent clauses, use a semicolon or a coordinating conjunction. A comma alone will create a comma splice: *Few old documents survive;* **in fact**, the oldest surviving news report is from 1541. ♣

Parenthetical expressions are "asides," additions to sentences that the writer thinks of as extra.

> The Spanish brought the first printing press in the New World to Mexico City in 1534, but, **surprisingly**, the earliest surviving pieces of work are from 1539. [parenthetical expression]

Expressions of contrast are set off with commas.

An early printing press at Lima turned out Indian- and Spanish-language religious material, **not political or news pamphlets**. [words of contrast]

The roots of the extensive modern Spanish-language press go back to these two printing centers, **rather than to Spain itself**. [words of contrast]

Words of direct address and tag questions should be set off with commas.

Did you know, **Rosa**, that your daily Spanish newspaper is part of a 400-year-old tradition? [direct address]

You are bilingual, **aren't you?** [tag question]

24g Using commas to set off quoted words from explanatory words

Use a comma to set off quoted words from short explanations in the same sentence, such as *she said, they replied*, and *he answered*.

According to a Chinese proverb, "A book is like a garden carried in the pocket."

"When I stepped from hard manual work to writing," said Sean O'Casey, "I just stepped from one kind of hard work to another."

"I can't write five words, but that I change seven," complained Dorothy Parker.

❖ COMMA CAUTION: When quoted words end with a question mark or an exclamation point, keep that punctuation and do not add a comma even if explanatory words follow. ❖

24h Using commas in dates, names, addresses, and numbers according to accepted practice

---

RULES FOR COMMAS WITH DATES

1. Use a comma between the date and the year: **November 24, 1859**.
2. Use a comma between the day and the date: **Thursday, November 24.**
3. Within a sentence, use commas after the day *and* the year in a full date.
   November 24, 1859, was the date of publication of Charles Darwin's *The Origin of Species*.
4. Don't use a comma in a date that contains only the month and year or only the season and year.
   Darwin's *The Origin of Species* was published in **winter 1859**.
5. An inverted date takes no commas.
   Charles Darwin's *The Origin of Species* was first published on **24 November 1859**.

RULES FOR COMMAS WITH NAMES, PLACES, AND ADDRESSES

1. When an abbreviated title (Jr., M.D., Ph.D.) comes after a person's name, set the abbreviation off with commas.

   The company celebrated the promotion of **Susan Cohen, M.B.A.**, to senior vice president.

2. When you invert a person's name, use a comma to separate the last name from the first: **Cohen, Susan.**

3. Use a comma between a city and state: **Cherry Hill, New Jersey**. In a sentence, use a comma after the state as well.

   Cherry Hill, New Jersey, is not far from Philadelphia.

4. When you write a complete address as part of a sentence, use a comma to separate all the items but the zip code, which follows the state. A comma does not follow the zip code.

   The check from U.R. Stuk, **1313 Erewhon Lane, Englewood Cliffs, New Jersey 07632** bounced.

RULES FOR COMMAS WITH LETTERS

1. For the opening of an informal letter, use a comma: **Dear Betty,**

2. For the close of a letter, use a comma: **Sincerely yours, Love, Best regards, Very truly yours,**

RULES FOR COMMAS WITH NUMBERS

1. Counting from the right, put a comma after every three digits in numbers over four digits: **72,867   156,567,066**

2. In a number of four digits, a comma is optional.

   $1776 or **$1,776**   **1776 miles** or **1,776 miles**

3. Don't use a comma for a four-digit year—**1990** (but **25,000 B.C.**); or in an address—**12161 Dean Drive**; or in a page number—**see page 1338**

4. Use a comma to separate related measurements written as words: **five feet, four inches**

5. Use a comma to separate a play's scene from an act: **Act II, scene iv**

6. Use a comma to separate a reference to a page from a reference to a line: **page 10, line 6**

24i Using commas to clarify meaning

Sometimes you will need to use a comma to clarify the meaning of a sentence, even though no other rule calls for one.

No	In his will power to run the family business was divided among his children.
Yes	In his will, power to run the family business was divided among his children.
No	People who want to register to vote without being reminded.
Yes	People who want to, register to vote without being reminded.

24j Avoiding misuse of the comma

Do not overuse commas by inserting them where they do not belong. Comma misuses are discussed throughout this chapter, signaled by ♣ COMMA CAUTION. ♣

Besides the misuses of commas discussed earlier, writers sometimes mistakenly use commas to separate major sentence parts.

No	Snowfalls over the last 20 million years, have created the Antarctic ice sheet. [Do not separate a subject from its verb with a single comma.]
Yes	Snowfalls over the last 20 million years have created the Antarctic ice sheet.
No	The massive ice sheet is, 16,000 feet deep. [Do not separate a verb from its complement with a single comma.]
Yes	The massive ice sheet is 16,000 feet deep.
No	The weight of the ice has pushed, the continent 2,000 feet into the water. [Do not separate a verb from its object with a single comma.]
Yes	The weight of the ice has pushed the continent 2,000 feet into the water.
No	Therefore, most of the continent lies below, sea level. [Do not separate a preposition from its object with a single comma.]
Yes	Therefore, most of the continent lies below sea level.

Using Commas in Compound Sentences

A: Rewrite the following sentences, inserting commas wherever coordinating conjunctions are used to join sentences. If a sentence does not need any additional commas, write *correct* on the line.

EXAMPLE   Some people consider slime molds protozoans but most scientists class them with the fungi.
Some people consider slime molds protozoans, but most scientists _____
class them with the fungi. _____

1. Slime molds move by creeping along and sometimes they seem to flow.
_____

2. They have a stationary stage, however and then they are more plantlike.
_____

3. An observer seldom sees much of the mold's body or plasmodium for it stays beneath decaying matter.
_____

4. The main part contains several nuclei but has no cell walls.
_____

5. Like an amoeba, its protoplasm moves in one direction and then it goes in another.
_____

6. Not only do slime molds come in many colors but they also come in many types.
_____

7. Some grow on long stalks while others are stalkless.
_____

8. Some kinds are very small and can only be seen through a microscope.
_____

9. Most slime molds grow on decaying wood yet some grow directly on the ground.
_____

10. A mold depends on water so it will dry up if it lacks moisture.

_____

11. Most mature molds change into sporangia and the sporangia each contain many spores.

_____

12. Scientists know that the wind carries the spores and that they eventually germinate and form new molds.

_____

13. The slime-mold species *Fuligo* has the largest sporangia and they dwarf others by comparison.

_____

14. Either they appear to be large sponges on the ground or they look like dark holes in the grass.

_____

B: Combine the following sentences by using the coordinating conjunctions given in parentheses. Remember to use a comma before each coordinating conjunction used to join two sentences.

EXAMPLE   Most slime molds live in the woods.
           They like soil with high humus content. (and)
           Most slime molds live in the woods, and
           they like soil with high humus content.

1. Some, however, leave the forest.
   They live on cultivated plants. (and)

_____

2. They can cause clubroot of cabbage.
   They can create powdery scab of potato. (or)

_____

3. Slime molds sound disagreeable.
   Some are quite attractive. (yet)

_____

4. One form produces unappealing stalks.
   The stalks are topped with tiny balls. (but)

_____

5. The balls appear to be woven.
   They look rather like baskets. (so)

   _____

6. The woven balls are really sporangia.
   They contain spores for distribution. (and)

   _____

7. Another form looks like tiny ghosts.
   Its white molds could be small sheeted figures. (for)

   _____

8. Serpent slime mold is yellow.
   It can look like a miniature snake on top of a decaying log. (and)

   _____

9. One would have to work hard to find it in New England.
   It is most common in the tropics. (for)

   _____

10. After one learns about slime molds, they no longer seem disgusting.
    They do not even seem disagreeable. (nor)

    _____

Using Commas after Introductory Elements

A: Applying the rules regarding commas and introductory elements, rewrite these sentences, inserting commas as needed. If any sentence does not need an additional comma, write *correct* on the line.

EXAMPLE Known as the Empty Quarter the Rub al-Khali is the largest of the deserts in Saudi Arabia.

Known as the Empty Quarter, the Rub al-Khali is the largest of the deserts in Saudi Arabia.

1. In fact it is the largest continuous body of sand in the world.

2. Extending over 250,000 square miles the Rub al-Khali comprises more than one third of Saudi Arabia.

3. As a point of comparison Texas is just slightly larger.

4. Because it is almost completely devoid of rain the Rub al-Khali is one of the driest places on the planet.

5. Despite the existence of a few scattered shrubs the desert is largely a sand sea.

6. However its eastern side develops massive dunes with salt basins.

7. Except for the hardy Bedouins the Rub al-Khali is uninhabited.

8. Indeed it is considered one of the most forbidding places on earth.

9. Until Bertram Thomas crossed it in 1931 it was unexplored by outsiders.

10. Even after oil was discovered in Arabia exploration in the Empty Quarter was limited.

11. Losing heavy equipment in the deep sand made such exploration expensive.

_____

12. To faciliate exploration huge sand tires were developed in the 1950s.

_____

13. Shortly thereafter drilling rigs began operating in the Rub al-Khali.

_____

14. We now know that the Empty Quarter sits on huge reserves of oil.

_____

15. As it turns out the Empty Quarter is not so empty after all.

_____

B: Applying the rules governing commas and introductory elements, insert commas as needed in this paragraph.

[1]As might be expected the Rub al-Khali is hot all year round. [2]In contrast the Gobi Desert is hot in the summer but extremely cold in the winter. [3]Located in China and Mongolia the Gobi is twice the size of Texas. [4]Unlike the Rub al-Khali the Gobi has some permanent settlers. [5]Nevertheless most of its inhabitants are nomadic. [6]To avoid the subzero winters the nomads move their herds at the end of summer. [7]When the harsh winters subside they return to the sparse desert vegetation.

Using Commas in Series and with Coordinate Adjectives

(24c-d)

A: In each sentence, first underline all items in series and all coordinate adjectives. Then rewrite each sentence, adding any necessary commas. If no commas are needed, explain why.

EXAMPLE   Vicunas guanacos llamas and alpacas are all South American members of the camel family.
Vicunas, guanacos, llamas, and alpacas are all South American
members of the camel family.

1. The vicuna, the smallest member of the camel family, lives in the mountains of Ecuador Bolivia and Peru.

_____

2. The guanaco is the wild humpless ancestor of the llama and the alpaca.

_____

3. The llama stands four feet tall is about four feet long and is the largest of the South American camels.

_____

4. A llama's coat may be white brown black or shades in between.

_____

5. Indians of the Andes use llamas to carry loads to bear wool and to produce meat.

_____

6. Llamas are foraging animals that live on lichens shrubs and other available plants.

_____

7. Because they can go without water for weeks, llamas are economical practical pack animals.

_____

8. The alpaca has a longer lower body than the llama.

_____

9. It has wool of greater length of higher quality and of superior softness.

_____

10. Alpaca wool is straighter finer and warmer than sheep's wool.

_____

324

B: Write complete sentences as described below. Take special care to follow the rules governing the use of commas in lists and between coordinate adjectives.

EXAMPLE   Mention three favorite holidays.
My favorite holidays are Christmas, New Year's Day, and Easter.

1. Give at least three reasons to spend those holidays with relatives.

   _____

   _____

2. List your three favorite fast foods.

   _____

   _____

3. Mention your four preferred vacation activities.

   _____

   _____

4. Using two or three coordinate adjectives, describe a pet.

   _____

   _____

5. Use a series of adjectives to describe a favorite movie.

   _____

   _____

6. Use a series of prepositional phrases to tell where the groom found rice after the wedding.

   _____

   _____

7. Using a series of verbs or verb phrases, tell what John does at his fitness center.

   _____

   _____

8. Use coordinate adjectives to describe John's improved appearance as a result of working out.

   _____

   _____

Using Commas with Nonrestrictive, Parenthetical, and Transitional Elements

Rewrite these sentences to punctuate nonrestrictive clauses, phrases, appositives, and transitional expressions. If a sentence needs no commas, write *correct* on the line.

EXAMPLE   Ballet a sophisticated form of dance is a theatrical art.
          Ballet, a sophisticated form of dance, is a theatrical art.

1. A ballet contains a sequence of dances that are performed to music.

   _____

   _____

2. The dances both solos and ensembles express emotion or tell a story.

   _____

   _____

3. The person who composes the actual dance steps is the choreographer.

   _____

   _____

4. A ballet's steps called its choreography become standardized over many years of performance.

   _____

   _____

5. The choreographer Marius Petipa created the blend of steps still used in most productions of *Swan Lake.*

   _____

   _____

6. The steps all with French names combine solos and groups.

   _____

   _____

7. The *corps de ballet* the ballet company excluding its star soloists may dance together or in small ensembles.

   _____

   _____

8. One soloist may join another for a *pas de deux* a dance for two.

_____

_____

9. Ensemble members not just soloists must be proficient at pliés and arabesques.

_____

_____

10. Children wanting to become professionals must practice for years.

_____

_____

11. It is important therefore to start lessons early.

_____

_____

12. In Russia which has some of the most stringent ballet training students begin at age three.

_____

_____

Expanding Sentences with Restrictive and Nonrestrictive Elements

Expand each sentence twice: first with a restrictive word, phrase, or clause, and then with a nonrestrictive word, phrase, or clause. Place commas as needed.

EXAMPLE   Comics are usually funny.
1. (restrictive) *Comics in the newspaper are usually funny.*
2. (nonrestrictive) *Comics, for all their absurdity, are usually funny.*

1. The dahlias did not bloom this year.

   _____

   _____

2. I dislike gossip.

   _____

   _____

3. The computer does not work.

   _____

   _____

4. The man would not go home.

   _____

   _____

5. The child can walk now.

   _____

   _____

6. The creek overflowed its banks.

   _____

   _____

7. I need to lose five pounds.

   _____

   _____

8. My cousin adores opera.

   _____

   _____

9. The teacher read the *Iliad* aloud.

_____

_____

10. He finally turned down the sound system.

_____

_____

Using Commas with Quotations

Using the rules governing the use of commas to attach quotations to their speaker tags, place commas in these sentences.

EXAMPLE   According to Herbert Samuel, "It takes two to make a marriage a success and only one to make it a failure."

1. "Marriage" said Joseph Barth "is our last, best chance to grow up."
2. Peter De Vries was right when he said "The difficulty with marriage is that we fall in love with a personality, but must live with a character."
3. According to André Maurois "A successful marriage is an edifice that must be rebuilt every day."
4. "Heaven" said Andrew Jackson "will be no heaven to me if I do not meet my wife there."
5. "Marriage resembles a pair of shears, so joined that they cannot be separated; often moving in opposite directions, yet always punishing any one who comes between them" observed Sydney Smith.
6. "Chains do not hold a marriage together" said Simone Signoret. "It is threads, hundreds of tiny threads which sew people together through the years."
7. An anonymous wise person said "If there is anything better than to be loved it is loving."
8. "The way to love anything is to realize that it might be lost" advised Gilbert K. Chesterton.
9. "Love gives itself; it is not bought" observed Longfellow.
10. "Love does not consist in gazing at each other" said Antoine de Saint-Exupéry "but in looking outward together in the same direction."

Using Commas in Dates, Names, Addresses, and Numbers

EXERCISE 24-7

(24h)

Rewrite the following sentences, inserting commas to punctuate dates, names, addresses, and numbers. If a sentence is correct as written, write *correct* on the line.

EXAMPLE   January 1 1975 was the beginning of a momentous year.
January 1, 1975, was the beginning of a momentous year.

1. In the northwest part of China, 6000 pottery figures were found.

2. Construction workers uncovered a terra cotta army in July 1975.

3. The life-sized warriors and horses had been buried for 2200 years.

4. The figures were in a huge tomb near the city of Xi'an China.

5. Archaeologists also unearthed almost 10000 artifacts from the excavation site.

6. It did not take John Doe Ph. D. to realize that this was an extraordinary find.

7. Some of the figures were displayed in Memphis Tennessee twenty years later.

8. Running from 18 April 1995 to 18 September 1995, the exhibit featured 250 objects from the imperial tombs of China.

9. The exhibit was open from 9 A.M. to 10 P.M. daily.

10. To get tickets, one could write to the Memphis Cook Convention Center 255 North Main Memphis TN 38103.

330

Adding Commas

A: Rewrite the following sentences, inserting commas as needed. If a sentence is correct as written, write *correct* on the line.

EXAMPLE   Ancient writers both Greek and Roman wrote about the seven wonders of the world.
Ancient writers, both Greek and Roman, wrote about the seven
wonders of the world.

1. One was the statue of Olympian Zeus which was covered with precious stones.

   _____

2. Unfortunately it was taken to Constantinople in 475 A. D. and there destroyed by fire.

   _____

3. The Hanging Gardens of Babylon built for Nebuchadnezzar were considered a wonder.

   _____

4. They were probably irrigated terraces connected by marble stairways.

   _____

5. To lift water from the Euphrates slaves had to work in shifts.

   _____

6. The Colossus of Rhodes was a huge impressive statue built to honor the sun god Helios.

   _____

7. Constructed near the harbor it was intended to astonish all who saw it.

   _____

8. Another wonder was the Lighthouse at Alexandria Egypt.

   _____

9. Because it stood on the island of Pharos the word *pharos* has come to mean lighthouse.

   _____

10. After the death of Mausolus king of Caria his widow erected a richly adorned monument to honor him.

_____

11. With sculptures by famous artists the Mausoleum at Halicarnassus amazed the ancient world.

_____

12. The Temple of Artemis at Ephesus an important Ionian city was also considered a wonder.

_____

13. It was burned rebuilt and burned again.

_____

14. Some wonders such as the Colossus and the Mausoleum were destroyed by earthquakes.

_____

15. Of the seven works that astounded the ancients only the pyramids of Egypt survive.

_____

B: Add commas as needed. You will not need to add any words or other marks of punctuation.

[1]St. Andrews Scotland is an old city. [2]Named for a Christian saint the city was once an object of devout pilgrimage. [3]Its cathedral the largest in Scotland is now a ruin. [4]It was destroyed in 1559 by followers of the reformer John Knox. [5]All the revered carefully preserved relics of St. Andrew disappeared. [6]Although the castle of St. Andrews also lies in ruins it preserves two fascinating remnants of medieval history. [7]One is a bottle-shaped dungeon and the other is a countermine. [8]When attackers tried to mine under castle walls defenders tried to intercept the tunnel with a countermine. [9]Interestingly one can actually enter both mine and countermine. [10]The University of St. Andrews which is the oldest university in Scotland was established in 1412. [11]From all parts of the globe students come to study there. [12]Nevertheless most people who think of St. Andrews associate it with golf. [13]Even golf at St. Andrews is old the first reference dating to January 25 1552. [14]The famous Old Course is only one of four courses from which the avid golfer may choose. [15]St. Andrews is still an object of pilgrimage but today's pilgrims come with drivers wedges and putters.

Eliminating Unnecessary
Commas

Rewrite this paragraph, omitting any unnecessary commas. You will not need to add any words or marks of punctuation.

[1]The Victoria Falls, were discovered by Dr. David Livingstone in 1855. [2]The waterfall is part of, the Zambezi River in Africa. [3]The falls are 355 feet high, and 4,495 feet wide. [4]Depending upon the time of year, up to 140 million cubic feet of water may pass over the falls each day. [5]The falls are, the result of an unusual geological condition. [6]The river bed abruptly funnels, into a deep crack. [7]The trapped water can escape, under great pressure, only through a narrow, crevice. [8]The rapidly moving water is divided by a number of small islands, and, each of the falls is named separately: the Devil's Cataract, the main falls, the Rainbow Falls, and the Eastern Cataract. [9]Once water has passed over the falls, it continues through narrow, savage, Batoka Gorge, and flows under the railroad bridge that joins Zimbabwe and Zambia. [10]The area has changed very little since, Livingstone's day. [11]Herds of wild animals live protected in the nearby, national parks, and the area is largely, undeveloped.

Adding and Deleting Commas

Rewrite this paragraph, adding or deleting commas as needed. You will not have to change any words or other marks of punctuation. Number each change you make, and on the lines below indicate the reason for each addition or omission.

     Mount Everest, the highest mountain in the world is located in the Himalayas on the border of Tibet, and Nepal. It is surrounded, by glaciers formed from the ice, and snow that fall from its peak. The first, successful climb up that peak was made by Edmund Hillary, and Tenzing Norgay a Sherpa
5 guide in 1953. Everest had been a challenge to, all climbers ever since 1852 when its height was first recorded, 29028 feet. The attempt to climb Everest began, in earnest in 1924, and continued right through 1952. On the first attempt two climbers Mallory and Irvine disappeared, leaving only an ice axe behind. Almost thirty years later the Royal Geographical Society team led by
10 Sir John Hunt, succeeded. As members of this team Hillary and Tenzing fulfilled a hundred-year-old dream. Since then there have been successful climbs by Indian Japanese United States and Swiss teams. Advanced equipment and the knowledge of the Hunt expedition have made them possible but climbing Everest still remains only for the strong the brave and the lucky.

Commas Added	*Commas Deleted*
_____	_____
_____	_____
_____	_____
_____	_____
_____	_____
_____	_____
_____	_____
_____	_____
_____	_____
_____	_____
_____	_____
_____	_____

25 | *The Semicolon*

25a Using a semicolon between closely related independent clauses

When independent clauses are related in meaning, you can separate them with a semicolon instead of a period. ♣ COMMA CAUTION: Do not use only a comma between independent clauses, or you will create a comma splice (see Chapter 14). ♣

> Independent clause; independent clause.

All changes are not growth; all movement is not forward.　　　　　—Ellen Glasgow

25b Using a semicolon before a coordinating conjunction joining independent clauses containing commas

You will usually use a comma to separate independent clauses linked by a coordinating conjunction (see 7h). When the independent clauses already contain commas, however, use a semicolon instead to separate the clauses.

> Independent clause, one that contains commas; coordinating conjunction
> independent clause.
> Independent clause; coordinating conjunction independent clause, one that contains
> commas.

Aim at the sun, and you may not reach it; but your arrow will fly far higher than if aimed at an object on a level with yourself.　　　　　—Joel Hawes

25c Using a semicolon when conjunctive adverbs or other transitional expressions connect independent clauses

Use a semicolon between two independent clauses when the second clause begins with a conjunctive adverb or other transitional word (4d). ♣ COMMA CAUTION: Do not use only a comma between independent clauses connected by a conjunctive adverb or other words of transition, or you will create a comma splice (see Chapter 14). ♣

> Independent clause; conjunctive adverb or other transition, independent clause.

A coelacanth, a supposedly extinct fish, was caught by an African fisherman in 1938; **as a result**, some scientists believe other "extinct" animals may still live in remote parts of the world.

♣COMMA ALERT: When you place a conjunctive adverb or a transition after the first word in an independent clause, set it off with commas: *This theory may be true; some people, **however**, even suggest the Loch Ness Monster may be a dinosaur.* ♣

25d Using a semicolon between long or comma-containing items in a series

When a sentence contains a series of words, phrases, or clauses, commas usually separate one item from the next. When the items are long and contain commas for other purposes, you can make your message clearer by separating the items with semicolons instead of commas.

> Independent clause that includes a series of items, each or all of which contain commas; another item in the series; another item in the series.

Many are always praising the by-gone time, for it is natural that the old should extol the days of their youth; the weak, the time of their strength; the sick, the season of their vigor; and the disappointed, the spring-tide of their hopes.

—CALEB BINGHAM

25e Avoiding misuse of a semicolon

Don't use a semicolon between a dependent clause and an independent clause; use a comma: *Because the price of new cars continues to rise, people are keeping their old cars.*

Don't use a semicolon to introduce a list; use a colon: *Keeping these old cars running can be expensive too: rebuilt engines, new transmissions, and replacement tires.*

EXERCISE **25-1**

Using the Semicolon

(25a–e)

A: Insert semicolons where needed. They may be placed where there is now no punctuation or they may replace commas. Some sentences may require more than one semicolon. If an item is correct, write *correct* in the left margin.

EXAMPLE   Vision is our most important sense; we get most of our information about the world by seeing.

1. The sclera is the outer cover of the eye, it helps the eye keep its shape because the sclera is fairly hard.
2. The choroid is just inside the sclera it keeps out unneeded light.
3. The pupil is the opening in the eye this is where the light enters.
4. The cornea is the clear cover of the pupil, therefore, light can enter the eye.
5. The pupil is opened or closed by muscles in the iris, in fact, in bright light the iris closes to decrease the amount of light entering, in low light, it opens to increase the light.
6. After passing through the pupil, light shines on the retina, which sends messages to the brain.
7. The retina contains cells, cones and rods, which are outgrowths of the brain when light strikes them, nerve impulses travel to the brain.
8. The optic nerve connects the eye to the brain, thus any damage to the nerve can cause blindness.
9. Cone cells give us color vision, they are most effective in the day.
10. Rods are sensitive to low light they are involved in night vision.

B: This paragraph is missing seven semicolons. Insert them where needed.

   Hearing is based on sound waves these are pressure changes spreading out from a vibrating source. If we could see sound waves, they might remind us of ripples on water like ripples, sound waves vary in number, size, and speed. When these waves reach us, our ears and brain translate them
5 into pitch, loudness, and timbre. Pitch is the number of wave vibrations per second it determines whether a tone is high or low, whether a singer is a soprano or an alto. Loudness is a measure of the intensity of the waves this is called their amplitude. When we turn up the volume on the stereo, we are raising the amplitude. Sound intensity is measured in decibels. Any sound
10 registering over 130 decibels is painful however, people still listen to loud music or live near railroad tracks. Timbre is hard to describe in everyday language in physics terms, however, timbre is the main wavelength plus any

other wavelengths that may come from a particular source. Timbre explains
why a note played on a violin sounds different from the same note played
15 on an electric guitar or why two people singing the same note sound different.
Physics defines *noise* as too many unrelated frequencies vibrating together
nevertheless, people still disagree over whether some sounds are noise or
exciting music.

Using the Semicolon and the Comma

Add commas or semicolons as needed to fill in the blanks appropriately.

EXAMPLE One out of every twenty-five people is colorblind __,__ unable to tell
certain colors apart.

1. Colorblindness is inherited _____ it appears more often in men than in
women.
2. The most common colorblindness is the inability to tell red from green
_____ but more than green and red are involved.
3. Different colors, the result of differences in light wavelengths, create a
spectrum _____ the spectrum of colors is red, orange, yellow, green, blue,
indigo, and violet.
4. People who are severely red-green colorblind cannot "see" any colors at
that end of the spectrum _____ that is _____ they cannot tell the difference
between blue-greens, reds, or yellow-greens.
5. Colorblindness varies from person to person _____ people who can
distinguish red from green a little are called color-weak.
6. Some people have no cone cells (the cells that send signals about color to
the brain) _____ so they are completely colorblind.
7. They have achromatism _____ a rare condition.
8. Such people can see only black, white, and grays _____ what a boring view
of the world.
9. However, their problem is much more serious than this _____ they also
have trouble focusing on objects.
10. The part of the eye that usually receives images is the fovea, which
contains the cone cells _____ achromatics' foveas are blank and cannot
receive images.
11. To compensate, they look at objects off center _____ to pick up images
with their rod (black and white) cells.
12. It is possible to be colorblind and not know it _____ how can people miss
what they have never known?
13. There are several tests for colorblindness _____ most involve seeing (or not
seeing) a number or word written on a background of a complementary
color _____ for example, a red *48* on a green background.

26 | *The Colon*

In sentence punctuation, the colon introduces what comes after it: a quotation, a summary or restatement, or a list. The colon also has a few separating functions.

26a Using a colon after an independent clause to introduce a list, an appositive, or a quotation

Use a colon to introduce a list or series of items announced by an independent clause.

In selecting a major, consider these factors: your talent for the subject, the number of years needed to qualify professionally, and the availability of jobs.

When you use phrases such as *the following* or *as follows*, a colon is usually required. A colon is *not* called for with the words *such as* or *including* (see 26d).

Woods commonly used in fine furniture include the following: black walnut, mahogany, oak, and pecan.

You can use a colon to lead into a final appositive—a word or group of words that renames a noun or pronoun.

A hot plate can enable any student to become a dormitory chef, preparing simple and satisfying meals: omelets, stir-fried vegetables, even stews.

Use a colon at the end of a grammatically complete statement that introduces a formal quotation.

Francis Bacon was referring to men and women when he wrote of the destructiveness of seeking vengeance: "A man that studieth revenge keeps his own wounds green."

26b Using a colon between two independent clauses

You can use a colon at the end of an independent clause to introduce statements that summarize, restate, or explain what is said in that clause.

The makers of some movies aimed at teenagers think that their audience is interested in little more than car chases, violence, and nudity: they sadly underestimate young people.

Independent clause containing words that introduce a quotation: "Quoted words."
Independent clause: summarizing or restating words.
Independent clause: listed items.

26c Using a colon to separate standard material

TITLE AND SUBTITLE
Broca's Brain: Reflections on the Romance of Science

HOURS, MINUTES, AND SECONDS
The lecture began at 9:15 A.M.

CHAPTERS AND VERSES OF THE BIBLE
Ecclesiastes 3:1

LETTER SALUTATION
Dear Ms. Winters:

MEMO FORM

TO:	Dean Elliot Gordon
FROM:	Professor Steven Wang
RE:	Honors and Awards Ceremony

26d Avoiding misuse of the colon

A colon must follow a complete independent clause except when it separates standard material (26c). Lead-in words must make a grammatically complete statement. When they do not, do not use a colon. Also do not use a colon after the words *such as* and *including* or forms of the verb *be*.

No   The shop sold: T-shirts, bumper stickers, posters, and greeting cards.

Yes   The shop sold T-shirts, bumper stickers, posters, and greeting cards.

No   Students work in many of the town's businesses, such as: the diner, the grocery, the laundromat, and the gas station.

Yes   Students work in many of the town's businesses, such as the diner, the grocery, the laundromat, and the gas station.

Yes   Students work in many of the town's businesses: the diner, the grocery, the laundromat, and the gas station.

Do not use a colon to separate a dependent clause from an independent clause.

No   When summer comes: the town is almost deserted.

Yes   When summer comes, the town is almost deserted.

Using the Colon

Rewrite the following sentences, adding colons as needed. If no colon is needed, write *correct* in the left margin.

EXAMPLE   A poll of Philadelphia schoolchildren identified their favorite first names David and Linda.

A poll of Philadelphia schoolchildren identified their favorite first *names*: **David and Linda.**

1. People believe that Napoleon was short, but he was average height 5'6".

2. According to an ABC News-Harris Survey, U.S. males' three favorite free-time activities are as follows eating, watching TV, and fixing things around the house.

3. According to the same survey, females' favorite activities include eating, reading books, and listening to music.

4. In case you were wondering, here are the most common street names in the United States Park, Washington, Maple, Oak, and Lincoln.

5. I plan to call my autobiography *Burrowing The Adventures of a Bookworm*.

6. The train, 20 minutes late, was due at 640.

7. John F. Hylan, mayor of New York in 1922, spoke for all of us "The police are fully able to meet and compete with the criminals."

8. When walking alone at night, remember one thing Be alert!

9. The nineteenth century was a bad time for Turkey it lost three wars to Russia and three to Egypt, and it lost control over Greece.

10. Few animals are man-eaters, but those that are include the following bears, crocodiles, giant squid, leopards, lions, piranhas, sharks, and tigers.

Writing Sentences with the Colon

Write complete sentences in answer to these questions. Use a colon in each sentence.

EXAMPLE   What time do you wake up?
             I wake up at 5:45.
_____

1. What is the full title and subtitle of one of your textbooks?

   _____

2. What are your favorite classes? (Use the expression *as follows*.)

   _____

3. What is your advice to someone going to a job interview?

   _____

4. Who are the star players on your favorite team?

   _____

5. What streets or geographical features mark the borders of your campus?

   _____

   _____

27 | *The Apostrophe*

The apostrophe plays three major roles: it helps to form the possessive of **nouns** and a few pronouns, it stands for omitted letters, and it helps to form the **plurals of** letters and numerals.

27a Using an apostrophe to form the possessive case of nouns and indefinite pronouns

The possessive case shows ownership (*the scientist's invention*) or close relationship (*the governor's policy, the movie's ending*). It indicates the same meaning as phrases beginning *of the* (*the invention of the scientist*).

When nouns and indefinite pronouns do not end in *-s*, add *'s* to show possession.

The **doctor's** diplomas are on her office wall. [singular noun not ending in *-s*]
The class studied the **women's** rights movement. [plural noun not ending in *-s*]
Good health is **everyone's** wish. [indefinite pronoun not ending in *-s*]

When singular nouns end in *-s*, add *'s* to show possession.

The **waitress's** tip was less than she expected.
Les's phone bill was enormous.

When a plural noun ends in *-s*, use only an apostrophe to show possession.

The **workers'** tools were all over the room.
Their **supervisors'** reports were critical of their sloppiness.

In compound words, add *'s* to the last word.

The **police chief's** retirement party was held in the hotel ballroom.
They held their wedding in her **sister-in-law's** backyard.

In individual possession, add *'s* to each noun.

Pat's and Lee's songs are hits. [Pat and Lee each wrote some of the songs; they did not write the songs together.]
Dali's and Turner's paintings were sold for record prices. [Dali and Turner painted different canvasses.]

In joint or group possession, add *'s* to only the last noun.

Pat and Lee's songs are hits. [Pat and Lee wrote the songs together.]
Dali and Turner's show at the art museum was a hit. [Dali and Turner are featured in the same show.]

27b Not using an apostrophe with the possessive forms of personal pronouns

Some pronouns have their own possessive forms. Do not use an apostrophe with these forms: *his, her, hers, its, our, ours, your, yours, their, theirs, whose.* Be especially careful in using *its/it's* and *whose/who's*, which are often confused. *It's* stands for *it is; its* is a personal pronoun showing possession. *Who's* stands for *who is; whose* is a personal pronoun showing possession.

No   The state will elect **it's** governor next week.

Yes   The state will elect **its** governor next week.

No   The candidate **who's** ads appear on television daily expects to win.

Yes   The candidate **whose** ads appear on television daily expects to win.

27c Using an apostrophe to stand for omitted letters, numbers, or words in contractions

In informal English, some words may be combined by omitting one or more letters and inserting apostrophes to signal the omission: *I'm (I am), aren't (are not), he'll (he will),* and others. These words are called **contractions**.

Apostrophes also indicate the omission of the first two numerals in years: *The professor spoke of the sit-ins of '68.* However, no apostrophe is used when you indicate a span of years: *1948–52.*

27d Using an apostrophe to form plurals of letters, numerals, symbols, and words used as terms

The child practiced writing her **Q's**.
The computer went berserk and printed out pages of **4's**.

In writing the plural form of years, two styles are acceptable: with an apostrophe (1990's) or without (1990s). Whichever form you prefer, use it consistently.

Using the Apostrophe in Possessive Nouns

Write the possessive forms, singular and plural, for each of the following words. If you are unsure how to form the plural of any word, see your dictionary or section 22c.

	Singular Possessive	Plural Possessive
EXAMPLE COW	cow's	cows'
1. sheep		
2. pony		
3. turkey		
4. lion		
5. mouse		
6. she		
7. gorilla		
8. goose		
9. gnu		
10. ox		
11. you		
12. buffalo		
13. zebra		
14. ibex		
15. fly		
16. I		
17. giraffe		
18. dodo		
19. zoo		
20. zoo keeper		
21. he		
22. farm		
23. farmer		
24. ranch		
25. it		

Using the Apostrophe in Possessive Expressions

Rewrite each of these noun phrases as a possessive noun followed by another noun.

EXAMPLE   the schedule of the student
          the student's schedule

1. the menu of the restaurant

2. the daughter of the boss

3. the waiting room of the doctor

4. the waiting room of the doctors

5. the guess of anyone

6. the scripts of the actor

7. the scripts of the actors

8. the crew of the ship

9. the reputation of someone

10. the tools of my father-in-law

Using Apostrophes in Contractions

Write contractions of the following expressions.

EXAMPLE   he + is =   *he's* _____

1. are + not = _____
2. will + not = _____
3. let + us = _____
4. he + had = _____
5. was + not = _____
6. you + would = _____
7. did + not = _____
8. I + will = _____
9. what + is = _____
10. I + am = _____
11. is + not = _____
12. would + not = _____
13. can + not = _____
14. does + not = _____
15. I + have = _____
16. you + are = _____
17. there + is = _____
18. we + would = _____
19. were + not = _____
20. they + are = _____
21. it + is = _____
22. we + have = _____
23. she + will = _____
24. we + are = _____
25. do + not = _____

Using Apostrophes

Insert apostrophes as needed. If no apostrophes are called for in a sentence, write *correct* in the left margin.

EXAMPLE   The detective storys roots go back to at least 1841.

The detective story's roots go back to at least 1841.

1. The modern detective story began with Edgar Allan Poes "The Murders in the Rue Morgue."

2. Its detective reappeared in "The Mystery of Marie Rogêt" in 1842–43.

3. The authors last pure detective story was "The Purloined Letter."

4. The three stories featured amateur detective C. August Dupins ability to solve crimes by using logic.

5. Poe didnt use the word *detective* in the stories.

6. The publics response was not enthusiastic, perhaps because the heros personality was unpleasant.

7. This may explain why there werent any more detective stories by Poe.

8. Twenty years later, in 66, a Frenchman revived the detective story, and this time it was a great success.

9. Soon after, Englishman Wilkie Collins published *The Moonstone.*

10. Collins book was the first full-length detective novel in English.

11. The books hero was a professional detective who grew roses when he wasnt working.

12. *The Moonstones* hero had a better personality than Dupin, so the publics acceptance of him is understandable.

13. Charles Dickens, Collins friend, was writing a mystery novel when he died.

14. The fragment of *The Mystery of Edwin Drood* has been studied for years, but no ones been able to figure out how Dickens planned to explain the mystery.

15. Its been one of my favorite literary puzzles for years.

16. Arthur Conan Doyles Sherlock Holmes made his debut in "A Study in Scarlet" in 1887.

17. Holmes popularity really dates from July 1891, when "A Scandal in Bohemia" was published.

18. Peoples attention was finally captured, and they demanded more and more stories featuring Holmes.

19. Conan Doyle became so tired of the character that he wrote about Holmes death, killing him in a fall over a waterfall.

20. The readers outcry was so great that Holmes was brought back for more stories in 1902.

21. Then in 1905, Holmes earlier absence was explained.

22. The explanation was weak, but the fans couldnt have been happier.

28 | *Quotation Marks*

Quotation marks most frequently enclose direct quotations—spoken or written words from an outside source. Quotation marks also set off some titles, and they can call attention to words used in special senses. Always use quotation marks in pairs. Be especially careful not to forget the second (closing) quotation mark.

28a Using quotation marks to enclose direct quotations of not more than four lines

Direct quotations present exact words copied from an original source. Use double quotation marks to enclose short quotations (no more than four lines).

SHORT QUOTATION

> According to Marvin Harris in *Cows, Pigs, Wars, and Witches*, "We seem to be more interested in working in order to get people to admire us for our wealth than in the actual wealth itself."

Longer quotations are not enclosed in quotation marks. They are displayed, starting on a new line, and all lines of the quotation are indented ten spaces.

When the words of a short quotation already contain quotation marks, use double quotation marks at the start and end of the directly quoted words. Then substitute single quotation marks (' ') wherever there are double quotation marks in your original source.

> Carl Sagan begins his essay called "In Defense of Robots" by telling us, "The word 'Robot,' first introduced by the Czech writer Karl Căpek, is derived from the Slavic root for 'worker.' "

When the words of a longer quotation already contain quotation marks, display the quotation without enclosing it in quotation marks. Then use quotation marks exactly as they were used in your original source.

Use double quotation marks to enclose a short quotation of poetry (no more than three lines of the poem). If you quote more than one line of poetry, use slashes to show the line divisions (see 29e).

> Not everyone would agree with Emily Dickinson's statement: "Success is counted sweetest / By those who ne'er succeed."

Quotation marks are also used to enclose speakers' words in **direct discourse**. Whether you are reporting the exact words of a real speaker or making up dialogue in, for example, a short story, quotation marks let your readers know which words belong to the speaker and which words do not. Use double quotation marks at the beginning and end of a speaker's words, and start a new paragraph each time the speaker changes.

> "The marks were some twenty yards from the body and no one gave them a thought. I don't suppose I should have done so had I not known the legend."
> "There are many sheep dogs on the moor?"
> "No doubt, but this was no sheep dog."
> "You say it was large?"
> "Enormous."
>
> —Sir Arthur Conan Doyle, *The Hound of the Baskervilles*

In contrast to direct discourse, **indirect discourse** reports only the spirit of what a speaker said. Do not enclose indirect discourse in quotation marks.

Direct Discourse	The professor said, "Your midterm is a week from Tuesday."
Indirect Discourse	The professor said that our midterm would be a week from Tuesday.

28b Using quotation marks to enclose certain titles

Use quotation marks around the titles of short published works, such as pamphlets and brochures. Also use them around song titles, episodes of television series, and titles of works that are parts of longer works or parts of collected works: poems, short stories, essays, and articles from periodicals.

Stephen Jay Gould examines what we know about dinosaur intelligence in the essay "Were Dinosaurs Dumb?"

Modern readers still enjoy Edgar Allan Poe's short story "The Tell-Tale Heart."

28c Using quotation marks for words used in special senses or for special purposes

Writers sometimes use quotation marks to indicate words or phrases that are not meant to be taken at face value.

The "free" records came with a bill for ten dollars—for postage and handling.

Writers sometimes put technical terms in quotation marks and define them the first time they are used. No quotation marks are used after such terms have been introduced and defined.

"Plagiarism"—the unacknowledged use of another person's words or ideas—can result in expulsion. Plagiarism is a serious offense.

Words being referred to as words can be either enclosed in quotation marks or underlined.

Yes   Do not confuse "then" and "than."

Yes   Do not confuse then and than.

28d Avoiding the misuse of quotation marks

Writers sometimes place quotation marks around words they are uncomfortable about using. Instead of resorting to this practice, find appropriate words.

No   Einstein's theory of relativity is very "heavy stuff."

Yes   Einstein's theory of relativity is very sophisticated.

Do not enclose a word in quotation marks merely to call attention to it.

No   The report is due on Friday, "or else."

Yes   The report is due on Friday, or else.

Do not put quotation marks around the title of your own papers (on a title page or at the top of the first page). The only exception is if your paper's title includes words that require quotation marks for one of the reasons discussed in 28a–c.

28e Following accepted practices for other punctuation with quotation marks

Place commas and periods inside closing quotation marks.

Besides writing such stories as "The Premature Burial," Edgar Allan Poe was also a respected literary critic and poet.

The bill read, "Registration fees must be paid in full one week before the start of classes."

Place colons and semicolons outside closing quotation marks.

The label on the ketchup said "low salt": it was also low taste.

Some people have trouble singing "The Star-Spangled Banner"; they think the United States should choose a different national anthem.

Place question marks, exclamation points, and dashes inside or outside closing quotation marks, according to the situation. If a question mark, exclamation point, or dash belongs with the words enclosed in quotation marks, put that punctuation mark *inside* the closing quotation mark.

"Where is Andorra?" asked the quiz show host.

Before her signal faded, we heard the CB'er say, "There is a radar trap on Route—"

If a question mark, exclamation point, or dash belongs with words that are *not* included in quotation marks, put the punctuation mark *outside* the closing quotation mark.

Do you know Adrienne Rich's poem "Aunt Jennifer's Tigers"?

Grieving for a dead friend, Tennyson spent seventeen years writing "In Memoriam A. H. H."!

Using Quotation Marks

Insert additional quotation marks as needed. Use double quotation marks unless single quotation marks are specifically needed. Remember to place quotation marks carefully in relation to other marks of punctuation. If a sentence needs no additional quotation marks, write *correct* in the left margin.

EXAMPLE   Speaking of an old friend, Winston Churchill said, In those days he was wiser than he is now; he used frequently to take my advice.

Speaking of an old friend, Winston Churchill said, "In those days he was wiser than he is now; he used frequently to take my advice."

1. According to Chesterfield, Advice is seldom welcome.
2. "If you are looking for trouble, offer some good advice, says Herbert V. Prochnow.
3. Marie Dressler was right: No vice is so bad as advice.
4. Someone once remarked, How we do admire the wisdom of those who come to us for advice!
5. "Free advice, it has been noted, is the kind that costs you nothing unless you act upon it."
6. "The only thing to do with good advice is to pass it on; it is never of any use to oneself," believed Oscar Wilde.
7. I sometimes give myself admirable advice, said Lady Mary Wortley Montagu, but I am incapable of taking it.
8. Says Tom Masson, " 'Be yourself! is the worst advice you can give to some people.
9. The Beatles' song With a Little Help from My Friends contains some good advice.
10. Do you seriously advise me to marry that man?
11. My uncle advised me, The next time you are depressed, read Lewis Carroll's poem *Jabberwocky.*
12. Do you recall the Beach Boys' words: Be true to your school?
13. Many marriage counselors advise us never to go to sleep angry with our mate.
14. However, comedienne Phyllis Diller suggests, Never go to bed mad. Stay up and fight.
15. Rachel Carson advised, The discipline of the writer is to learn to be still and listen to what his subject has to tell him.
16. If I had to give students advice in choosing a career, I would tell them to select a field that interests them passionately.

Writing Direct Quotations

Rewrite these indirect quotations as direct quotations. You will need to add commas, colons, capitals, and quotation marks. If necessary, change pronouns and verbs to suitable forms.

EXAMPLE   The chair said that she had an important announcement.
   The chair said, "I have an important announcement."

1. She said that the committee had received an anonymous donation.

2. She told them the donation was $5000.

3. She ended by saying that the big problem was deciding how to spend the money to help the community. [Make this a split quotation.]

4. The treasurer suggested that the money should be used to repair town hall.

5. Someone shouted out that that was stupid.

6. After much discussion, the committee agreed, and the minutes read that the money would be used to make the library handicapped-accessible.

Writing Properly Punctuated Dialogue

Write an original dialogue using proper punctuation and appropriate pronouns and verb tenses. Select one of the following situations, letting each person speak at least three times. Remember to start a new paragraph each time the speaker changes. Use your own paper.

1. You are asking your boss for a raise.
2. You are asking one of your parents for advice.
3. You are trying to talk a traffic officer out of giving you a ticket.
4. You and your boyfriend/girlfriend are trying to decide what movie to see.
5. You are trying to convince your younger brother/sister not to drop out of high school.

29 | *Other Marks of Punctuation*

29a Using the dash

The dash, or a pair of dashes, lets you interrupt a sentence to add information. Dashes are like parentheses in that they set off extra material at the beginning, in the middle, or at the end of a sentence. Unlike parentheses, dashes emphasize the interruptions. Use dashes sparingly—so that their dramatic impact is not blunted.

Use a dash or dashes to emphasize explanations, including appositives, examples, and definitions.

EXAMPLES

In general, only mute things are eaten alive—plants and invertebrates. If oysters shrieked as they were pried open, or squealed when jabbed with a fork, I doubt whether they would be eaten alive.

—MARSTON BATES

DEFINITIONS

Personal space—"elbow room"—is a vital commodity for the human animal, and one that cannot be ignored without risking serious trouble.

—DESMOND MORRIS, "Territorial Behavior"

APPOSITIVES

Many's the long night I've dreamed of cheese—toasted, mostly.

—ROBERT LOUIS STEVENSON

Use a dash or dashes to emphasize a contrast.

I know a lot of people didn't expect our relationship to last—but we've just celebrated our two months' anniversary.

—BRITT EKLAND

Use a dash or dashes to emphasize an "aside." Asides are writers' comments within the structure of a sentence or paragraph.

These five passages have not been picked out because they are especially bad—I could have quoted far worse if I had chosen—but because they illustrate various of the mental vices from which we now suffer.

—GEORGE ORWELL, "Politics and the English Language"

Commas, semicolons, colons, and periods are not used next to dashes, but if the words you put between a pair of dashes would take a question mark or an exclamation point written as a separate sentence, use that punctuation before the second dash.

> The tour guide—do you remember her name?—recommended an excellent restaurant.

Use a dash to show hesitating or broken-off speech.

> "Yes," he said. "That is why I am here, you see. They thought we might be interested in that footprint."
> "That footprint?" cried Dorothy. "You mean—?"
> "No, no; not your footprint, Miss Brant. Another one."
>
> —CARTER DICKSON, "The Footprint in the Sky"

29b Using parentheses

Parentheses let you interrupt a sentence's structure to add information of many kinds. Parentheses are like dashes in that they set off extra or interrupting words. However, unlike dashes, which make interruptions stand out, parentheses de-emphasize what they enclose.

Use parentheses to enclose interrupting words, including explanations, examples, and asides.

EXPLANATIONS

On the second night of his visit, our distinguished guest (Sir Charles Dilke) met Laura in the passage on her way to bed; he said to her: "If you will kiss me, I will give you a signed photograph of myself." To which she answered: "It's awfully good of you, Sir Charles, but I would rather not, for what on earth should I do with the photograph?"

—MARGOT ASQUITH

EXAMPLES

Many books we read as children (*Alice in Wonderland*, for example) may be even more enjoyable when we reread them as adults.

ASIDES

I have heard of novelists who say that, while they are creating a novel, the people in it are ever with them, accompanying them on walks, for all I know on drives (though this must be distracting in traffic), to the bath, to bed itself.

—ROSE MACAULAY

Use parentheses for certain numbers and letters of listed items. When you number listed items within a sentence, enclose the numbers (or letters) in parentheses.

> I plan to do four things during summer vacation: (1) sleep, (2) work to save money for next semester's tuition, (3) catch up on my reading, and (4) have fun.

In business and legal writing, use parentheses to enclose a numeral repeating a spelled-out number.

The monthly fee to lease a color television is forty dollars ($40).

Never put a comma before an opening parenthesis even if what comes before the parenthetical material requires a comma. Put the parenthetical material in, and then use the comma immediately after the closing parenthesis.

Even though I grew up in a big city (New York), I prefer small-town life.

You can use a question mark or an exclamation point with parenthetical words that occur within the structure of a sentence.

We entered the old attic (what a mess!) and began the dirty job of organizing the junk of three generations.

Use a period, however, only when you enclose a complete statement in parentheses outside the structure of another sentence. In this case, use a capital letter as well.

We entered the old attic and began the dirty job of organizing the junk of three generations. (The place was a mess.)

29c Using brackets

When you work quoted words into your own sentences, you may have to change a word or two to make the quoted words fit into your structure. You may also want to add explanations to quoted material. Enclose your own words within brackets.

According to John Ackerman, "He [Dylan Thomas] was aware of the extent to which his temperament and his imagination were the products of his Welsh environment."

When you find a mistake in something you want to quote—for example, a wrong date or a misspelled word—you cannot change another writer's words. So that readers do not think you made the error, insert the Latin word *sic* (meaning "so" or "thus") in brackets next to the error. Doing this indicates that this is exactly what you found in the original.

The student wrote that, "The Vikings came to North America long before Columbus's arrival in 1942 [*sic*]."

You can also use brackets to enclose very brief parenthetical material inside parentheses.

From that point on, Thomas Parker simply disappears. (His death [c. 1441] is unrecorded officially, but a gravestone marker is mentioned in a 1640 parish report.)

29d Using the ellipsis

An ellipsis is a series of three spaced dots. In quotations, it is used to show that you have left out some of the writer's original words. Ellipses can also show hesitant or broken-off speech.

Ellipses can show that you have omitted words from material you are quoting.

ORIGINAL

My aunt has survived the deaths of her husband and my parents in typical, if I may say so, West Indian fashion. Now in her 70s, and no longer principal of a New York City public school, she rises at 5 A.M. every day to prepare for another day of complicated duties as the volunteer principal of a small black private academy.

—JUNE JORDAN, "Thank You, America"

SOME MATERIAL USED IN A QUOTATION

My aunt has survived the deaths of her husband and my parents.... Now in her 70s, and no longer principal of a New York City public school, she rises at 5 A.M. every day to prepare for another day ... as the volunteer principal of a small black private academy.

If an omission occurs at the beginning of your quoted words, you do not need to use an ellipsis. Also, you do not need to use an ellipsis at the end as long as you end with a complete sentence. If an ellipsis occurs after a complete sentence, use a fourth dot to represent the period of that sentence (for an example of this, see the first ellipsis in the above quotation).

Also, you can use ellipses to show broken-off speech.

"And, anyway, what do you know of him?"
"Nothing. That is why I ask you ..."
"I would prefer never to speak of him."

—UMBERTO ECO, *The Name of the Rose*

29e Using the slash

If you quote more than three lines of a poem in writing, set the poetry off with space and indentations as you would a prose quotation of more than four lines. For three lines or less, quote poetry—enclosed in quotation marks—in sentence format, with a slash to divide one line from the next. Leave a space on each side of the slash.

Robert Frost makes an important point when he writes, "Before I built a wall I'd want to know / What I was walling in or walling out, / And to whom I was like to give offense."

Capitalize and punctuate each line as it is in the original, with this exception: end your sentence with a period, even if the quoted line of poetry does not have one.

If you have to type numerical fractions, use a slash between the numerator and denominator and a hyphen to attach a whole number to its fraction: *1/16, 1-2/3, 2/5, 3-7/8.*

You will not use word combinations such as *and/or* often, but where use is acceptable, separate the words with a slash. Leave no space before or after the slash. *He/she* is one option available to you in avoiding sexist language (see 11q and 21b).

Using Dashes, Parentheses, Brackets, Ellipses, and Slashes

Add dashes, parentheses, brackets, ellipses, or slashes as needed. If more than one kind of punctuation is possible, choose the one you think best. Be prepared to explain your decision.

EXAMPLE   "I'll pay by Do you accept checks?"

"I'll pay by—Do you accept checks?"

1. Chicago is not the windiest city in the United States Great Falls, Montana, is.

2. The next windiest cities are 2 Oklahoma City, Oklahoma, 3 Boston, Massachusetts, and 4 Cheyenne, Wyoming.

3. Chicago is relatively calm average wind speed equals 10.4 mph.

4. Greenland the largest island in the world was given its name by Eric the Red in 985.

5. The name was a masterstroke of publicity convincing settlers to come to what was actually an ice-covered wasteland.

6. Let's go to New Orleans for Mardi Oops! I have exams that week.

7. The most expensive part of a trip the airfare can be reduced by careful planning.

8. Contest rules say "The winner must appear to claim his her prize in person."

9. "Broadway my favorite street is a main artery of New York—the hardened artery," claimed Walter Winchell. [Note: *my favorite street* is not part of the quotation.]

10. Punctuate the shortened version of the following quotation: "Too often travel, instead of broadening the mind, merely lengthens the conversation," said Elizabeth Drew. "Too often travel merely lengthens the conversation," said Elizabeth Drew.

11. New Jersy sic has some spectacular parks for camping.

12. Once a camper has been there, he she will always want to return.

13. I can say only one thing about camping I hate it.

14. We leave as soon as Have you seen the bug spray? we finish packing.

15. "Let's take Interstate 80 across" "Are you crazy?"

16. Finding an inexpensive hotel motel isn't always easy.

17. Motels named from a combination of *motorist* and *hotel* are usually cheaper than regular hotels.

18. When traveling, always remember to a leave a schedule with friends, b carry as little cash as possible, and c use the hotel safe for valuables.

Using Assorted Punctuation

A: Add missing punctuation or change mistaken punctuation as needed. There may be more than one choice possible. If so, use the punctuation mark you think best. Be prepared to explain your answers.

The cheetah, is the fastest animal on earth, it can accelerate from one mile an hour to forty miles an hour in under two seconds. Briefly reaching speeds of up to seventy miles an hour. Its stride, may during these bursts of speed, be as much as (23 feet). To help it run at these speeds: the cheetah is built unlike any of the other large cats—powerful heart, oversized liver, long, thin leg bones, relatively small teeth, and a muscular tail (used for balance. Unlike other cats; it cannot pull in its claws. They are blunted by constant contact (with the earth), and so are of little use, in the hunt. The cheetah—instead, makes use of a strong dewclaw on the inside of its front, legs to grab and hold down prey.

B: Add whatever punctuation is needed to this completely unpunctuated paragraph. Be sure to add capital letters as needed too. If more than one kind of punctuation is suitable, select the best one. Be prepared to explain your choices.

Have you ever wondered how instant coffee is made first the coffee beans are prepared as they would be for regular coffee they are roasted blended and ground at the factory workers brew great batches of coffee 1800 to 2000 pounds at a time the coffee is then passed through tubes under great pressure at a high temperature this causes much of the water to boil away creating coffee liquor with a high percentage of solids at this point a decision must be made about what the final product will be powdered instant coffee or freeze dried coffee powdered instant coffee is made by heating the coffee liquor to 500°F in a large drier this boils away the remaining water and the powdered coffee is simply gathered from the bottom of the drier and packed if freeze dried coffee is being made the coffee liquor is frozen into pieces which are then broken into small granules the granules are placed in a vacuum box a box containing no air which turns the frozen water into steam which is removed all that is left are coffee solids some people say they prefer freeze dried coffee because the high temperature used to make regular instant coffee destroys some of the flavor either way the coffee is more convenient than home-brewed coffee

30 | *Capitals, Italics, Abbreviations, and Numbers*

CAPITALS

30a Capitalizing the first word of a sentence

Always capitalize the first letter of the first word in a sentence, a question, or a command.

> Pain is useful because it warns us of danger.
> Does pain serve any purpose?
> Never ignore severe pain.

Whether to capitalize the first letter of a complete sentence enclosed in parentheses depends upon whether that sentence stands alone or falls within the structure of another sentence. Those that stand alone start with a capital letter; those that fall within the structure of another sentence do not start with a capital letter.

> I didn't know till years later that they called it the Cuban Missile Crisis. But I remember Castro. (We called him Castor Oil and were awed by his beard—beards were rare in those days.) We might not have worried so much (what would the Communists want with our small New Hampshire town?) except that we lived 10 miles from an air base.
>
> —JOYCE MAYNARD, "An 18-Year-Old Looks Back on Life"

30b Capitalizing listed items correctly

A **run-in list** works its items into the structure of a sentence. When the items in a run-in list are complete sentences, capitalize the first letter of each item.

> Three groups attended the town meeting on rent control: (1) Landlords brought proof of their expenses. (2) Tenants came to complain about poor maintenance. (3) Real estate agents came to see how the new rules would affect them.

When the items in a run-in list are not complete sentences, do not begin them with capital letters.

Three groups attended the town meeting on rent control: (1) landlords, (2) tenants, and (3) real estate agents.

361

30c Capitalizing the first letter of an introduced quotation

When you quote another person's words, do not capitalize the first quoted word if you have made the quoted words part of the structure of your own sentence.

Thomas Henry Huxley called science "trained and organized common sense."

However, if your own words in your sentence serve only to introduce quoted words or if you are directly quoting speech, capitalize the first letter of the quoted words.

According to Thomas Henry Huxley, "Science is nothing but trained and organized common sense."

Do not capitalize a partial quotation or a quotation you resume within a sentence.

"We," said Queen Victoria, "are not amused."

30d Capitalizing *I* and *O*

Once upon a midnight dreary, while **I** pondered, weak and weary, . . .

—EDGAR ALLAN POE, "The Raven"

Temper, **O** fair Love, Love's impetuous rage.

—JOHN DONNE, "On His Mistress"

30e Capitalizing nouns and adjectives according to standard practice

Capitalize proper nouns (7a) and adjectives made from them.

PROPER NOUNS	PROPER ADJECTIVES
Korea	the Korean language
Hollywood	a Hollywood studio

Notice that the articles (*the, a, an*) are not capitalized.

Do not capitalize common nouns (nouns that name general classes of people, places, or things) unless they start a sentence: *a country, the movies, friends, planes*. Many common nouns are capitalized when names or titles are added to them. For example, *lake* is not ordinarily capitalized, but when a specific name is added, it is: *Lake Erie*. Without the specific name, however, even if the specific name is implied, the common noun is not capitalized.

I would like to visit the **Erie Canal** because the **canal** played a big part in opening up the Northeast to trade.

On the next page is a list to help you with capitalization questions. Although it cannot cover all possibilities, you can apply what you find in the list to similar items.

CAPITALIZATION GUIDE

	CAPITALS	LOWER-CASE LETTERS
Names	Bob Ojeda	
	Mother (name)	my mother (relationship)
Titles	the President (usually reserved for the U.S. president in office)	a president
	Professor Edgar Day	the professor
Groups of Humankind	Caucasian (race)	black (or Black)
	African American (race)	white (or White)
	Oriental (race)	
Organizations	Congress	congressional
	the Rotary Club	the club
Places	Los Angeles	
	India	
	the South (a region)	turn south (a direction)
	Main Street	the street
Buildings	Carr High School	the high school
	the China Lights	the restaurant
Scientific Terms	Mars, Martian	the moon, the sun
	the Milky Way galaxy	the galaxy
Languages	Portuguese	
School Courses	Chemistry 342	the chemistry course
Names of Things	the *Times-Union*	the newspaper
	Purdue University	the university
	the Dodge Omni	
Time Names	Friday	spring, summer, fall, autumn, winter
	August	
Historical Periods	World War II	the war
	the Great Depression	the depression (any other depression)
Religious Terms	God	a god, a goddess
	Buddhism	
	the Torah	
Letter Parts	Dear Ms. Tauber:	
	Sincerely yours,	
Titles of Works	"The Lottery"	
	Catcher in the Rye	
Acronyms	IRS	
	NATO	
	AFL-CIO	

30f

ITALICS (UNDERLINING)

In printed material, **roman type** is the standard. Type that slants to the right is called **italic**. Words in italics contrast with standard roman type, so italics create an emphasis readers can see. In typewritten and handwritten manuscripts, underline to indicate italics.

30f Using standard practice for underlining titles and other words, letters, or numbers

Some titles require underlining: long written works, names of ships, trains, and some aircraft, film titles, titles of television series. Underlining also calls readers' attention to words in languages other than English and to letters, numbers, and words used in ways other than for their meaning. The list below shows these uses. It also shows (and explains) some titles that call for quotation marks and some names and titles neither underlined nor in quotation marks.

GUIDE TO UNDERLINING

Titles: Underline	Titles: Do Not Underline
<u>The Bell Jar</u> (a novel)	
<u>Death of a Salesman</u> (a play)	
<u>Collected Works of O. Henry</u> (a book)	"The Last Leaf" (one story)
<u>Simon & Schuster Handbook for Writers</u> (a book)	"Writing Argument" (one chapter)
<u>Contexts for Composition</u> (a collection of essays)	"Science and Ethics" (one essay)
<u>The Iliad</u> (a long poem)	"Design" (a short poem)
<u>The African Queen</u> (a film)	
the <u>Los Angeles Times</u>	
<u>Scientific American</u> (a magazine)	"The Molecules of Life" (an article)
<u>Twilight Zone</u> (a television series)	"Terror at 30,000 Feet" (an episode of a television series)
<u>The Best of Bob Dylan</u> (an album)	"Blowin' in the Wind" (one song)

(continued on next page)

GUIDE TO UNDERLINING *(continued)*

Other Words: Underline	Other Words: Do Not Underline
the <u>Intrepid</u> (a ship; don't underline preceding initials like U.S.S.)	aircraft carrier (a general class of ship)
<u>Voyager 2</u> (names of specific aircraft, spacecraft, and satellites)	Boeing 747 (general names shared by classes of aircraft, spacecraft, and satellites)
<u>summa cum laude</u> (term in a language other than English)	burrito, chutzpah (widely used and commonly understood words from languages other than English)
the plural pronoun <u>they</u> (a word used as a term instead of for the meaning it conveys)	
the <u>abc's</u>; confusing <u>3</u>'s and <u>8</u>'s (letters and numbers referred to as symbols rather than for the meaning they convey)	

30g Underlining sparingly for special emphasis

Instead of counting on underlining to deliver impact, try to make word choices and sentence structures convey emphasis. Reserve underlining for special situations.

ABBREVIATIONS

30h Using abbreviations with time and symbols

What you are writing and who will read that writing should help you to determine whether to use an abbreviation or a spelled-out word. A few abbreviations are standard in any writing circumstance.

A.M. AND P.M. WITH SPECIFIC TIMES

8:20 A.M. or 8:20 a.m.   9:35 P.M. or 9:35 p.m.

A.D. AND B.C. WITH SPECIFIC YEARS

A.D. 576 [A.D. precedes the year.]   33 B.C. [B.C. follows the year.]

Symbols are seldom used in the body of papers written for courses in the humanities. You can use a percent symbol (%) or a cent sign (¢), for example, in a table, graph, or other illustration, but in the body of the paper spell out *percent* and *cent*. You can, however, use a dollar sign with specific dollar amounts: *$1.29, $10 million*.

Let common sense and your readers' needs guide you. If you mention temperatures once or twice in a paper, spell them out: *ninety degrees, minus twenty-six degrees*. If you mention temperatures throughout a paper, use figures (see 30k) and symbols: *90°, −26°*.

30i Using abbreviations with titles, names and terms, and addresses

TITLES OF ADDRESS BEFORE NAMES

Dr. P. C. Smith   Mr. Scott Kamiel

Ms. Rachel Wang   Mrs. Ann Wenter

ACADEMIC DEGREES AFTER NAMES

Jean Loft, Ph.D.   Peter Kim, J.D.

Asha Rohra, M.D.   Verna Johnson, D.D.

♣ ABBREVIATION CAUTION: Do not use a title of address before a name *and* an academic degree after a name. Use one or the other. ♣

If you use a long name or term often in a paper, you can abbreviate it. The first time you use it, give the full term, with the abbreviation in parentheses right after the spelled-out form. After that you can use the abbreviation alone.

Volunteers in Service to America (VISTA) began at about the same time as the Peace Corps, but VISTA participants do not go to exotic foreign countries.

You can abbreviate *U.S.* as a modifier (*the U.S. economy*), but spell out *United States* when you use it as a noun.

If you include a full address—street, city, and state—in the body of a paper, you can use the postal abbreviation for the state name, but spell out any other combination of a city and a state.

No   **Miami, FL**, has a thriving Cuban community.

YES   **Miami, Florida**, has a thriving Cuban community.

30j Using *etc.*

Etc. is the abbreviation for the Latin *et cetera*, meaning *and the rest*. Do not use it in academic writing; acceptable substitutes are *and the like*, *and so on*, or *and so forth*.

The Greenlawn Resort offers water sports such as snorkeling, scuba diving, wind-surfing, **and the like** [not *etc.*].

NUMBERS

30k Using spelled-out numbers

Depending on how often numbers appear in a paper and what they refer to, you will sometimes express numbers in words and sometimes in figures. The guidelines here are those used in the humanities. For the guidelines that other disciplines follow, ask your instructor or consult style manuals written for specific fields.

If numerical exactness is not a prime purpose in your paper and you mention numbers only a few times, spell out numbers that can be expressed in one or two words.

Most people need to take the road test for their driver's license **two or three** times.

Eating **one** extra slice of bread a day can lead to a weight gain of about **seven** pounds per year.

♣ HYPHENATION ALERT: Use a hyphen between spelled-out two-word numbers from *twenty-one* through *ninety-nine*. ♣

If you use numbers frequently in a paper, spell out numbers from *one* to *nine* and use figures for numbers *10* and above.

| two shirts | 12 blocks |
| third base | 21st year |

Never start a sentence with a figure. If a sentence starts with a number, spell it out or revise so that the number does not come first.

Thirteen is known as a baker's dozen because bakers used to give an extra roll or pastry to customers who placed large orders.
Nineteen fifty saw the start of the Korean War.
The Korean War started in 1950.

301 Using numbers according to standard practice

Give specific numbers—dates, addresses, measurements, identification numbers—in figures.

GUIDE FOR USING SPECIFIC NUMBERS

Dates	August 6, 1941 1732–1845 34 B.C. to A.D. 230
Addresses	10 Downing Street 237 North 8th Street (*or* 237 North Eighth Street) Export Falls, MN 92025
Times	8:09 A.M.; 3:30 (*but* half past three, quarter of seven, six o'clock)
Decimals and Fractions	5.55; 98.6; 3.1415; ⅞; 12¼ (*but* one quarter, one half, two thirds)
Chapters and Pages	Chapter 27; page 245
Scores and Statistics	a 6–0 score; a 5 to 3 ratio; 29 percent
Identification Numbers	94.4 on the FM dial; call 1-212-555-0000
Measurements	2 feet; 67.8 miles per hour; 1.5 gallons; 2 level teaspoons; 3 liters; 8½″ × 11″ paper or 8½-×-11-inch paper
Act, Scene, and Line Numbers	act II, scene 2, lines 75–79
Temperatures	43°F; −4° Celsius
Money	$1.2 billion; $3.41; 25 cents

Using Capital Letters

A: Select the passage in each pair that needs capital letters. Then rewrite the passage correctly on the line provided.

EXAMPLE (a) going to the city next summer
         (b) going to milwaukee in june
         (b) going to Milwaukee in June

1. (a) president truman
   (b) the thirty-third president

2. (a) the ancient gods
   (b) god's love

3. (a) the federal communications commission
   (b) a government agency

4. (a) a meeting in the afternoon
   (b) a meeting on friday

5. (a) my favorite aunt
   (b) my aunt clara

6. (a) when i graduate
   (b) when we graduate

7. (a) the rising sun
   (b) the sun is rising

8. (a) mother terésa
   (b) my mother

9. (a) dinner at a fine restaurant
   (b) dinner at the steak palace

10. (a) english 202
    (b) a literature course

11. (a) across the main street
    (b) across main street

12. (a) the los angeles lakers
    (b) a basketball team

13. (a) the election officials
    (b) election day

14. (a) northeast of town
    (b) a town in the northeast

15. (a) a college in florida
    (b) a college on the coast

16. (a) "the gift of the magi"
    (b) a story about sacrifice

17. (a) learning a second
       language
    (b) learning french

18. (a) nassau county medical
       center
    (b) the local hospital

19. (a) stars shining in the sky
    (b) the moon and venus
       shining in the sky

20. (a) the hudson river
    (b) the polluted river

B: Rewrite these sentences on the lines provided, adding or deleting capital letters as needed. If no capitals are needed, write *correct* on the line.

EXAMPLE   My uncle Peter and my Aunt are visiting.
          My Uncle Peter and my aunt are visiting.

1. The Spring semester starts in february.

2. They live six miles North of Elm street.

3. The Hotel has 450 rooms.

4. Green, the Ambassador, had a meeting with Foreign Minister Ramirez.

5. I want to visit lake Tahoe to go Skiing.

6. The bible is full of great adventures.

7. They plan to open an italian restaurant Downtown.

8. The league of women voters believes in the democratic system.

9. The teachers' union campaigned for better textbooks.

10. Springfield high school has a large pta.

11. Texans will always Remember the Alamo.

_____

12. Traveling around the cape of Good Hope is dangerous.

_____

13. Rembrandt's "Aristotle contemplating the bust of Homer" is one of his best-known paintings.

_____

14. The Smithsonian institution is in Washington, d.c.

_____

15. Tickets to the super bowl were not available at the Stadium.

_____

Using Italics

A: Select the passage in each of these pairs that needs italics added. Then rewrite the passage correctly on the line provided, using underlining to indicate italics.

EXAMPLE   (a) My favorite movie is a mystery.

(b) My favorite movie is Citizen Kane.

My favorite movie is Citizen Kane.

_____

1. (a) a book about war and peace
   (b) War and Peace

_____

2. (a) the humor of Bill Cosby
   (b) The Bill Cosby Show

_____

3. (a) The Washington Post
   (b) a Washington newspaper

_____

4. (a) a cruise ship
   (b) The Queen Elizabeth II

   _____

5. (a) a space ship
   (b) the U.S.S. Enterprise

   _____

6. (a) We are Homo sapiens.
   (b) We are human beings.

   _____

7. (a) pay particular attention
   (b) nota bene

   _____

8. (a) Many words have the common root, cycle.
   (b) Many words come from the same source.

   _____

9. (a) Don't tease your pets.
   (b) Never tease a hungry crocodile.

   _____

10. (a) The Orient Express was the setting of a famous mystery novel.
    (b) Amtrak goes all over the United States.

   _____

B: Rewrite these sentences on the lines provided, adding italics (underlining) as needed. If no italics are needed, write *correct* on the line.

EXAMPLE   How do you pronounce chamois?
          How do you pronounce chamois? [sham'ē]

1. The word cool has many meanings.

   _____

2. The new hospital is shaped like the letter H.

   _____

3. Scientifically the chimpanzee is called Pan troglodytes and the gorilla is Gorilla gorilla.

   _____

4. I'm feeling muy bien after seeing the play Man of La Mancha.

   _____

5. The H.M.S. Bounty was a real ship.

_____

6. The troubles of its crew are told in the book Mutiny on the Bounty.

_____

7. I subscribe to a Memphis newspaper.

_____

8. William Randolph Hearst began his career in journalism in 1887 running his father's paper, the San Francisco Examiner.

_____

9. By the end of his career, he had a nationwide chain of papers, and his policies had given rise to the term "yellow journalism."

_____

10. The movie Citizen Kane (1941) was an unflattering portrait of a thinly disguised Hearst.

_____

EXERCISE **30-3**

Using Abbreviations

(30h-i)

A. Rewrite each of these sentences, replacing inappropriate abbreviations with their full forms. If a sentence is correct as given, write *correct* on the line.

EXAMPLE   It takes years to become a dr.
It takes years to become a doctor. _____

1. The Chang bros. are opening a fishing charter co.

_____

2. It will be off pier no. 17, not far from L.A., Calif.

_____

3. They plan to go after game fish, e.g., shark, some of which are as much as 45 ft. long.

_____

4. Election Day is always the 2nd Tues. in Nov.

   _____

5. What did you get for Xmas?

   _____

6. Everyone ought to know the story of Wm. Henry Harrison, 9th pres. of the U.S.

   _____

7. He is mentioned in my textbook on the hist. of poli. sci. and philo.

   _____

8. The prof. says the midterm will cover chaps. 1–5.

   _____

9. The midterm & final each count 40%.

   _____

10. The body contains about 10 pts. of blood.

    _____

11. Some people sell their blood for a few $'s.

    _____

12. A kilo. equals 2.2 lbs.

    _____

13. The counselor had an MSW degree from NYU.

    _____

14. She had put herself through school working as an assist. mgr. in a fast-food rest.

    _____

15. Mr. and Mrs. McDonald live on Maple Ave. in Duluth, Minn.

    _____

B: Rewrite each of these sentences, replacing inappropriate full forms with standard abbreviations. It may be necessary to slightly rearrange some sentences.

EXAMPLE   Americans celebrate independence on the fourth day of July.
           Americans celebrate independence on July 4th. _____

1. The bank's loan officer awoke at 2:00 *ante meridiem.*

   _____

2. He was thinking about the family that had applied for a loan of thirty thousand dollars.

   _____

3. Doctor Jones had given them a letter of reference.

   _____

4. Bill Smith, a Certified Public Accountant, had also sent a letter.

   _____

5. For collateral, they offered a Spanish doubloon dated 1642 *Anno Domini.*

   _____

6. The doubloon had been in the family since nineteen nineteen.

   _____

7. Mister and Missus Grossman wanted to use the money to set up a company to make precision measuring devices.

   _____

8. They already had a contract with the National Aeronautics and Space Administration.

   _____

9. The banker wanted to give his okay, but loans this big had to be co-authorized by the bank president.

   _____

10. However, the president had taken her Self-Contained-Underwater-Breathing-Apparatus and gone on a vacation.

   _____

Using Figures

Rewrite each of these sentences, replacing inappropriate figures with words or inappropriate words with figures. If a sentence is correct as given, write *correct* on the line.

EXAMPLE   He is six feet four and a half inches.
          He is 6'4½".
_____

1. There are a hundred and seven women in the freshman class at the law school this year.

   _____

2. Ten years ago there were only 47.

   _____

3. ⅓ the faculty is female now compared with ⅒ then.

   _____

4. Many students share apartments in a building that charges six hundred dollars for two rooms, $700 for three rooms, and $775 for 4 rooms.

   _____

5. The semester begins on September fourteenth.

   _____

6. The entering class will graduate on June first, nineteen ninety-six.

   _____

7. Entrance requirements are on pages thirty to thirty-five.

   _____

8. The average law student is expected to drink 1½ gallons of coffee a day over the next 3 years.

   _____

9. The drop-out rate is about twenty-nine percent.

   _____

10. The law school is located at Fifteen Clark Street.

    _____

31 | *Using Sources: Avoiding Plagiarism and Quoting, Paraphrasing, and Summarizing*

For many writing assignments, you are expected to draw upon outside sources—books, articles, videos, interviews, or even computer bulletin boards—to explain and support your ideas. **Paraphrasing, summarizing**, and **quoting** are three techniques that writers use (1) to take notes from sources and (2) to incorporate into their own writing the ideas and sometimes the words of sources.

GUIDELINES FOR USING OUTSIDE SOURCES IN YOUR WRITING

1. Apply the concepts and skills of critical thinking, reading, and writing.
2. Avoid plagiarism by always giving credit for ideas and words not originally yours.
3. Document sources accurately and completely.
4. Know how and when to use the techniques of paraphrase, summary, and quotation.

31a Avoiding plagiarism

To plagiarize is to present another person's words or ideas as if they were your own. Plagiarism is stealing. It is a serious offense that can be grounds for failure of a course or expulsion from a college. Plagiarism can be intentional, as when you deliberately copy or borrow from the work of other people in your writing without mentioning and documenting the source. Plagiarism can be unintentional—but no less serious an offense—if you are unaware of what must be acknowledged and how to go about documenting. In college, all students are expected to know what plagiarism is and how to avoid it. If you are not absolutely clear about what is involved, take time *now* to learn the rules so that you never expose yourself to charges of plagiarism.

You are not expected to document (give the source of) *common knowledge*—for example, that Columbus's ships landed in America in 1492. You might have to look up the date on which Neil Armstrong walked on the moon, but such material is common knowledge nevertheless. Similarly, you should not document *personal knowledge*—for example, that your grandmother was born June 6, 1916.

What should you document? You must acknowledge the source of any words you quote. Along with your documentation, you must always use quotation marks or, if the material is more than three lines, an indented format. In addition, you must give your source when you present someone else's ideas in your own words.

31b Understanding the concept of documentation

Basic to paraphrasing, summarizing, and quoting is documentation—acknowledging your sources by giving full and accurate information about the author, title, and date of publication, and related facts. For information about how to document properly in a particular discipline, ask your instructor or refer to the *Simon & Schuster Handbook for Writers*.

31c Using quotations effectively

Quotations have special impact in your writing. While paraphrase and summary put one step between your source and your readers, quotations give your readers the chance to encounter directly the words of your source. A carefully chosen, brief quotation from an expert can establish the validity of what you say.

GUIDELINES FOR WORKING QUOTATIONS INTO YOUR WRITING

1. Set off quotations with quotation marks; otherwise you will be plagiarizing.
2. Do not use quotations in more than a third of your paper; rely mostly on paraphrase and summary to report information from sources.
3. Use quotations to *support* what you say, not to present your thesis and main points.
4. Choose a quotation if
   a. its language is particularly appropriate.
   b. its thought is particularly difficult to rephrase accurately.
   c. the authority of the source is especially important as support for your thesis and main ideas.
   d. the source's words are open to interpretation.
5. Quote accurately.
6. Select quotations from authorities in your subject.
7. Select quotations that fit your meaning.
8. Keep long quotations to a minimum.
9. Work quotations smoothly into your writing.
10. Document your source.

31d Paraphrasing accurately

When you **paraphrase**, you re-create in your own words a passage written by another author. Your paraphrasings offer an account of what various authorities have to say, not in their words but in yours. These ideas give substance and believability to your message. Also, paraphrasing forces you to read closely and to get the words' precise meaning into your notes. To do so, use words that come naturally to you, even if it means using more words than the author does. Use synonyms for the author's words wherever you can, but make sure that the sentences in your paraphrase make sense.

GUIDELINES FOR WRITING A PARAPHRASE

1. Say what the source says, but no more.
2. Reproduce the source's order of ideas and emphases.
3. Use your own words and phrasing to restate the message. If certain synonyms are awkward, quote the material—but do this very sparingly.
4. Read over your sentences to make sure that they make sense and do not distort the source's meaning.
5. Expect your material to be as long as, and possibly longer than, the original.
6. Avoid plagiarism.
7. Write down all documentation facts so that you can document your source when you use it in your writing.

31e Summarizing accurately

Summary reviews the main points of a passage. A summary gives you a written overview of what you have read. It is probably the most frequently used device in note-taking for papers.

To summarize a paragraph, a passage, or a chapter, you isolate its main points and write a general statement about each topic. A formal summary is composed of these sentences tied together with appropriate transitions. In an informal summary for your notes, you can worry less about transitions because the notes are meant only to give you the essence of the source.

31e

GUIDELINES FOR WRITING A SUMMARY

1. Identify the main points.
2. Condense the main points without losing the essence of the material.
3. Use your own words to condense the message. If words have been coined by the source or if certain synonyms are awkward, quote the words—but do this very sparingly.
4. Keep your summary short.
5. Avoid plagiarism.
6. Write down all documentation facts so that you can document your source when you use it in your writing.

Quoting

A. Select the portion of this passage that could be usefully quoted in a report. Carefully and accurately copy that portion of the passage. Be prepared to explain why quoting, rather than summarizing or paraphrasing, is called for.

The problem with cosmetics exists only when women feel invisible or inadequate without them. The problem with working out exists only if women hate ourselves when we don't. When a woman is forced to adorn herself to buy a hearing, when she needs her grooming in order to protect her identity, when she goes hungry in order to keep her job, when she must attract a lover so that she can take care of her children, that is exactly what makes "beauty" hurt. Because what hurts women about the beauty myth is not adornment, or expressed sexuality, or time spent grooming, or the desire to attract a lover. Many mammals groom, and every culture uses adornment. "Natural" and "unnatural" are not the terms in question. The actual struggle is between pain and pleasure, freedom and compulsion.

—NAOMI WOLF, *The Beauty Myth*

B. Select any sample paragraph in Chapter 4 and write a paraphrase that includes the most important passages as quotations.

C. Select a paragraph from one of your textbooks or any other nonfiction work, and take notes that combine paraphrase with careful, selective quotation.

Paraphrasing

A. Paraphrase the following paragraph.

The Rites of Beauty also seduce women by meeting their current hunger for color and poetry. As they make their way into male public space that is often prosaic and emotionally dead, beauty's sacraments glow brighter than ever. As women are inundated with claims on their time, ritual products give them an alibi to take some private time for themselves. At their best, they give women back a taste of mystery and sensuality to compensate them for their days spent in the harsh light of the workplace.

—NAOMI WOLF, *The Beauty Myth*

B. Select any sample paragraph in Chapter 4 and paraphrase it.

C. Select a paragraph from one of your textbooks or any other nonfiction work and paraphrase it.

Summarizing

A. Summarize the following paragraph.

During the past decade, women breached the power structure; meanwhile, eating disorders rose exponentially and cosmetic surgery became the fastest-growing medical specialty. During the past five years, consumer spending doubled, pornography became the main media category, ahead of legitimate films and records combined, and thirty-three thousand American woman told researchers that they would rather lose ten to fifteen pounds than achieve any other goal. More women have more money and power and scope and legal recognition than we have ever had before; but in terms of how we feel about ourselves *physically*, we may actually be worse off than our unliberated grandmothers. Recent research consistently shows that inside the majority of the West's controlled, attractive, successful working women, there is a secret "underlife" poisoning our freedom; infused with notions of beauty, it is a dark vein of self-hatred, physical obsessions, terror of aging, and dread of lost control.

—NAOMI WOLF, *The Beauty Myth*

B. Select any sample paragraph in Chapter 4 and summarize it.

C. Select a paragraph from one of your textbooks or any other nonfiction work and summarize it.

ESL-1 | *Singulars and Plurals*

HOW TO USE CHAPTER ESL-1 EFFECTIVELY
This chapter corresponds to Chapter 41-ESL in the *Simon & Schuster Handbook for Writers*.

1. Use this chapter together with these workbook sections:
    - 7a nouns
    - 8c *-s* forms of verbs
    - 11a-11l subject-verb agreement
    - 12f nouns as modifiers
2. Use any cross-references (usually given in parentheses) to find full explanations.

ESL-1a Understanding the concept of count and noncount nouns

Count nouns name items that can be counted: *hand, ball, ring, interpretation*. Count nouns can be singular or plural (*hands, balls*).

Noncount nouns name things that are thought of as a whole and not separated into individual parts: *flour, heritage*. (Noncount nouns are used in the singular form only.) The following chart lists eleven categories of uncountable items, and it gives examples of noncount nouns in each category.

UNCOUNTABLE ITEMS

Groups of similar items making up "wholes":

baggage, fruit, garbage, hardware, makeup, and others

Abstractions

education, evidence, patience, luck, and others

Liquids

tea, milk, oil, ginger ale, wine, and others

Gases

air, hydrogen, nitrogen, oxygen, pollution, and others

Materials

gold, iron, paper, silver, wood, and others

Food

cheese, chicken, lamb, pasta, venison, and others

Particles or grains

corn, grass, pepper, rye, sand, and others

Sports, games, activities

baseball, bridge, checkers, football, tennis, and others

Languages

French, German, Japanese, Latin, Thai, and others

Fields of study

architecture, chemistry, engineering, geology, nursing, and others

Events in nature

darkness, dew, fog, snow, lightning, and others

If you want to check whether a noun is count or noncount, look it up in a dictionary such as the *Longman Dictionary of Contemporary English* or the *Oxford Advanced Learner's Dictionary*. These two dictionaries use the terms *countable* and *uncountable*. Noncount nouns are indicated by the letter *U*. Nouns without a *U* are always count.

Some nouns, including some listed in the previous Chart, can be countable or uncountable. Most such nouns name things that can be meant individually or as "wholes" made up of individual parts depending on the meaning you want to deliver in each sentence.

COUNT	Our instructor expects ten **papers** this semester. [In this sentence, *papers* is meant as individual, countable items.]
NONCOUNT	I ran out of **paper** before I finished. [In this sentence, *paper* is meant as a whole.]
COUNT	The **chickens** escaped from the coop. [In this sentence, *chickens* is meant as individual, countable items.]
NONCOUNT	Fried **chicken** is John's favorite food. [In this sentence, *chicken* is meant as a whole.]

When you are editing your writing (see section 3d), be sure that you have not added a plural *-s* to any noncount nouns, for they are always singular in form. ❖ VERB ALERT: Be sure to use a singular verb with any noncount noun that functions as a subject in your sentences. ❖

ESL-1b Using determiners with singular and plural nouns

Determiners, also called *expressions of quantity*, are a group of words that traditionally are called adjectives but that are used to tell "how much" or "how many" about nouns. Additional names for determiners include *limiting adjectives, noun markers,* and *articles.* (For information about articles—the words *a, an,* and *the*—which occur in English more often than any other determiners, see Chapter ESL-2.)

Choosing the correct determiner with a noun depends first on whether the noun is count or noncount (see ESL-1a). For count nouns, you must also decide whether the noun is singular or plural. The following Chart lists many determiners and singular count nouns, noncount nouns, plural (count) nouns that they can accompany.

❖ USAGE ALERT: The phrases *a few* and *a little* convey the meaning "some": *I have a few worries* means "I have some worries." *The Joneses spend a little time with their children* means "The Joneses spend some time with their children."

Without the word *a, few* and *little* convey the meaning "almost none" or "not enough": *I have few* [or *very few*] *worries* means "I have almost no worries." *The Joneses spend little time with their children* means "The Joneses spend almost no time with their children." ❖

DETERMINERS TO USE WITH COUNT AND NONCOUNT NOUNS

With every **singular count noun**, always use one of the determiners listed in Group 1.

> **No**   We live in **apartment** in large, white **house**.

> **Yes**   We live in **an apartment** in **that** large white **house**.

GROUP 1: DETERMINERS FOR SINGULAR COUNT NOUNS

a, an, the

a chair	**an apple**	**the room**

one, any, some, every, each, either, neither, another, the other

any chair	**each apple**	**another room**

my, our, your, his, her, its, their, nouns with 's or s'

your chair	**its apple**	**Connie's room**

this, that

this chair	**that apple**	**this car**

one, no, the first, the second, and so on

one chair	**no apple**	**the fifth room**

With every **plural count noun**, use one of the determiners listed in Group 2. Count nouns are sometimes used without determiners, as discussed fully in Chapter ESL-2.

> **Yes**   Be sure that the tomatoes you select are ripe.

> **Yes**   Tomatoes are tasty in salad.

GROUP 2: DETERMINERS FOR PLURAL COUNT NOUNS

the

the signs	**the rugs**	**the headaches**

some, any, both, many, more, most, few, fewer, the fewest, a number of, other, several, all, all the, a lot of

some signs	**many rugs**	**all headaches**

my, our, your, his, her, its, their, nouns with 's or s'

our signs	**her rugs**	**students' headaches**

these, those

these signs	**those rugs**	**these headaches**

no, two, three, four, and so on, the first, the second, the third, and so on

no signs	**four rugs**	**the first headaches**

With every **noncount noun** (always singular), use one of the determiners listed in Group 3. Noncount nouns can also be used without determiners, as discussed in Chapter ESL-2.

> **Yes**   I bought **the fish** we ate for supper.

> **Yes**   I bought **fish** for supper.

DETERMINERS TO USE WITH COUNT AND NONCOUNT NOUNS *(continued)*

GROUP 3: DETERMINERS FOR NONCOUNT NOUNS

the

the cream	**the light**	**the progress**

some, any, much, more, most, other, the other, little, less, the least, enough, all, all the, a lot of

enough cream	**a lot of light**	**more progress**

my, our, your, his, her, its, their, nouns with '*s* or *s*'

their cream	**its light**	**your progress**

this, that

this cream	**that light**	**this progress**

no, the first, the second, the third, and so on

no cream	**the first light**	**no progress**

ESL-1c Using correct forms in *one of* constructions, for nouns used as adjectives, and with *States* in names or titles

One of *Constructions*

One of constructions include *one of the* and *one of* followed by a pronoun in the possessive case (*one of my, one of your, one of his, one of her, one of its one of their*). Always use a plural noun as the object when you begin a phrase with *one of*.

No   One of our **goal** is progress.
YES   One of our **goals** is progress.

No   One of his **pet** has died.
YES   One of his **pets** has died.

The verb in *one of* constructions is always singular. The verb agrees with *one*, not with a plural noun: *One of the most important inventions of the twentieth century* **is** [not *are*] *television.*

Nouns Used as Adjectives

Some words that function as nouns can also function as adjectives.

The bird's wingspan in ten **inches**. [*Inches* functions here as a noun.]
The bird has a ten-**inch** wingspan. [*Inch* functions here as an adjective.]

Adjectives in English do not have plural forms. When you use a noun as an adjective, therefore, do not add -s or -es to the adjective even when the noun or pronoun it modifies is plural.

No Many **Americans** students are basketball fans.

Yes Many **American** students are basketball fans.

Names and Titles that Include the Word States

The word *states* is always plural. However, names such as the *United States* or the *Organization of American States* refer to singular things—a country and an organization—so they are singular nouns and therefore require singular verbs.

No The United **State** has a large entertainment industry.

No The United **States have** a large entertainment industry.

Yes The United **States has** a large entertainment industry.

ESL-1d Using nouns with irregular plurals

Some English nouns have irregular spellings. Here are some categories of nouns that often cause difficulties.

Plurals of Foreign Nouns and Other Irregular Nouns

Whenever you are unsure whether a noun is plural, look it up in a dictionary. If no plural is given for a singular noun, add an -s.

Many nouns from other languages that are used unchanged in English have only one plural. If two plurals are listed in the dictionary, look carefully for differences in meaning. Some words for example, keep the plural form from the original language for scientific usage and have another English-form plural that is used in non-science contexts. Examples include *antenna, antennae, antennas; formula, formulae, formulas; appendix, appendices, appendixes; index, indices, indexes; medium, media, mediums; cactus, cacti, cactuses;* and *fungus, fungi, funguses.*

Words of Latin origin that end in -*is* in their singular form become plural by substituting -*es*: *parenthesis, parentheses; thesis, theses; oasis, oases,* for example.

Other Words

Medical terms for diseases involving an inflammation end in -*itis*: *tonsillitis, appendicitis.* They are always singular.

The word *news*, although it ends in -s, is always singular: *The news is encouraging.* The words *people, police,* and *clergy* are always plural even though they do not end in -s: *The police are prepared.*

390

Name _____   Date _____

Identifying Nouns

Divide the following list of words into count and noncount nouns. Give the plural forms of the count nouns. List in all columns any words that can be both count and noncount.

advice	fern	jewelry	paragraph
book	flour	library	physics
calculator	gold	lightning	pollution
chocolate	hair	man	rain
desk	happiness	news	report
earring	homework	novel	storm
essay	honesty	occupation	time
experiment	information	paper	weather

	Noncount	Count	Plural
1.			
2.			
3.			
4.			
5.			
6.			
7.			
8.			
9.			
10.			
11.			
12.			
13.			
14.			
15.			
16.			
17.			
18.			
19.			

20. _____ _____ _____

21. _____ _____ _____

22. _____ _____ _____

23. _____ _____ _____

24. _____ _____ _____

25. _____ _____ _____

26. _____ _____ _____

27. _____ _____ _____

28. _____ _____ _____

29. _____ _____ _____

30. _____ _____ _____

31. _____ _____ _____

32. _____ _____ _____

Name _____ Date _____

Correct Forms

Choose the correct forms of the nouns in parentheses and write them on the lines at the right.

EXAMPLE Some _____ (hiker) return to   _____*hikers*_____
_____ (nature) by walking the   _____*nature*_____
Appalachian Trail.

1. Hikers with little _____ (money) but much   _____
_____ (fortitude) can begin the hike in Georgia   _____
and continue to Maine.
2. The 2,015-_____ (mile) trail extends through   _____
fourteen _____ (state).   _____
3. The trail passes cultivated _____ (farm) and   _____
untamed _____ (wilderness).   _____
4. Since 1968 it has been one of two federally   _____
protected _____ (trail) in the United   _____
_____ (state).
5. Few _____ (hiker) have anything but praise for   _____
their ____ _____ (experience) on the trail.   _____
6. Many _____ (youngster) would gladly give   _____
up _____ (piano) lessons or _____   _____
(homework) to be climbing wooded _____   _____
(path).   _____
7. The Appalachian Trail is one of the nation's   _____
_____ (treasure).

ESL-2 | *Articles*

HOW TO USE CHAPTER ESL-2 EFFECTIVELY
This chapter corresponds to Chapter 42-ESL in the *Simon & Schuster Handbook for Writers.*

Use this chapter together with these workbook sections:
- 7a articles
- ESL-1a singulars and plurals with count nouns and noncount nouns
- ESL-1b singulars and plurals with expressions of quantity

ESL-2a Using *a*, *an*, or *the* with singular count nouns

The words *a* and *an* are called **indefinite articles**. The word *the* is called a **definite article**. Articles are one type of determiner. (For other types of determiners, see the Chart ESL-1b.) Articles signal that a noun will follow and than any modifiers between the article and the noun refer to that noun.

a sandwich
a fresh tuna sandwich
the guest
the welcome guest

Every time you use a singular count noun, the noun requires some kind of determiner. To choose between *a* or *an* and *the*, you need to determine whether the noun is **specific** or **nonspecific**. A noun is considered specific when anyone who reads your writing can understand from the context of your message exactly and specifically to what the noun is referring.

For nonspecific singular count nouns, use *a* (or *an*). When a singular noun is specific, use *the* or some other determiner. Use the following Chart to help you determine when a noun is specific and therefore requires the article *the*.

One common exception affects Rule 4 in the Chart. Even when a noun has been used in an earlier sentence, it may require *a* (or *an*) if one or more descriptive adjectives come between the article and the noun: *I bought a computer today. It was a* [not *the*] *used computer.* Other information may make the noun specific so that *the* is correct. For example, *it was the used computer that I saw advertised on the bulletin board* uses *the* because the *that* clause lets a reader know which specific used computer is meant.

♣USAGE ALERT: Use *an* before words that begin with a vowel sound. Use *a* before words that begin with a consonant sound. Words that begin with *h* or *u* can have either a vowel or a consonant sound. Make the choice based on the sound of the first word after the article even if that word is not the noun.

a cat	**an** axiom	**a** fine day
a unicorn	**an** underpass	**a** united front
a heretic	**an** herb	**a** happy smile ♣

FOUR RULES: WHEN A SINGULAR COUNT NOUN IS SPECIFIC AND REQUIRES *THE*

Rule 1: A noun is specific and requires *the* when it names something unique or generally known.

> **The stars** lit his way. [Because *stars* is a generally known noun, it is a specific noun in the context of this sentence.]

Rule 2: A noun is specific and requires *the* when it names something used in a representative or abstract sense.

> **The termite** is actually a fascinating insect. [Because *termite* is a representative reference rather than a reference to a particular termite, it is a specific noun in the context of this sentence.]

Rule 3: A noun is specific and requires *the* when it names something defined elsewhere in the same sentence or in an earlier sentence.

> **The disease bilharzia** is a serious threat in some parts of the world. [The word *bilharzia* means a specific disease.]

> **The face in the painting** startled me. [*In the painting* defines exactly which face is meant, so *face* is a specific noun in this context.]

> I know **a good place** to eat. **The place** is near my home. [*Place* is not specific in the first sentence, so it uses *a*. In the second sentence *place* has been made specific by the first sentence, so it uses *the*.]

Rule 4: A noun is specific and requires *the* when it names something that can be inferred from the context.

> **The chef** is excellent. [If this sentence follows the two sentences about a place in Rule 3 above, *chef* is specific in this context.]

One common exception affects Rule 3 in the Four Rules Chart. A noun may still require *a* (or *an*) after the first use if one or more descriptive adjectives comes between the article and the noun: *I bought **a sweater** today. It was **a*** [not *the*] **red sweater.**

Other information may make the noun specific so that *the* is correct. For example, *It was **the red sweater that I saw in the store yesterday*** uses *the* because the *that* clause makes specific which red sweater is meant.

ESL-2b Using articles with plural nouns and with noncount nouns

With plural nouns and noncount nouns, you must decide about articles whether to use *the* or to use no article at all. (For guidelines about using determiners other than articles with nouns, see the Chart in ESL-1b.)

What you learned in section ESL-2a about nonspecific and specific nouns can help you make the choice between using *the* or using no article. The Four Rules Chart in section ESL-2a explains when a singular count noun's meaning is specific and calls for *the*. Plural nouns and noncount nouns with specific meanings usually use *the* in the same circumstances. However, a plural noun or a noncount noun with a general or nonspecific meaning usually does not use *the*.

I need **nuts** and **chocolate chips** for this recipe. I also need **flour**.

Plural Nouns

A plural noun's meaning may be specific because it is widely known.

The crops may not survive the drought. [Because the meaning of *crops* is widely understood, *the* is correct to use. This example is related to Rule 1 in the Four Rules Chart.]

A plural noun's meaning may also be made specific by a word, phrase, or clause in the same sentence.

I don't know **the students** in my apartment building. [Because the phrase *in my apartment building* makes *students* specific, *the* is correct to use. This example is related to Rule 3 in the Four Rules Chart.]

A plural noun's meaning usually becomes specific by being used in an earlier sentence.

We have begun doing **exercises**. We hope **the exercises** will develop our stamina. [*Exercises* is used in a general sense in the first sentence, without *the*. Because the first sentence makes *exercises* specific, *the exercises* is correct in the second sentence. This example is related to Rule 4 in the Four Rules Chart.]

A plural noun's meaning may be made specific by the context.

The aerobics should be particularly beneficial. [In the context of the sentences about exercises, *aerobics* is specific and calls for *the*. This example is related to Rule 4 in the Four Rules Chart.]

Noncount Nouns

Noncount nouns are always singular in form (see ESL-1a). Like plural nouns, noncount nouns use either *the* or no article. When a noncount noun's meaning is specific, use *the* before it. If its meaning is general or nonspecific, do not use *the*.

Li served us **tea**. He had brought **the tea** from China. [*Tea* is a noncount noun. This example is related to Rule 4 in the Four Rules Chart. By the second sentence, *tea* has become specific, so *the* is used.]

Li served us **the tea that he had brought from China**. [*Tea* is a noncount noun. This example is related to Rule 3 in the Four Rules Chart: *Tea* is made specific by the clause *that he had brought from China*, so *the* is used.]

Generalizations with Plural or Noncount Nouns

Rule 2 in the Four Rules Chart tells you to use *the* with singular count nouns used in a general sense. With generalizations using plural or noncount nouns, omit *the*.

| No | **The elephants** live longer than **the zebras**. |
| Yes | **Elephants** live longer than **zebras**. |

ESL-2c Using *the* with proper nouns and with gerunds

Proper Nouns

Proper nouns name specific people, places, or things (see 7a). Most proper nouns do not require articles: *I spent my holidays with Asda at Cape Cod.* As shown in the following Chart, however, certain types of proper nouns do require *the*.

PROPER NOUNS THAT USE *THE*

Nouns with the pattern *the . . . of . . .*

    the United States **of** America
    the Isle **of** Wight
    the Fourth **of** July
    the University **of** Illinois

Plural proper nouns

    the Randalls   **the** Atlanta Braves
    the Trossachs
    the Smoky Mountains   [but Mount Everest]
    the Virgin Islands   [but Staten Island]
    the Great Lakes   [but Lake Titicaca]

Collective proper nouns (nouns that name a group)

    the Lions Club
    the League of Women Voters

Some (but not all) geographical features

    the Amazon River   **the** Gobi Desert
    the Indian Ocean

Two countries and one city

    the Congo   **the** Sudan
    the Hague [capital of the Netherlands]

Gerunds

Gerunds are present participles (the *-ing* form of verbs) used as nouns: ***Skating* *is challenging*.** Gerunds usually are not preceded by *the*.

    No   **The constructing** new bridges is necessary to improve traffic flow.
    YES   **Constructing** new bridges is necessary to improve traffic flow.

Use *the* before a gerund when two conditions are met: (1) the gerund is used in a specific sense and (2) the gerund does not have a direct object.

No   **The designing** fabric is a fine art. [*Fabric* is a direct object of *designing*, so *the* should not be used.]

Yes   **Designing** fabric is a fine art. [*Designing* is a gerund, so *the* is not used.]

Yes   **The designing** of fabric is a fine art. [*The* is used because *fabric* is the object of the preposition *of* and *designing* is meant in a specific sense.]

Articles

In the following blanks write *a*, *an*, or *the* as needed. If no article is necessary, put a *0* in the blank.

In 1872 _____ Congress passed _____ Yellowstone Act, establishing _____ Yellowstone as _____ first national park in _____ United States and indeed in _____ world. For centuries _____ wealthy set aside _____ private preserves for their own recreational use, but except for _____ few public parks in _____ major cities, setting aside _____ vast area for _____national enjoyment was _____ novel idea. It became _____ popular one. Since _____ founding of _____ Yellowstone, forty-nine other national parks have been established in _____ United States and its territories.

_____ Yellowstone is _____ largest of this country's national parks. It occupies 3,472 square miles at _____ juncture of _____ states of _____ Wyoming, _____ Montana, and _____ Idaho. Although _____ Native American habitation goes back 800 years, _____ park's remoteness from _____ centers of _____ population left it undiscovered by _____ white settlers until _____ nineteenth century.

_____ John Colter is thought to be _____ first explorer to venture into _____ area. Colter was _____ member of _____ Lewis and Clark Expedition. When _____ expedition returned to _____ St. Louis, he remained in _____ region of _____ upper Missouri River to become _____ mountain man. In 1807 he explored _____ Yellowstone Basin. When he later wrote about _____ thermal wonders of _____ area, many people did not believe such natural phenomena existed. They continue to amaze _____ tourists today.

Yellowstone is truly _____ natural fantasy land. Its features include _____ geysers, _____ hot springs, and _____ mud volcanoes along with _____ forests, _____ lakes, _____ mountains, and _____ waterfalls. _____ most famous of _____ park's attractions is _____ "Old Faithful," _____ geyser which erupts on _____ average of every 65 minutes. It shoots _____ steaming water from 120 to 170 feet into _____ air. Each eruption lasts approximately four minutes and spews out 10,000 _____ gallons of _____ water.

Other active geysers in _____ six geyser basins may be less predictable but are no less spectacular. Some of _____ more than 200 just emit _____ steam and _____ spooky underground noises. _____ silica in _____ geyser water builds up around _____ walls of _____ geyser craters, making _____ craters very colorful and beautiful to view even when _____ geysers are not spouting.

_____ hot springs are another Yellowstone attraction. There are more than 3,000 of them ranged throughout _____ park. Some, such as _____ Emerald Spring, are remarkable because of their color. _____ Morning Glory Spring looks like its flower namesake.

_____ Yellowstone Lake, _____ Golden Gate Canyon, and _____ Tower Falls are just some of _____ features that combine with _____ geysers and _____ hot springs to make _____ Yellowstone National Park _____ extraordinary place to visit.

ESL-3 | *Word Order*

HOW TO USE CHAPTER ESL-3 EFFECTIVELY
This chapter corresponds to Chapter 43-ESL in the *Simon & Schuster Handbook for Writers*.

Use this chapter together with these workbook sections:
- 7k–7o sentence patterns
- 7e adjectives
- 7p sentence types
- 7f adverbs
- 7m modifiers
- 11f verbs in inverted word order
- 7o clauses

ESL-3a Understanding standard and inverted word order in sentences

In **standard word order**, the most common pattern for declarative sentences in English, the subject comes before the verb. (To better understand these concepts, review sections 7k–7o).

    SUBJECT   VERB
       ↓   ↓
   My schedule   is full.

With **inverted word order**, the main verb or an auxiliary verb comes before the subject. The most common use of inverted word order in English is forming direct questions. Questions that can be answered with "yes" or "no" begin with a form of *be* used as a main verb, or with an auxiliary verb (*be, do,* or *have*), or with a modal auxiliary (*can, should, will,* and others—see Chapter ESL-6).

ESL-3a

QUESTIONS THAT CAN BE ANSWERED WITH YES OR NO

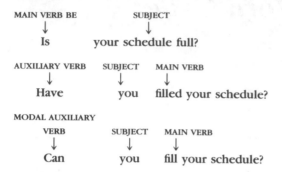

MAIN VERB BE   SUBJECT
↓   ↓
Is   your schedule full?

AUXILIARY VERB   SUBJECT   MAIN VERB
↓   ↓   ↓
Have   you   filled your schedule?

MODAL AUXILIARY
VERB   SUBJECT   MAIN VERB
↓   ↓   ↓
Can   you   fill your schedule?

To form a **yes/no question** with a verb other than *be* as the main verb and when there is no auxiliary or modal as part of a verb phrase, use the appropriate form of the auxiliary verb *do*.

AUXILIARY VERB   SUBJECT   MAIN VERB
↓   ↓   ↓
Does   Mako   wear only black?

You may sometimes see a question formed with the main verb at the beginning.

MAIN VERB   SUBJECT
↓   ↓
Has   she   no other option?

It is equally correct and more common to see the question formed with *do* as an auxiliary and *have* as a main verb, following the pattern of auxiliary verb-subject-main verb: *Does she have no other option?*

A question that begins with a question-forming word like *why, when, where,* or *how* cannot be answered with "yes" or "no": *Why did the doorbell ring?* Such a question communicates that information must be provided to answer it; the answer cannot be "*yes*" or "*no*." Information is needed: for example, *Suki rang it.*

Most information questions follow the same rules of inverted word order as yes/no questions.

INFORMATION QUESTIONS: INVERTED ORDER

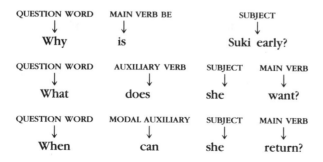

QUESTION WORD   MAIN VERB BE   SUBJECT
↓   ↓   ↓
Why   is   Suki early?

QUESTION WORD   AUXILIARY VERB   SUBJECT   MAIN VERB
↓   ↓   ↓   ↓
What   does   she   want?

QUESTION WORD   MODAL AUXILIARY   SUBJECT   MAIN VERB
↓   ↓   ↓   ↓
When   can   she   return?

When **who** or **what** functions as the subject in a question, however, use standard word order.

INFORMATION QUESTIONS: STANDARD ORDER

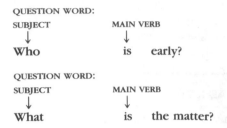

QUESTION WORD:
SUBJECT   MAIN VERB
↓   ↓
Who   is   early?

QUESTION WORD:
SUBJECT   MAIN VERB
↓   ↓
What   is   the matter?

♣ ALERT: When a question has more than one auxiliary verb, put the subject after the first auxiliary verb:

FIRST   SECOND
AUXILIARY   SUBJECT   AUXILIARY   MAIN VERB
↓   ↓   ↓   ↓
Could   she   have   returned later? ♣

The same rules apply to emphatic exclamations: *Was that soup delicious! Did it hit the spot!*

Also, when you use negatives such as *never, hardly ever, seldom, rarely, not only* or *nor* to start a clause, use **inverted order**. These sentence pairs show the differences:

I have never been so embarrassed.
(**standard order**)
Never have I been so embarrassed!
(**inverted order**)

Jo is not only a chemist but also a writer.
Not only is Jo a chemist, but he is also a writer.

Paul did not study, and his brother didn't either.
Paul did not study, and neither did his brother.

♣USAGE ALERT: With indirect questions, use standard word order: *She asked when Suki could return* (not *She asked when could Suki return*.)♣

♣STYLE ALERT: Word order deliberately inverted can be effective, when used sparingly, to create emphasis in a sentence that is neither a question nor an exclamation (also see 19f). ♣

ESL-3b Understanding the placement of adjectives

Adjectives modify—that is, they describe or limit—nouns, pronouns, and word groups that function as nouns (see section 7e). In English, an adjective comes directly before the noun it describes. However, when more than one adjective describes the same noun, several sequences may be possible. The following Chart shows the most common order for positioning several adjectives.

WORD ORDER FOR MORE THAN ONE ADJECTIVE

1. **Determiners, if any:** *a, an, the, my, your, Jan's, this, that, these, those,* and so on
2. **Expressions of order, including ordinal numbers, if any:** *first, second, third, next, last, final,* and so on
3. **Expressions of quantity, including cardinal (counting) numbers, if any:** *one, two, three, few, each, every, some,* and so on
4. **Adjectives of judgment or opinion, if any:** *pretty, happy, ugly, sad, interesting, boring,* and so on
5. **Adjectives of size and/or shape, if any:** *big, small, short, round, square,* and so on
6. **Adjectives of age and/or condition, if any:** *new, young, broken, dirty, shiny,* and so on
7. **Adjectives of color, if any:** *red, green, blue,* and so on
8. **Adjectives that can also be used as nouns, if any:** *French, Protestant, metal, cotton,* and so on
9. **The noun**

1	2	3	4	5	6	7	8	9
A		few		tiny		red		ants
The	last	six					Thai	carvings
My			fine		old		oak	table

ESL-3c Understanding the placement of adverbs

Adverbs modify—that is, describe or limit—verbs, adjectives, other adverbs, or entire sentences (see section 7f). Adverbs are usually positioned first, in the middle, or last in a clause. The following chart summarizes adverb types, what they tell about the words they modify, and where each type can be placed.

TYPES OF ADVERBS AND WHERE TO POSITION THEM

ADVERBS OF MANNER

- describe how something is done
- usually are in middle or last position

> Boris **thoroughly** cleaned his car.
> Boris cleaned his car **thoroughly.**

ADVERBS OF TIME

- describe when or how long about an event
- usually are in the first or last position

> **First**, he scrubbed the wheels.
> He scrubbed the wheels **first**.

- include *just, still*, and *already*, and similar adverbs, which usually are in the middle position

> He had **already** vacuumed the interior.

ADVERBS OF PLACE

- describes *where* an event takes place
- usually are in the last position

> He cleaned the car **outdoors**.

ADVERBS OF FREQUENCY

- describe *how often* an event takes place
- usually are in the middle position

> Boris **rarely** takes the car to a car wash.

- are in the first position when they modify an entire sentence (see Sentence adverbs below)

> **Occasionally**, he waxes the car.

ADVERBS OF DEGREE OR EMPHASIS

- describe how much or to what extent about other modifiers
- are directly before the word they modify

> Boris is **extremely** proud of his car. [*Extremely* modifies *proud*.]

- include *only*, which is easy to misplace (see 15b–1)

TYPES OF ADVERBS AND WHERE TO POSITION THEM *(continued)*

SENTENCE ADVERBS

- modify the entire sentence rather than just one word or a few words
- include transitional words and expressions (see 4d–1) as well as *maybe probably, possibly, fortunately, unfortunately, incredibly,* and others
- are in first position

Surprisingly, he doesn't mind loaning it.

❖ PUNCTUATION ALERT: Unless they are very short (fewer than five letters), adverbs in the first position are usually followed by a comma. ❖

❖ USAGE ALERT: Do not let an adverb in a middle position separate a verb from its direct object or indirect object (see section 15b–3). ❖

Question Form

Convert the following sentences into questions.

EXAMPLE   We should have called first.
          Should we have called first?

1. That pizza is enough for all of us.

   _____

2. Henri understood the lesson.

   _____

3. You have my lab manual. (two ways)

   _____

   _____

4. Juanita will have finished by the time we return.

   _____

5. Everyone in the room can see the screen.

   _____

Order in Adjectives and Adverbs

Rewrite the following sentences using correct word order.

EXAMPLE   Our English class took a field final trip to an auction large house.
<u>Our English class took a final field trip to a large auction house.</u>

1. Katrina purchased two Limoges lovely boxes.

   _____

2. A black leather comfortable chair appealed to Nils.

   _____

3. He waited to bid on it patiently.

   _____

4. We left unfortunately before it was auctioned.

   _____

5. Marios wanted a wooden old table but bought a silver worn spoon.

   _____

6. Suchen outbid someone for a green round interesting hatbox.

   _____

7. She was delighted extremely to get it.

   _____

8. She has wanted often one.

   _____

9. The English entire class bought something except Ingrid.

   _____

10. Because she brought an empty small purse, she bought nothing at all.

   _____

ESL-4 | *Prepositions*

HOW TO USE CHAPTER ESL-4 EFFECTIVELY
This chapter corresponds to Chapter 44-ESL in the *Simon & Schuster Handbook for Writers.*

Use this chapter together with these workbook sections:
- 7g prepositions
- 21a using appropriate language

Prepositions function with other words in prepositional phrases. Prepositional phrases usually indicate **where** (direction or location) **how** (by what means or in what way), or **when** (at what time or how long), about the words they modify.

This chapter can help you with several uses of prepositions, which function in combination with other words in ways that are often idiomatic. An idiom's meaning differs from the literal meaning of each individual word (see 20a). For example, *Yao-Ming broke into a smile* means that a smile appeared on Yao-Ming's face. However, the dictionary definitions of *break* and *into* imply that *broke into a smile* means "shattered the form of" a smile. Knowing which preposition to use in a specific context takes much experience reading, listening to, and speaking the language. A dictionary like the *Longman Dictionary of Contemporary English* or the *Oxford Advanced Learner's Dictionary* can be especially helpful when you need to find the correct preposition to use in cases not covered by this chapter.

ESL-4a

ESL-4a Recognizing Prepositions

The following chart shows many common prepositions.

COMMON PREPOSITIONS		
about	despite	out
above	down	out of
according to	during	outside
across	except	over
after	except for	past
against	excepting	regarding
along	for	round
along with	from	since
among	in	through
apart from	in addition to	throughout
around	in back of	till
as	in case of	to
as for	in front of	toward
at	in place of	under
because of	inside	underneath
before	in spite of	unlike
behind	instead of	until
below	into	up
beneath	like	upon
beside	near	up to
between	next	with
beyond	of	within
but	off	without
by	on	
by means of	onto	
concerning	on top of	

ESL-4b Using prepositions with expressions of time and place

The following Chart shows how to use the prepositions *in, at,* and *on* to deliver some common kinds of information about time and place. The chart, however, does not convey every preposition that indicates time or place, nor does it cover all uses of *in, at,* and *to.* For example, it does not explain the subtle different in meaning delivered by the prepositions *at* and *in* in these two correct sentences: *I have a checking account **at** that bank and I have a safe-deposit box **in** that bank.* Also, the chart does not include expressions that operate outside the general rules. (Both these sentences are correct: *You ride **in** the car and You ride **on** the bus.*)

USING *IN, AT,* AND *ON* TO SHOW TIME AND PLACE

TIME

***in* a year or a month** (*during* is also correct but less common)

    in 1995   **in** May

***in* a period of time**

    in a few months (seconds, days, years)

***in* a period of the day**

    in the morning (afternoon, evening)
    in the daytime (morning, evening), but **at** night

***on* a specific day**

    on Friday   **on** my birthday

***at* a specific time or period of time**
    at noon   **at** 2:00
    at dawn   **at** nightfall
    at takeoff (the time a plane leaves)
    at breakfast (the time a specific meal takes place)

→

USING *IN, AT,* AND *ON* TO SHOW TIME AND PLACE *(continued)*

PLACE

in **a location surrounded by something else**

> **in** the province of Alberta
> **in** Utah   **in** downtown Bombay
> **in** the kitchen   **in** my apartment
> **in** the bathtub

at **a specific location**

> **at** your house   **at** the bank
> **at** the corner of Third Avenue and Main Street

on **the top or the surface of something**

> **on** page 20   **on** the mezzanine
> **on** Washington Street   **on** street level
> **on** the second floor, but **in** the attic or **in** the basement

---

ESL-4c Using prepositions in phrasal verbs

Phrasal verbs, also called *two-word verbs* and *three-word verbs*, are verbs that combine with prepositions to deliver their meaning.

In some phrasal verbs, the verb and the preposition should not be separated by other words: *Look **at** the moon* [not ***Look** the moon **at***].

In **separable phrasal verbs**, other words in the sentence can separate the verb and the preposition without interfering with meaning: *I threw away my homework* is as correct as *I threw my homework away*.

Here is a list of some common phrasal verbs. The ones that cannot be separated are marked with an asterisk (*).

LIST OF SELECTED PHRASAL VERBS

ask out	get along with*	look into
break down	get back	look out for*
bring about	get off*	look over
call back	go over*	make up
drop off	hand in	run across*
figure out	keep up with*	speak to*
fill out	leave out	speak with*
fill up	look after*	throw away
find out	look around	throw out

Position a pronoun object between the words of a separable phrasal verb: *I threw **it** away*. Also, you can position an object phrase of several words between the parts of a separable phrasal verb: *I threw **my research paper** away*. However, when the object is a clause, do not let it separate the parts of the phrasal verb: *I threw away **all the papers that I wrote last year***.

Many phrasal verbs are informal and are used more in speaking than in writing. For academic writing, a more formal verb may be more appropriate than a phrasal verb. In a research paper, for example, *propose* or *suggest* might be better choices than *come up with*. For academic writing acceptable phrasal verbs include *believe in, benefit from, concentrate on, consist of, depend on, dream of* (or *dream about*), *insist on, participate in, prepare for,* and *stare at*. None of these phrasal verbs can be separated.

ESL-4d Using prepositions in common expressions

In many common expressions, different prepositions convey great differences in meaning. For example, four prepositions can be used with the verb *agree* to create five different meanings:

agree to = to give consent (*I cannot **agree to** buy you a new car.*)

agree about = to arrive at a satisfactory understanding (*We **agree about** your needing a car.*)

agree on = to arrive at a satisfactory understanding (*You and the seller must **agree on** a price for the car.*)

agree with = to have the same opinion (*I **agree with** you that you need a car.*)

agree with = be suitable or healthful (*The idea of having such a major expense does not **agree with** me.*)

You can find entire books filled with English expressions that include prepositions. This list shows a few that you are likely to use often.

LIST OF SELECTED EXPRESSIONS WITH PREPOSITIONS

ability in
access to
accustomed to
afraid of
angry with *or* at
authority on
aware of
based on
capable of
certain of
confidence in
dependent on

different from
faith in
familiar with
famous for
frightened by
happy with
in charge of
independent of
in favor of
influence on *or* over
interested in
involved in [*something*]

involved with [*someone*]
knowledge of
made of
married to
opposed to
patience with
proud of
reason for
related to
suspicious of
time for
tired of

In, At, On

In the following blanks, use *in*, *at*, or *on* to show time or place.

EXAMPLE   The University of Virginia, located _____ Charlottesville,
was founded by Thomas Jefferson.
The University of Virginia, located _____*in*_____ Charlottesville,
was founded by Thomas Jefferson.

1. Others wanted to put the new university _____ Staunton or Lexington.
2. _____ August 1818, Jefferson convinced legislators to place it _____ Albermarle County.
3. Jefferson designed the university so that students and faculty lived together _____ an "academical village."
4. A rotunda building for classes sits _____ one end of a lawn.
5. _____ both sides of the lawn are sets of student rooms.
6. Faculty members lived _____ pavilions between the sets of student rooms.
7. The university opened _____ 1825.
8. _____ his last visit to the university, Jefferson stood _____ a window _____ the rotunda and surveyed the campus.
9. _____ his deathbed, Jefferson included founding the university as one of the three accomplishments for which he hoped to be remembered.
10. Today students at the University of Virginia consider it an honor to live _____ the rooms Jefferson designed.

Phrasal Verbs

A: Fill in each blank with a phrasal verb from page 415. Use each phrasal verb only once. More than one phrasal verb may be appropriate for some blanks.

EXAMPLE   Walid cannot _____ why it takes so long to register.
            Walid cannot ___*figure out*___ why it takes so long to register.

1. Ravi will _____ Walid and explain.
2. First he must _____ all the forms.
3. He must _____ all his records to make sure he does not _____ anything.
4. He must then _____ the forms at the registrar's office.
5. Should he _____ the forms without some vital information, the registrar will _____ him _____ to get it.
6. Walid will have to _____ the forms and _____ what is missing.
7. He must not _____ any records until he has finished the procedure.

B: Now rewrite the sentences using as many formal verbs as possible.

ESL-5 | *Gerunds, Infinitives, and Participles*

HOW TO USE CHAPTER ESL-5 EFFECTIVELY
This chapter corresponds to Chapter 45-ESL in the *Simon & Schuster Handbook for Writers*.

Use this chapter together with these workbook sections:
- 7d verbals
- 11a subject-verb agreement
- 7k–l subjects and objects
- 18a–c parallelism
- 8b principal parts of verbs

Participles are verb forms (see 8b). A verb's *-ing* form is its present participle. The *-ed* form of a *regular verb* is its past participle; irregular verbs form their past participles in various ways (for example, *bend, bent; eat, eaten; think, thought*—for a complete list, see the chart in section 8d). Participles can function as adjectives (*a **smiling** face, a **closed** book*).

A verb's *-ing* form can also function as a noun (***sneezing** spreads colds*), which is called a **gerund**. Another verb form, the **infinitive**, also functions as a noun. An infinitive is a verb's simple or base form usually preceded by the word *to* (*Tell everyone **to smile***). Verb forms—participles, gerunds, and infinitives—functioning as nouns or modifiers are called **verbals**, as explained in section 7d.

ESL-5a Using gerunds and infinitives as subjects

Gerunds are used more commonly than infinitives as subjects. Sometimes, however, either is acceptable.

Choosing the best instructor is difficult.

To choose the best instructor is difficult.

✤ VERB ALERT: When a gerund or an infinitive is used alone as a subject, it is singular and requires a singular verb. When two or more gerunds or infinitives create a compound subject, they require a plural verb. (See sections 7k and 11d.) ✤

ESL-5b Using a gerund, not an infinitive, as an object after certain verbs

Some verbs must be followed by gerunds used as direct objects. Other verbs must be followed by infinitives. Still other verbs can be followed by either a gerund or an infinitive. (A few verbs can change meaning depending on whether they are followed by a gerund or an infinitive; see ESL-5d.) The following Chart lists common verbs that must be followed by gerunds, not infinitives.

Sasha **considered** *dropping* [not *to drop*] her accounting class.

She **was having trouble** *understanding* [not *to understand*] the teacher.

Her advisor **recommended** *hiring* [not *to hire*] a tutor.

VERBS AND EXPRESSIONS THAT USE GERUNDS AFTER THEM

acknowledge	detest	mind
admit	discuss	object to
advise	dislike	postpone
anticipate	dream about	practice
appreciate	enjoy	put off
avoid	escape	quit
cannot bear	evade	recall
cannot help	favor	recommend
cannot resist	finish	regret
complain about	give up	resent
consider	have trouble	resist
consist of	imagine	risk
contemplate	include	suggest
defer from	insist on	talk about
delay	keep (on)	tolerate
deny	mention	understand

Gerund After go

Go is usually followed by an infinitive: *We can **go to hear** [not go hearing] a band after the show.* Sometimes, however, *go* is followed by a gerund in phrases such as *go swimming, go fishing, go shopping,* and *go driving: I will **go swimming** [not go to swim] after class.*

Gerund After be + Complement + Preposition

Many common expressions use a form of the verb *be* plus a complement plus a preposition. In such expressions, use a gerund, not a infinitive, after the preposition. Here is a list of some of the most frequently used expressions in this pattern.

LIST OF SELECTED *BE* + COMPLEMENT + PREPOSITION EXPRESSIONS

be (get) accustomed to	be interested in
be angry about	be prepared for
be bored with	be responsible for
be capable of	be tired of
be committed to	be (get) used to
be excited about	be worried about

Hari **is tired of** *waiting* [not *to wait*] for his grades.
Katrina **is bored with** *learning* [not *to learn*] to ski.

♣ USAGE ALERT: Always use a gerund, not an infinitive, as the object of a preposition. Be especially careful when the word *to* is functioning as a preposition in a phrasal verb (see ESL–4c): *We are **committed to changing*** [not *to change*] the rules. ♣

ESL-5c Using an infinitive, not a gerund, as an object after certain verbs

The following Chart lists selected common verbs and expressions that must be followed by infinitives, not gerunds, as objects.

Niki **hoped** *to go* [not *hoped going*] home for the holidays.
Astrid **decided** *to remain* [not *remaining*] in the dormitory.

VERBS AND EXPRESSIONS THAT USE INFINITIVES AFTER THEM			
afford	claim	hope	promise
agree	consent	intend	refuse
aim	decide	know how	seem
appear	decline	learn	struggle
arrange	demand	like	tend
ask	deserve	manage	threaten
attempt	do not care	mean	volunteer
be left	expect	offer	vote
beg	fail	plan	wait
cannot afford	give permission	prepare	want
care	hesitate	pretend	would like

Infinitives After be + Complement

Gerunds are common in constructions that use forms of the verb *be*, a complement, and a preposition (see ESL-5b). However, use an infinitive, not a gerund, when *be*

plus a complement is not followed by a preposition.

> We **are glad** *to see* [not *seeing*] you so happy.
> Maria **is ready** *to learn* [not *learning*] to cook.

Infinitives to Indicate Purpose

Use an infinitive in expressions that indicate purpose: *I wore an old shirt **to gather** berries.* This sentence means "I wore an old shirt for the purpose of gathering berries." *To gather* delivers the idea of purpose more concisely (see Chapter 16) than expressions such as "so that I can" or "in order to."

Infinitives with the first, the last, the one

Use an infinitive after the expressions *the first, the last,* and *the one: Colin is the first **to start** [not starting] and the last **to quit** [not quitting] on this project.*

Unmarked Infinitives

Infinitives used without the word *to* are called **unmarked infinitive** or **bare infinitives**. An unmarked infinitive may be hard to recognize because it is not preceded by *to*. Some common verbs followed by unmarked infinitives are *feel, have, hear, let, listen to, look at, make,* (meaning "compel"), *notice, see,* and *watch.*

> Please make your son **behave** [not *to behave*]
> > [unmarked infinitive]
>
> I asked your son **to behave**.
> > [marked infinitive]

The verb *help* can be followed by either a marked or an unmarked infinitive. Either is correct: *Help me **count** [or **to count**] the receipts.*

♣ USAGE ALERT: Be careful to use parallel structure (see Chapter 18) correctly when you use two or more gerunds or infinitives after verbs. If two or more verbal objects follow one verb, put the verbals into the same form.

> **No**   We like **skating** and **to ski**.
> **Yes**   We like **skating** and **skiing**.
> **Yes**   We like **to skate** and **to ski**.

Conversely, if you are using verbal objects with compound predicates, be sure to use the kind of verbal that each verb requires.

> **No**   We enjoyed **scuba diving** but do not plan **sailing** again. [*Enjoyed* requires a gerund object and *plan* requires an infinitive object; see the Charts in ESL-4b and ESL-5b.]
> **Yes**   We enjoyed **scuba diving** but do not plan **to sail** again. ♣

ESL-5d Knowing how meaning changes when certain verbs are followed by a gerund or an infinitive as an object

With Stop

The verb *stop* followed by a gerund means "finish, quit." *Stop* followed by an infinitive means "stop or interrupt one activity to begin another."

> We **stopped eating**. [We finish our meal.]
> We **stopped to eat**. [We stopped another activity, such as driving, in order to eat.]

With remember *and* forget

The verb *remember* followed by an infinitive means "not to forget to do something": *I must **remember to talk** with Isa. Remember* followed by a gerund means "recall a memory": *I **remember talking** in my sleep last night.*

The verb *forget* followed by an infinitive means "to not do something": *If you **forget to put** a stamp on that letter, it will be returned. Forget* followed by a gerund means "to do something and not recall it": *I **forget having put** the stamps in the refrigerator.*

With try

The verb *try* followed by an infinitive means "made an effort": *I **tried to find** your jacket. Followed by a gerund, try* means "experimented with": *I **tried jogging** but found it too difficult.*

ESL-5e Understanding that meaning does not change whether a gerund or an infinitive follows certain sense verbs

Sense verbs include words such as *see, notice, hear, observe, watch, feel, listen to,* and *look at.* The meaning of these verbs is usually not affected whether it is followed by a gerund or an infinitive as an object. *I **saw** the water **rise*** and *I **saw** the water **rising*** both have the same meaning in American English.

ESL-5f Choosing between *-ing* forms and *-ed* forms for adjectives

Deciding whether to use the *-ing* form (*present participle*) or the *-ed* (*past participle of a regular verb*) as an adjective in a specific sentence can be difficult. For example, *I am amused* and *I am amusing* are both correct in English, but their meanings are very different. To make the right choice, decide whether the modified noun or pronoun is causing or experiencing what the participle describes.

Use a present participle (*-ing*) to modify a noun or pronoun that is the agent or the cause of the action.

> Mica described your **interesting** plan. [The noun *plan* causes what its modifier describes—*interest*; so *interesting* is correct.]
>
> I find your plan **exciting**. [The noun *plan* causes what its modifier describes—*excitement*; so *exciting* is correct.]

Use a past participle (*-ed* in regular verbs) to modify a noun or pronoun that experiences or receives whatever the modifier describes.

> An **interested** committee wants to hear your plan. [The noun *committee* experiences what its modifier describes—*interest*; so *interested* is correct.]
>
> **Excited** by your plan, I called a board meeting. [The noun *I* experiences what its modifier describes—*excitement*; so *excited* is correct.]

Here is a list of some frequently used participles that require your close attention when you use them as adjectives. To choose the right form, decide whether the noun or pronoun experiences or causes what the participle describes.

amused, amusing	frightened, frightening
annoyed, annoying	insulted, insulting
appalled, appalling	offended, offending
bored, boring	overwhelmed, overwhelming
confused, confusing	pleased, pleasing
depressed, depressing	reassured, reassuring
disgusted, disgusting	satisfied, satisfying
fascinated, fascinating	shocked, shocking

Use of Verbals

Complete each sentence with the appropriate gerund, infinitive, or participle form of the verb in parentheses.

EXAMPLE Most students at a university hope _____ (prepare) themselves for a career.
Most students at a university hope ___*to prepare*___ themselves for a career.

1. They are worried about _____ (get) jobs after graduation.
2. They may want _____ (study) for the pure enjoyment of learning.
3. They may even dream about _____ (be) philosophers or writers.
4. However, many parents refuse _____ (support) students who lack a definite career goal.
5. They are happy _____ (help) their children reach their goals.
6. They resist _____ (aid) children who lack direction.
7. Yet _____ (read) widely in the liberal arts is one way for students _____ (know) themselves.
8. Students of the humanities are the first _____ (see) the value of a liberal education.
9. When they hear their parents _____ (complain) about wasting money, students try _____ (explain) their positions.
10. They recommend _____ (learn) about life before _____ (train) for a specific job.

ESL-6 | *Modal Auxiliary Verbs*

HOW TO USE CHAPTER ESL-6 EFFECTIVELY
This chapter corresponds to Chapter 46-ESL in the *Simon & Schuster Handbook for Writers*.

Use this chapter together with these workbook sections:
- 7c recognizing verbs
- 8j progressive tenses
- 8e auxiliary verbs
- 8g verb tense
- 8l–m subjunctive mood

Auxiliary verbs are known as *helping verbs* because adding an auxiliary verb to a main verb helps the main verb convey additional information (see 8e). For example, the auxiliary verb *do* is important in turning sentences into questions. *You have to sleep* becomes a question when *do* is added: *Do you have to sleep?* The most common auxiliary verbs are forms of *be, have,* and *do.*

The charts in section 8e list the forms of these three verbs.

Modal auxiliary verbs are one type of auxiliary verb. They include *can, could, may, might, should, had better, must, will, would,* and others discussed in this chapter. They have only two forms: the present-future and the past. Modals differ from *be, have,* and *do* used as auxiliary verbs in the ways discussed in the following Chart.

SUMMARY OF MODALS AND THEIR DIFFERENCES FROM OTHER AUXILIARY VERBS

Modals in the present or future are always followed by the simple form of a main verb

> I might **go** tomorrow.

One-word modals have no -s ending in the third-person singular

> She **could** go with me, you **could** go with me, they **could** go with me. (The two-word modal *have to* changes form to agree with its subject: *I **have to** leave, she **has to** leave.)*

→

SUMMARY OF MODALS AND THEIR DIFFERENCES FROM OTHER AUXILIARY VERBS *(continued)*

Auxiliary verbs other than modals usually change form for third-person singular

> I **have** talked with her, he **has** taked with her.

Some modals change form in the past. Others (*should, would, must* when it conveys probability, and *ought to*) use *have* + a past participle: *I* **can** *do it* becomes *I* **could** *do it* in past-tense clauses about ability. *I* **could** *do it* becomes *I* **could have** *done it* in clauses about possibility.

Modals convey meaning about ability, advisability, necessity, possibility, and other conditions: for example, *I can go* means *I am able to go*. Modals do not indicate actual occurrences.

ESL-6a Conveying ability, necessity, advisability, possibility, and probability with modals

Conveying Ability

The modal *can* conveys ability now (in the present) and *could* conveys ability before (in the past). These words deliver the meaning of "able to." For the future, use *will be able to*.

> Luis **can** beat Pepe at tennis. [*Can* conveys present ability.]
>
> He **could** beat him last month too. [*Could* conveys past ability.]
>
> If he practices, he **will be able to** beat him next month. [*Will be able to* conveys future ability.]

Adding *not* between a modal and the main verb makes the clause negative: *Mondana* **can not** (or **cannot**) *attend the study session; she* **could not** *attend last night; she* **will not be able** *to attend next Monday.*

♣ USAGE ALERT: You will often see negative forms of modals turned into contractions: *can't, couldn't, won't, wouldn't,* and others. Because contractions are considered informal usage by some instructors, you will never be wrong if you avoid them in academic writing except for reproducing spoken words. ♣

Conveying Necessity

The modals *must* and *have to* convey the message of a need to do something. Both *must* and *have to* are followed by the simple form of the main verb. In the present tense, *have to* changes form to agree with its subject.

> You **must** turn your paper in on time.
> You **have to** meet the minimum requirements.

In the past tense, *must* is never used to express necessity. Instead, use *had to*.

PRESENT TENSE	We **must** submit out papers today.
	We **have to** abide by the rules.
PAST TENSE	We **had to** [not *We must*] write our first paper yesterday.

The negative forms of *must* and *have to* also have different meanings. *Must not* conveys that something is forbidden; *do not have to* conveys that something is not necessary.

> You **must not** miss the lecture. [Missing the lecture is forbidden.]
> You **do not have to** miss the lecture. [Missing the lecture is not necesary. You can watch it on television.]

Conveying Advisability or the Notion of a Good Idea

The modals *should* and *ought to* express the idea that doing the action of the main verb is advisable or is a good idea.

> You **should** write in your journal daily.

In the past tense, *should* and *ought to* convey regret or knowing something through hindsight. They mean that good advice was not taken.

You **should have** written in it yesterday.
I **ought to have** written in mine too.

The modal *had better* delivers the meaning of good advice or warning or threat. It does not change form for tense.

You **had better** start writing before you get behind.

Need to is often used to express strong advice, too. Its past-tense form is *needed to.*

You **need to** be a more conscientious student.

Conveying Possibility

The modals *may, might,* and *could* can be used to convey an idea of possibility or likelihood.

We **may** travel during our fall break.
We **could** leave Friday after classes end.

The past-tense forms for *may, might,* and *could* use these words followed by *have* and the past participle of the main verb.

We **could have** traveled during the summer, but we both attended summer school.

Conveying Probability

The modal *must* can convey probability or likelihood in addition to its conveying necessity (see Conveying Necessity). It means that a well-informed guess is being made.

Shakir **must** be a gregarious person. Everyone on campus seems to know him.

When *must* conveys probability, the past tense is *must have* plus the past participle of the main verb.

We hoped Marisa would come to the party; she **must have** had to study.

ESL-6b Conveying preferences, plans, and past habits with modals

Conveying Preferences

The modals *would rather* and *would rather have* express a preference. *Would rather* (present tense) is used with the simple form of the main verb and *would rather have* (past tense) is used with the past participle of the main verb.

> Carlos **would rather** work on the computer than sleep.
> He **would rather have** had an earlier class.

Conveying Plan or Obligation

A form of *be* followed by *supposed to* and the simple form of a main verb delivers a meaning of something planned or of an obligation.

> Lucia **was supposed to be** here an hour ago.

Conveying Past Habit

The modals *used to* and *would* express the idea that something happened repeatedly in the past.

> Inger **used to** dream of studying in the States.
> She **would** imagine what it would be like.

✿ USAGE ALERT: Both *used to* and *would* can be used to express repeated actions in the past, but *would* cannot be used for a situation that has lasted for a duration of time in the past.

> **No**   I **would** be a physics major.
> **Yes**   I **used to** be a physic major. ✿

ESL-6c Recognizing modals in the passive voice

Modals use the active voice, as shown in sections ESL-6a and ESL-6b. In the active voice, the subject does the action expressed in the main verb (see 8m–8o).

Modals can also use the passive voice. In the passive voice, the doer of the main verb's action is either unexpressed or is expressed as an object in a prepositional phrase starting with the word *by*.

PASSIVE	The rooftop **can be reached** from a door in the east tower.
ACTIVE	I **can reach** the rooftop from a door in the east tower.
PASSIVE	The assignment **must be completed** by Friday.
ACTIVE	Everyone **must complete** the assignment by Friday.

Modal Auxiliaries

Fill in the blanks with the correct modal auxiliary forms.

EXAMPLE   _____ (present ability) you imagine a more interesting place to visit than New Orleans?

_____*Can*_____ you imagine a more interesting place to visit than New Orleans?

1. I _____ (present advisability, negative) brag, but I went there for spring vacation.

2. You _____ (present possibility, negative) know it, but New Orleans was founded in 1718 by two brothers from Montreal.

3. They _____ (past probability) been looking for a warmer climate.

4. They _____ (past advisability) looked for higher ground.

5. Much of New Orleans is below sea level and _____ (present passive necessity) kept dry by using dikes and pumps.

6. Early settlers _____ (past necessity) build with cypress timbers.

7. Because cypress wood came from the surrounding swamps, it _____ (past ability) withstand the moisture of the climate.

8. Owners of plantations near the Mississippi River _____ (past habit) expect to be flooded occasionally.

9. They _____ (past possibility) moved, but they preferred to keep their rich soil and their beautiful view.

10. I _____ (preference) visit New Orleans than any other city in the South.

Index

Section numbers are in bolface type, and page numbers are in regular type. This listing **7a**: 63 thus refers you to page 63, which is in section 7a.

Index